JOHN ONO LENNON
Volume 2 1967–1980

JOHN
ONO
LENNON

VOLUME 2 1967–1980

RAY COLEMAN

SIDGWICK & JACKSON
LONDON

First published in 1984 in Great Britain
by Sidgwick and Jackson Limited

Copyright © 1984 by Ray Coleman

ISBN 0-283-99082-1

Phototypeset by Falcon Graphic Art Ltd
Wallington, Surrey
Printed in Great Britain by
R.J. Acford, Industrial Estate, Chichester, Sussex
for Sidgwick and Jackson Limited
1 Tavistock Chambers, Bloomsbury Way
London WC1A 2SG

For Sean Lennon

CONTENTS

ACKNOWLEDGEMENTS

The author and publishers gratefully acknowledge the permission of David Sheff and Barry Golson, and *Playboy* magazine, New York, for reproduction of parts of their 1980 interview with John Lennon and Yoko Ono; *Melody Maker* for permission to reproduce parts of several interviews conducted with the Lennons; Patrick Humphries, who contributed part of the chapter on John's music; Roger Scott and Capital Radio, London, for the statements by Paul McCartney on the break-up of the Beatles contained in Chapter 2 and L. G. Wood, former managing director of E.M.I. Records, for the loan of John Lennon's letter and a list of his songs.

The words to the songs 'Strawberry Fields Forever', 'Lucy In The Sky With Diamonds', 'A Day In The Life', 'Across The Universe', 'Revolution', 'Glass Onion', 'Julia', 'The Ballad Of John and Yoko', 'Give Peace A Chance', 'Cold Turkey', 'Mother', 'God', 'Isolation', 'Working Class Hero', 'My Mummy's Dead', 'Imagine', 'Crippled Inside', 'Jealous Guy', 'Give Me Some Truth', 'How Do You Sleep?' and 'Oh Yoko!' are copyright © Northern Songs and are reproduced by kind permission of A.T.V. Music, 19 Upper Brook Street, London W.1. The words to 'Out The Blue', 'Scared', 'Steel and Glass', and 'Nobody Loves You (When You're Down and Out)' are copyright © Lennon Music/A.T.V. Music and are reproduced by kind permission of A.T.V. Music. The words to 'Woman Is The Nigger Of The World', 'The Luck Of The Irish', 'Attica State', and 'Sunday Bloody Sunday' are copyright © Ono Music/Lennon Music and are reproduced by kind permission of Warner Bros. Music and A.T.V. Music. The words to 'Beautiful Boy (Darling Boy)', 'Watching The Wheels', and 'Woman' are copyright © Lenono Music/Warner Bros. Music and are reproduced by kind permission of Warner Bros. Music. The words to 'Borrowed Time' and 'Grow Old With Me' are copyright © Ono Music and are reproduced by kind permission of Warner Bros. Music.

LIST OF ILLUSTRATIONS

AUTHOR'S NOTE

'Here I am, rich and famous as I always wanted to be, and *nothing's happening*,' John Lennon said to me at his home in Weybridge, Surrey in 1965.

Hundreds of superficial pop stars have been satisfied with fame and fortune but ephemeral success was never going to satisfy John Lennon. Part of John's philosophy was, ironically, voiced on his penultimate album *Double Fantasy*, when he sang: 'Life is what happens to you when you're busy making other plans.' John Lennon wrote these words for 'Beautiful Boy', the song to his son Sean. He wrote the song fifteen years after talking about his disaffection with life as a Beatle, when as a pop star he had been gaining weight, gaining money, gaining adulation from millions, but losing himself.

He did not have to wait long for his life to change dramatically. Within a year of his restlessness the Beatles stopped touring and he met Yoko Ono. As man and woman, husband and wife, and artists who were both competitive and compatible, they began a journey unheard of for a pop star. Eventually they captivated millions. At first reviled as 'the woman who broke up the Beatles', taking cuddly John from the world, Yoko Ono, with John's help, confounded the bigots with her patience, grace, and imagination, and by propounding a message that everyone understood but few articulated so well: peace and love. John, understandably, was intensely angry at the hatred poured on his wife. It was, he said, an insult to him as well as to Yoko.

Many of us who knew John Lennon in Liverpool, London, and New York, during three key phases of a rich life, saw an

xiii

extraordinary evolution, from ambitious student, through the years of desperate, embryonic pop star to a mature artist and family man. Few achieved that transformation with such distinction or with such heartfelt affection from the people. This book aims to capture the frenzy, the turbulence, the achievements and the joy of those years. The people who helped me shape it had a unique perspective of John Ono Lennon and I thank them warmly.

Yoko Ono Lennon's continual encouragement and unending patience has been an inspiration as well as a great practical help in recapturing their work, their marriage, and their extraordinary chemistry. Elliot Mintz, John's closest male friend in America from 1971, gave, unstintingly, hours of his time, contributing perceptive insights into John's moods and movements, particularly during his years of seclusion.

Leon Wildes, John's lawyer during his four-year immigration battle has been a great help during my New York researches; Vincent Urwand, the café owner who had a unique friendship with John for four years, provided important recollections; and photographer Bob Gruen's observations on the many moods of the man have been a great help.

My special thanks to Julian Lennon for his enthusiastic involvement in the book and loan of illuminating postcards from his father; and to John's first wife, Cynthia, for describing the sequence of events leading up to their divorce. John's Aunt Mimi's memories have been a powerful reminder, throughout both volumes, of the man's roots and her co-operation was irreplaceable.

The chronology of John's life at the end of this volume was compiled by Mark Lewisohn, who also undertook most of the picture research; his help and guidance has been invaluable. I thank Jane Birdsell, my astute editor at Sidgwick & Jackson, who has marshalled both volumes through many trials; and Christina Masterman who typed the final manuscript.

In a life that touched millions with its honesty and style, John Lennon became the victim of many myths. Chief among these was that he was an uncaring, rumbustious rock 'n' roller with little compassion. The reverse is true, as his music demonstrated from 'If I Fell', which he wrote in 1964, right through to 'Imagine' (1971) and 'Woman' (1980). His anthems, 'Imagine', 'All You Need Is Love', 'Give Peace A Chance', and 'Jealous Guy' bear testimony to his sincerity and search for his own truths: self-deflating but never self-hating, optimistic, a force for good.

As an artist he understood the full range of human emotions. As a man he was the bravest I have ever known.

Ray Coleman
Shepperton, England
April 1984

1
DIVORCE

'When I met Yoko, I had to drop everything!'

'I think,' says Yoko Ono, 'that I was probably the successor to
Aunt Mimi in John's life.' Her comparison of herself with the
formidable but intensely caring woman who raised John Lennon
through his entire childhood is both brave and astute. The
qualities in his stern Aunt Mimi, which John grew to admire and
respect, were to be re-created in a much more bizarre fashion by
Yoko Ono. And she too had a profound, devastating effect on
him.

Their first meeting set the pattern of their loving, creative and
often tempestuous relationship. At London's Indica art gallery in
late 1966 one of the exhibits in Yoko's show as an avant-garde
artist was an apple which she had on sale for £200. John was
taken aback by the absurdity of it. 'Look, I don't have to pay all
that money for an apple,' he said, smiling cynically with that
familiar curled bottom lip. He appreciated the dry humour in her
work immediately. Yoko Ono had won her point: she had elicited
a firm response. For the artist in her, contact had been made.

Next she asked John to climb a stepladder and hammer an
imaginary nail into the wall. This, she said, would cost him five
shillings. John's retort was as swift as one might have expected
from a no-nonsense Liverpudlian: 'I'll give you an imaginary five
shillings,' he said, 'If you'll let me hammer the imaginary nail.' The
joke was that there were no nails left. Yoko permitted herself a
rare smile. John said later that he regarded the event as 'nutty'. But
Yoko remembers that they both felt a certain electricity in the air
as they 'connected'. Lennon was a sucker for experimentation.
Yoko says she recognized in him that evening an artistic sense of

humour that placed him apart from his professional role as Millionaire Beatle. She was anyway totally unimpressed by the fact that he was rich and famous: 'I was a conceptual artist and had no interest in pop music. The Beatles' thing, rock 'n' roll, had passed me by.' Lennon, conversely, was drawn to the art world like a magnet. The restlessness that simmered underneath the pop star at the end of 1966 had resulted from his deep involvement with drugs.

The evening he first met Yoko he had been up for three nights, stoned on marijuana and L.S.D. His demeanour virtually reflected his inner self: confused and dissatisfied with the mad whirl of Beatlemania. Crucially, at the time of his meeting with Yoko he was looking for a new force in his life. With the uncanny sixth sense of communication that was to manifest itself between them as the years unfolded, Yoko realized after that odd encounter at the Indica Gallery that something had happened to her too. 'He played exactly the same mind game as me,' she says.

John's account of that first meeting is somewhat longer but just as immediate. 'Imagine two cars of the same make heading towards each other and they're gonna crash, head-on. Well, it's like one of those scenes from a film – they're doing a hundred miles an hour, they both slam their brakes on and there's smoke everywhere on the floor and they stop just in the nick of time with their bumpers almost touching but not quite. That's what it was like from the first time I got to know her.' The analogy was perfect.

There was a problem, however. Both John Winston Lennon and Yoko Ono were married . . .

Back at home in Weybridge, Surrey, John's wife Cynthia firmly believed her role was to continue as before Beatlemania: as the rock-solid, unquestioning, loving, home-building wife and devoted mother to their three-year-old son Julian. John's absence as a travelling Beatle had forced her to shoulder all the domestic chores. Passive, maternal, at all times understanding, except on the subject of drugs, Cynthia was still the contented, tasteful, resilient Hoylake girl who had first won John's heart at art college. Being the wife of a millionaire star whose face was in the newspapers and on television every week had not changed her one scrap. The problem was that John *had* changed. And he regretted that Cyn had not changed with him. He was looking

John in 1967, posing for a promotional picture to launch the *Sgt Pepper* album at his home in Weybridge

for new action. And he wanted it quickly, like everything else.

'There was nothing basically wrong with my marriage to Cyn,' John told me. 'It was just like an amber light. It wasn't on go and it wasn't on stop. I suppose that me being away so much during the early years of our marriage, I never did feel like the average married man.'

His artistic flirtation with Yoko took months, and a determined pursuit by her, before it developed; in the beginning he was sceptical of her strange world but intrigued too. Soon after their meeting Yoko sent John a copy of her small book, *Grapefruit*. Its simplicity infuriated him but it played on his imagination just as Yoko had intended. Effectively it was a continuation of the odd images conjured up in the catalogue which he had smiled over at the Indica Gallery. *Grapefruit* featured Yoko's instructions to: 'Cut a hole in a bag filled with seeds and place the bag where there is wind.' One entry read: 'Hide until everybody goes home. Hide until everybody forgets about you. Hide until everybody dies.'

John read *Grapefruit* in bed at night. Beside him lay Cynthia, who once asked what he was reading. 'Oh, something that weird artist woman sent me,' he replied. Neither husband nor wife realized that within two years that same 'weird artist woman' would radically re-shape both their lives and that John would write as his introduction to the reprinted version of *Grapefruit*: 'Hi, my name is John Lennon. I'd like you to meet Yoko Ono.' Alongside the terse message would be his drawing of the woman who by then had won his heart as well as his head.

John was no saint and Cynthia knew it. The temptations for a Beatle, who was one of the most famous people in the world in 1966, adored, mentally and physically, by thousands of women, would have been almost impossible for a full-blooded male to resist.

'But I had blind faith,' says Cynthia. 'I couldn't imagine John being involved with another woman. And even if he had, I would have ignored it because he always came back. Whatever John did outside our marriage, he didn't flaunt anything. So when I learned later about the temptations he had succumbed to, I had the satisfaction of knowing he had protected me at the time, just like he had since we first met.'

Cynthia says she had more fears about his desirability when he was a student than when he was a Beatle. 'Once he became famous, he was like a national institution, not easy to be picked off for flings – well, easy maybe, but he had to be careful about it, be careful who knew.'

Honesty, one of John's most endearing characteristics, forced him to confess to Cynthia one day early in 1967. Cynthia was washing the dishes when John came behind her, put his arms around her waist and said: 'I want to get it off my chest, Cyn. There have been hundreds of other women.'

It could have been an explosive moment. But such was Cynthia's love and devotion to John that his honesty and his tender way of breaking the news of his affairs developed into one of the frankest moments in their marriage since the turbulence of Beatlemania and drugs had pulled them apart. 'Strangely,' says Cynthia, 'it was a very loving moment. I was in tears, not of anger or shock, but tears of happiness that he could tell me, that we'd once again got close enough for him to get rid of it, talk it through and put it on a different level. Perhaps it would have been better if I'd been able to be a bit more aggressive. But I was so happy that at last he felt he could open his heart and tell me what was on his mind.'

Their marriage had been 'rolling along nicely with no fireworks,' she recalls. Although she had suspected that John had been involved with other women, she had shut herself away from the possibility, preoccupied with running a house, bringing up Julian and cosseting John when he returned from work. His extra-marital affairs did not concern her.

Mentally the rift between them had begun more than a year before with John's increased interest in drugs and Cynthia's steadfast refusal to join him on his trips. Now, in 1967, the full flowering of John's personality was to take shape; his own confrontation with his marriage was a central part of this.

'When John told me he'd had all these affairs, I felt as though we were being brought together again,' says Cynthia. 'He'd been leading his life as a musician and pop star and I'd led mine as a wife and mother. Conversation had become very thin on the ground. He was doing so many things I wasn't involved in.'

John's confession had a strange irony. A few weeks earlier he and Cynthia had been watching television when a programme mentioned the number of times a week an average married couple would make love. They fell far short of it, says Cynthia, because John was away so much. He said to her: 'God, we're just like brother and sister, aren't we?' But their marriage had ticked over until that crucial session of owning up. And that was the major problem. John's mind was expanding so fast by then that he did not want anything in his life to 'tick over'.

'Our relationship was one of friendship – we were always mates and we'd gone through a lot together,' says Cynthia. 'But I did know we couldn't pretend it was like the student days once he'd made it to the top. Once Julian was born, we were parents, responsible people and John was a big star. If any of John's agony, self-torment or torture was worrying him, then he kept it hidden from me. I wasn't aware of it.'

John's admission of other women in his life might have been therapeutic for both him and Cynthia but the physical flings were only a surface indication of something which ran much deeper. What he would not say to her, because he did not want to hurt her, was that he was desperately looking for some new milestone in his life. He did not feel comfortable in his Weybridge mansion in the stockbroker belt. The house was merely a status symbol, bought hurriedly to hide from fans thronging their central London flat. The roller-coaster of Beatlemania had lost its attraction for him. Drugs were increasing their hold over him and the continuing clash with Cynthia over his use of L.S.D. rocked their marriage still further. He became increasingly irritable when, as he took L.S.D. at home, Cynthia said: 'Please, John, it would be wise for you not to do it. You will go mental if you're not careful. Think about Julian, think about everything.'

Cynthia comments: 'But his reasoning power over what was important had gone. Whatever anyone said when he was taking L.S.D. was not to be treated seriously. Me, I didn't get involved because I saw my role as his wife, and Julian's Mum, as running the house and being the mainstay of his life when he was there.' She regrets not having been more positive, perhaps even slightly more aggressive, to counter John's excesses. 'I couldn't change my character, though, could I?' But Cynthia had miscalculated the degree of intellectual stimulus John was now seeking.

In midsummer 1967 the Beatles' manager Brian Epstein, threw a small party at his house at 24 Chapel Street, Belgravia, to mark a very special event in the career of the four men to whom he still paternally referred as 'the boys'. Few of the guests, including me, expected the new album from the Beatles to be so revolutionary. The record that blared out from behind tables groaning with exquisitely chosen gourmet food was *Sgt Pepper's Lonely Hearts Club Band*. The music perfectly captured the mood of that psychedelic, flowerpower summer when swinging London, mini skirts, Carnaby Street's fashion liberation and love and peace were precursors of a generation's change. It became a soundtrack for psychedelia.

John at the party at Brian Epstein's home in Belgravia to launch *Sgt Pepper's Lonely Hearts Club Band*. He was taking a lot of drugs at this time, and looked gaunt and under-nourished

There was no indication that the Beatles had gone so far down the road with drugs. A few months earlier John's song 'Strawberry Fields Forever' – one of his finest – evoked nothing more spiky than his childhood memories of ice-creams in a Salvation Army children's fete, while Paul's 'Penny Lane', on the reverse side, completed the Liverpool connection with flashbacks to the bus shelter where John and Paul, as fiendish schoolboys, would meet and eye the girls. But *Sgt Pepper* was different, a triumphant leap forward in songwriting ideas by John and Paul. Two Lennon songs in particular – 'A Day In The Life' and 'Lucy In The Sky With Diamonds' – were revolutionary even for the ever-questing John, the first being banned by the B.B.C. for its implied condoning of drugs, the second being a haunting stream-of-consciousness song which John had written after Julian had come home from school (Heath House, Weybridge) one afternoon and shown him a picture he had drawn, inspired by his friend Lucy.

At Epstein's party John looked haggard, old, ill, and hopelessly addicted to drugs. His eyes were glazed, his speech slow and slurred. I had a brief chat with him about music and he said he was worried that they had gone too far for public taste with the new album. 'Will they buy it? I like it, we all feel it's another step up, but will it sell?' I was astonished at his coherence while he was clearly under the influence of drugs. We spoke a little about the state of the music scene and he said there was one 'dope' record which he couldn't get off his mind. He couldn't remember the title. All other pop music of the period was 'crap', one of his favourite words at the time. John said he wasn't eating much and was on a vegetarian diet.

He smoked and drank wine incessantly. Talking later to Brian Epstein I said how horrifying and worrying John's physical state seemed. 'Don't worry. He's a survivor,' said Brian.

Next day John phoned me. 'I remembered after I'd gone what the record is that I can't stop playing,' he said. 'It's that dope song, Procol Harum's "Whiter Shade Of Pale". It's the best song I've heard for a while. You play it when you take some acid and . . .whoooooooooooooo.' What was most surprising about the phone call was that he'd actually remembered our conversation the previous evening. As he was later to prove, his eye and ear for detail and his memory, even when on drugs, would surprise anyone who thought him inattentive.

Talking of the making of *Sgt Pepper*, producer George Martin says: 'That was an incredible thing because it took on its own character, it grew despite us. It was a complete change of life, a

very long and arduous series of recordings and I suppose that
looking back on it, *Pepper* would never have been formed in
exactly that way if the boys hadn't got into the drug scene, and if I
hadn't been a normal person. I don't think it would have been as
coherent. . . . I just had to be patient. You can't do much with a
guy when he's giggling all the time. If they hadn't been on drugs,
it's possible something like *Pepper* would have happened but not
quite so flowery, maybe.'

Drugs, *Sgt Pepper*, his psychedelically painted Rolls-Royce, the
gipsy caravan in his garden at Weybridge, and his total embrace of
a more freewheeling way of life hardened John's attitude to his
home environment. Yoko both fascinated and annoyed him. A
steady stream of letters arrived at Weybridge from her and for a
period, postcards arrived daily, saying: 'Dance' or 'Breathe' or
'Watch all the lights until dawn.' John alternately found them
intriguing or simply dismissed them.

At this point in his life John was at his most vulnerable. The
Beatles had stopped touring and had just produced an album
which was critically acclaimed as setting new standards for
popular music, lifting Lennon and McCartney into a new echelon
of composers. This crossroads in the Beatles' position, coupled
with his foundering marriage and his enthusiasm for drugs, made
him easy prey to anything that offered new kicks.

As for the other Beatles, George Harrison had succumbed to
Eastern mysticism, entranced by the sitar-playing of his tutor and
new friend, Ravi Shankar. Paul McCartney, with actress Jane
Asher at his side, moved ever upwards in the social whirl of
London hip society, which held no appeal for John. Ringo, living a
few minutes away on the same estate at Weybridge, enjoyed
dispensing drinks from his private bar, the Flying Cow, and was
useful to John when he wanted to lock into light-heartedly playing
the Beatle role. But when Pattie Harrison, George's wife, said she
had heard from a friend about transcendental meditation, which
encouraged a deeper, cooler form of consciousness and awareness,
John was hooked. Together with Cynthia, George and Pattie, and
Paul and Jane he attended a lecture on meditation by the Maharishi Mahesh Yogi at London's Hilton Hotel.

By now the phone calls from Yoko had increased; she sought his
support for her artistic ventures and even visited his home when
neither he nor Cynthia was there. The housekeeper, Dorothy
Jarlett, allowed her in one day to make a phone call and next day

Yoko phoned John to say she must return because she had left her 'very precious' ring by the phone. John was getting used to her unpredictable behaviour and her spacey conversation attracted him, especially when he was high on drugs. Cynthia was blissfully ignorant that their relationship had any potential until that night after their baptism into transcendental meditation. Yoko was also at the meeting – alone.

As John and Cynthia climbed into their chauffeur-driven Rolls-Royce afterwards Yoko followed them into the car. 'John and I both looked at each other as though we'd gone crazy,' says Cynthia. 'I said to him: "What's going on?" He said: "I dunno." Neither of us had the courage to say: "Excuse me, madam, but where are you going?" She got in the car and asked to be dropped off down the road, which we duly did. For all I knew, there could have been something going on between John and Yoko even then but I don't think so judging from the look on his face. It was pure shock. It couldn't have been put on.' Yoko was dressed all in black. With her long hair and tiny figure even Cynthia admits she was fascinating. 'We thought it was quite amusing afterwards,' she recalls. 'We joked about it.' When John introduced Yoko to Cynthia, Yoko almost immediately propelled herself into talking about *Grapefruit*. Cynthia drew long and hard on her ever-present cigarette and pondered the weird woman in black who, according to John's reports, 'kept popping up all over the place' in his life.

At home later that evening Cynthia confronted John about Yoko and her strange behaviour.

'What is it with Yoko then?'

John replied: 'Oh nothing, she's crackers, she's just a weirdo artist. Don't worry about it.'

Cynthia persisted: 'Well what's all the phoning about, all these letters and leaving rings behind and knocking at the door?'

'Oh don't worry about it,' John insisted, 'it's not important. Crazy crazy crazy, Cyn! She's another nutter wanting money for all that avant-garde bullshit.'

Cynthia recalls: 'There was, though, something coming across constantly. It was worrying me but I had no tangible evidence . . . Although he and I didn't properly argue about it, the fact that he was smoking and taking L.S.D. made it hard to communicate. He kept pleading with me to join him and take it, but I wanted to keep my sanity. . . . During one of these scenes, I said to him: "Perhaps Yoko's the one for you, John." I remember he said: "Don't be stupid. That weird artist!" '

The day after that bizarre encounter John went with the other

En route to North Wales for a weekend of meditation in August 1967, John leans out of the carriage at Euston Station to see a forlorn Cynthia narrowly missing the train

Beatles to Bangor, North Wales to be properly taught transcendental meditation during a Bank Holiday weekend seminar. After a frantic dash to London's Euston Station Cynthia arrived to see the train leaving and John, hanging from the window, a face in the distance. The moment flashed before both John and Cynthia's eyes as strangely underlining the split in their marriage. When she eventually arrived alone John sarcastically berated her for 'always being late' and brought Cynthia to the brink of tears during what was supposed to be a weekend of tranquillity. The weekend, as well as widening the rift in John's marriage, proved to be a turning point for the Beatles.

On 27 August 1967, a day before he was due to travel north to join the Beatles for the meditation course, Brian Epstein died, a victim of an accidental drug overdose at his London home. Amid his beads and robes and peace in the North Wales countryside John reacted to the news with the same pent-up emotion which he had felt at the deaths of his mother, his Uncle George, and his best friend Stuart Sutcliffe. Lennon did not believe in prolonged grief. The Beatles returned to London to face the Press and try to marshal their thoughts about the millionaire, thirty-two-year-old manager who had steered them to the dizziest heights of world fame.

His death, so unexpected in the context of his success, was a puzzle. Brian was a complex, narcissistic man, very much a loner, and yet in a mere six years he had converted four scruffy rock 'n' rollers from Liverpool to legendary status and international social phenomena. It was a stupendous achievement. John had a love-hate feeling about Brian's triumph. He wanted the riches and fame which Brian's zeal had made possible, but he resented the fact that Epstein had cleaned them up and robbed them of their raw roots. Even so, John often demonstrated his big heart, sending Brian flowers or little gifts when Eppy was low.

That Bank Holiday Monday afternoon John invited me over to Weybridge to talk about the impact of Brian's death. Robed in white and lazing with Ringo by the pool, he seemed dazed as the words came together slowly.

'We all feel very sad but it's controlled grief, controlled emotion. As soon as I find myself feeling depressed, I think of something nice about him. But you can't hide the hurt – you know, I went to the phone book and saw his name and it hit me a few minutes ago. The memory must be kept nice but of course there's something inside us that tells us that Brian's death is sad.

'It hurts when someone close dies and Brian was very close. You know, we've all been through that feeling of wanting a good cry. But that wouldn't get us anywhere, would it?

'We all feel it but these talks on transcendental meditation have helped us to stand up to it so much better. You don't get upset, do you, when a young kid becomes a teenager or a teenager becomes an adult or when an adult gets old? Well, Brian is just passing into the next phase.

'His spirit is still around and always will be. It's a physical memory we have of him and as men we will build on that memory. It's a loss of genius, but other genius's bodies have died as well, and the world gains from their spirits.

'It's up to us now to sort out the way we, and Brian, wanted things to go. He might be dead physically but that's a negative way of thinking. He helped to give us the strength to do what we did and the same urge is still alive. It's a drag he didn't come up to the meditation course with the Maharishi.'

I asked John for his evaluation of Epstein's role in the Beatles' success and whether they would still have broken through without him. 'Not the same as we know it, no. But if he hadn't come along, we would all – the four of us and Brian – have been working towards the same thing, even though it might have been with different aims. We all knew what we wanted to get over; he helped us and we helped him.

'We're all going to India soon for a couple of months to study transcendental meditation properly. The only plans we had, before Brian died, were to make a record, do a T.V. show, and make a film. But meeting the Maharishi changed our thoughts a bit and Brian's death has changed it a lot. It makes it more worthwhile, now, somehow, to go to India.

'We want to learn the meditation thing properly so we can propagate it and sell the whole idea to everyone. This is how we plan to use our power now – they've always called us leaders of youth and we believe this is a good way to give a lead. We want to set up an academy in London and use all the power we've got to get it moving. And all the people who are worried about youth and drugs and that scene – all these people with the short back and sides, they can come along and dig it, too.

'It's no gospel, Bible-thumping, singalong thing and it needn't be religion if people don't want to connect it with religion. It's all in the mind.

'It strengthens understanding, makes people relaxed. The whole world wants to relax more and the people who get to know a bit about meditation will see it's not just a fad or a gimmick but the way to calm down tensions. You learn about thoughts, the meaning of thoughts, how to trace your thoughts – and it's much better than acid.

'We have no idea of whether we'll get a new manager. We have always been in control of what we're doing and we'll have to do what we have to, now. We know what we should do and what we shouldn't do. Brian was a natural guide and we'll certainly miss him.

'If Brian had been in on the lectures on meditation he would have understood. This is the biggest thing in my life now and it's come at the time when I need it most. It's nothing to do with mysticism. It's about *understanding*.

'Brian has died only in body and his spirit will always be working with us. His power and force were everything, and that will linger on. When we were on the right track he knew it, and when we were on the wrong track he told us so and he was usually right. But anyway, he isn't really dead.'

Just before he died Epstein had tried, unsuccessfully, to persuade the Beatles to re-consider their decision to stop touring. But John and George were resolute in their determination that the 1966 American trail had been the last. Brian died a dispirited man, empty at the realization that 'the boys' no longer needed him and that they did not respond to his requests. If they were to be a group that existed mostly for recording, John's whiplash tongue would see to it that, like any other visitor to their sessions, Brian kept silent when the music was being rehearsed or completed. Epstein had simply been left with an untenable role – a manager with no power and little control. His 'boys' had become men: rich, independent individuals with positive plans, widening horizons, and the talent to move on.

Or so it seemed that heady midsummer in 1967. That year, as the message of love and peace wafted from California to London on a tidal wave of good vibrations, as Scott McKenzie sang 'If you go to San Francisco be sure to wear some flowers in your hair' and John Lennon chewed gum before 400 million people on world television singing 'All You Need Is Love', John stayed cool. But later he would be forced to admit, 'The Beatles were finished when Eppy died. I knew, deep inside me, that that was it. Without him, we'd had it.'

As John and Cynthia left Heathrow Airport for the concrete chalets of Rishikesh, India, early in 1968 to accompany George and Pattie Harrison at the Maharishi's meditation academy, he looked, felt and spoke like a man with problems gnawing away inside him. He was no longer the lovable moptop Beatle whose steely wit had won the admiration of millions.

In Rishikesh the meditation was a healing influence and the changed environment was good for John but Cynthia noticed his jittery behaviour. 'Every morning he would be up and out of our room before me, at seven o'clock, saying he was off to meditate alone,' she says. 'He cut me dead in the mornings. The first week we were in India he was fine, but after that, he cut me off from himself. We'd always done things together . . . "Hang on wait for me John," I said.

' "No, no, I'm off," was his answer. I couldn't understand why at the time; I put it down to being away and his changed attitudes to meditation and the beauty that there were now no drugs. Meditation had killed the pushers stone dead, which I was thrilled about because it was getting to a very dangerous state. I thought heroin had to be the next stage. But now he was on edge. I realized later that he was going to collect the morning mail with letters from Yoko, but at the time I had no idea.

'It got to the stage when we were in the same room together that we would get on each others' nerves. Meditation has different patterns and I would sometimes go into deep meditation when John wasn't in the mood, and when we shared the same room, it was bad for both of us. . . . He seemed very isolated and would spend days on end with the Maharishi, emerging bleary-eyed and not wanting to communicate with me or anyone. So I believe he underwent a big change in Rishikesh. He went so deeply within himself through meditation that he separated himself from everything.'

John took meditation very seriously. He and George believed in its calming powers far more than the others in the party. For eight hours a day John would meditate and for the rest of the time during the eight weeks spent at the academy he wrote fifteen songs.

Yoko's flow of letters, some handwritten, others which she had typed immaculately, struck just the right mood for John's relaxed frame of mind. 'I'm a cloud. Watch for me in the sky', she wrote. John, who quickly moved to a separate bedroom from Cynthia reflected on her hypnotic words back in Weybridge: 'Perhaps Yoko's the one for you.' Perhaps, he decided, she was dead right. He could hardly wait to see her again.

Coupled with this was a growing disaffection with the Maharishi's behaviour and personality (although not with his methods). John and Cynthia announced they were leaving two weeks ahead of their original plan. Paul and Jane Asher, and Ringo and his wife Maureen had already returned home. There were too many Indian flies in the air for Maureen and Ringo commented with his dry humour that the academy resembled a Butlin's holiday camp. Lennon, asked by the Maharishi, whom he had grown to distrust, why he was leaving early, replied tersely: 'If you're so bloody cosmic, you'll know why.'

With his interest in Yoko growing rapidly John was eager to get back to England. On his return, however, he was bedevilled by problems which even he found hard to face.

With no manager, he and the other three Beatles decided to launch their own company, Apple, and a new album was also in the offing. By far the biggest issue in his mind, however, was his relationship with Cynthia. It wasn't that they were quarrelling much. It was more of a communication barrier. The mental rift caused by drugs was now increased by the meditation scene. 'We went through some bad times,' Cynthia says. 'It was very confusing, coming back to reality after meditating in India.'

John said to her that as he had an album to prepare and business to attend to he would be in the studios a lot. 'Cyn, why don't you get away for a couple of weeks on that holiday in Greece that Jenny and Alex are going on?' he said. Jenny Boyd was the sister of Pattie Harrison; Alex was 'Magic Alex' (his real name was John Alexis Mardas), a Greek-born electronics wizard who had inveigled himself into John's life and was a constant visitor to the Lennon home.

Cynthia agreed. 'We both needed space to breathe,' she says. 'I don't think he was intentionally getting rid of me. He just wanted to sort himself out, after India, just as I did. He was unsure of himself and the way his life was going. He felt he'd been let down by the Maharishi, the Beatles were obviously going to have to re-consider everything now Brian Epstein was dead, and then there were the uncertainties between us. It seemed a good thing for me to get away and let him concentrate on work.'

John's first major sign to Cynthia that he was going through agonizing decisions came the day she was packing for her Greek holiday. 'He was upstairs lying, fully clothed, on our bed, staring

Top: Garlands of flowers from the Maharishi Mahesh Yogi greet Paul and John as they arrive at Bangor railway station in August 1967 for a weekend of transcendental meditation

Above: John and Julian, aged four, with the Lennon Rolls-Royce that became a major talking-point in Britain during the psychedelic era. The picture was taken at Weybridge in June 1967

into space, not saying a word. It was as though he had so much on his mind he couldn't speak. Normally he'd have come down and waved me off in the taxi, but he was on a different planet that day I left. There was no getting through to him. He'd obviously got to the brink of planning what he wanted from his life and what was going to happen a week later with me on holiday. And what John wanted, he usually got.'

Cynthia left Weybridge under a cloud. John had decided that it was now or never with Yoko Ono. It was time to resolve their clandestine relationship and follow up the stream of curious, intriguing letters.

The only other person living at Weybridge during Cynthia's absence was his old schoolfriend from Quarry Bank, Liverpool. Pete Shotton was a little surprised when John said he thought he would invite Yoko Ono over for an evening the night before Cynthia's return. Shotton said he was going to bed anyway. John phoned Yoko in her London flat and his chauffeur-driven Rolls-Royce was sent to bring her, clad in her customary black, up the gravel drive into Kenwood by mid-evening.

John was apprehensive; he realized this might not be another of his fast affairs. He and Yoko sat talking nervously downstairs in the lounge for several hours: he about the pressures of being a famous millionaire Beatle and how he now no longer felt the same sense of challenge as before; she about the frustrations of being an artist. 'Yoko and I were on the same wavelength right from the start, from that first night,' John told me years later. 'That first night convinced me I'd have to end my marriage to Cyn.'

John took Yoko to his upstairs den with its two tape recorders on which he had first practised some of his songwriting gems like 'Nowhere Man', 'I'm A Loser' and the classic 'Norwegian Wood' which told of his affair with a prominent woman journalist. John and Yoko introduced each other to their different worlds. Lennon had always experimented with sounds and was interested in electronic effects and comedy; Yoko's interest was the human voice and extending its potential beyond the realms of orthodox singing. 'We improvised for many hours,' she recalls. 'He used the two tape recorders and put through them any sounds that came into his hands, you know: old recorded sounds. I sat down and did the voice. We were both involved and enjoying the uncertainty of how it would all turn out. And that was it. We called it *Unfinished Music*. The idea is that the listener can take from it, or add to it in his mind, or her mind.' Challenging her public was a central theme in Yoko's work. John was mesmerized by her sense of artistic

adventure. From his guitar and pen, everything had been channelled into straightforward commercial songs. Yoko's world, he
suddenly decided, was not 'avant-garde crap' as he had earlier
feared. It opened up real possibilities. They went to bed together at
dawn as the birds were waking. 'It was very beautiful', John
recalled. 'I had no doubt I'd met The One.'

Next morning Pete Shotton became the first person to know.
John told him that he was going to look for a new house in which
he and Yoko could live. A flabbergasted Shotton asked him what
he was talking about. John replied that he had met the person he'd
been looking for and was prepared to cash in everything, whatever
the cost, to be with her. Beatles, houses, money, fame – nothing
counted except his future with Yoko Ono. The chemistry between
them was unbelievable; her physical attraction was strengthened
by her intuitive knowledge of what fired John's thoughts. If there
was one moment when John Lennon ceased to be a committed
Beatle and chose, instead, to become an artist, it was that spring
night and dawn in May 1968. And, as always when John decided
on something, it was irrevocable.

By mid-afternoon, a joyful, refreshed Cynthia arrived home. After
her holiday she was bubbling and optimistic that the short
separation might now improve her life with John. Mysteriously
the outside porch light was on and all the curtains were drawn. 'It
was eerily silent,' she recalls. 'Normally there would be a gardener
around, or Dot the housekeeper, or Julian playing, but it was
deserted, as if there had been an all-night party. I had no idea what
would confront me when I got in. I knocked on the door like mad
at first but there was no reply. The whole of the front of the house
was in darkness but looking through to the big lounge there was a
light coming through, rather eerily.'

Once inside Cynthia, followed by Jenny Boyd and Magic Alex,
walked slowly around shouting: 'Is anybody there? John? Julian?
Dot?' Still there was no sound. Cynthia ran round all the rooms on
the ground floor, until finally reaching the dining-room and
kitchen. Off this, in the sun-room, the sight that faced her left her
'dumbstruck'. John, in his green-and-white-striped towelling robe,
hair dishevelled, mug of tea in his hand, sat on the small settee,
facing Cynthia as she walked in. Yoko, her mass of black hair
cascading down the back of a chair, making her instantly recogniz-
able, sat on a chair facing John. She was motionless, her back to
Cynthia who had stopped dead at the doorway. 'It was like

walking into a brick wall, as if I didn't belong any more. I felt absolutely shut out from communication,' says Cynthia. Within seconds Jenny and Alex were standing behind her, open-mouthed.

John broke the silence of what seemed hours and was probably a minute. 'Oh hi,' he said coolly, taking a drag from his cigarette. He might have been addressing the gardener or a waiter.

Cynthia, feeling the unreality of the situation, was shattered and lost for words. She attempted to pacify the ugliness of the experience. 'Oh hi,' she said to John. 'I had this great idea,' she went on quietly. 'We had breakfast in Greece, lunch in Rome and Jenny and Alex and I thought it would be great if we all went out to dinner in London to carry on the whole holiday.'

With no expression in his voice, John answered bluntly: 'No thanks.'

At this point Yoko turned round and gave Cynthia 'a very positive, confident look'. She was dressed in a black silk kimono. 'I suppose I should have been prepared for it but I wasn't,' says Cynthia. 'It took my breath away. I wasn't angry. I was just absolutely shattered at the vision. John wasn't talking to anybody – not just me, but to nobody. He was just staring, expressionless. So instead of starting a battle and asking questions about what was going on, I felt I had to get out of that house immediately.' She went upstairs and, in the panic, re-packed the kind of things she had just returned with from her holiday in the sun: toothbrush, shoes, make-up, coat, toilet bag. Passing the guest bedroom, Cynthia saw a pair of Japanese slippers outside the door: the final, crushing evidence, if she needed it, that Yoko had spent a night there.

Seized by a need to get out of the house as soon as she could, Cynthia was ready to leave within fifteen minutes of her arrival and confrontation. 'I decided John had been almost willing me to go. I took his silence as saying, "Don't interrupt this fantastic situation. Get lost. You're spoiling things." I got the message immediately without any more words.' She says she travelled faster than the speed of sound.

Cynthia went to stay with Jenny Boyd and Alex Mardas at their mews house in central London. 'I knew Julian would be safe with Dot, the housekeeper. He often went there,' she says. Three days later, having collected her thoughts, Cynthia warily phoned Kenwood. Dorothy Jarlett, the loyal housekeeper, now in an impossible situation, answered. No, she said, John was not in. Cynthia enquired if Julian was all right and said she was returning home that day.

To her amazement John greeted her as if nothing had happened. 'I can't understand why you went off,' he said. 'What have you been up to?' Cynthia apologized and said she couldn't cope with seeing him and Yoko looking so together. John insisted that their liaison was purely intellectual, Yoko and he had 'messed around with tapes all night' and it was quite wrong for Cynthia to misconstrue the situation. He would not talk about his association with Yoko. Cynthia says: 'It was strange that he would talk about the other women he'd been involved with, but with Yoko he stopped the conversation flat.'

Superficially, a warm, welcoming John gave Cynthia the impression all was well with their marriage. 'But I noticed his unease when I said, several times: "I see a great similarity between you and Yoko. John, there's something about her that's just like you. Look, you may say these things about Yoko, that she's crazy, just a weird artist, but there's an aura about her that's going to click with you." ' Cynthia succeeded only in irritating John when she said: 'I can see more into your situation with her than you can.' As she says: 'I knew immediately I saw them together that they were right for each other. I knew I'd lost him.'

Despite John's assurances, Cynthia knew in her heart that their relationship was now threatened. Superficially, however, life seemed to return to normal and she had no reason to fear an immediate marriage crisis. For several weeks during their reunion she asked if she should cancel the family holiday in Italy she had planned for herself, Julian, and her mother. 'No, no, you go ahead and have a lovely time,' said John. But he became increasingly distant as the time neared for them to go to Pesaro. There was no chance of his going with them: he had work to do, and besides, the prospect of John going on holiday with his mother-in-law was unthinkable. They had always kept their distance and he told several people how much he resented the intrusion of Lilian Powell into his domain.

Cynthia felt that she should press on with the holiday 'for Julian's sake'. If she had feared that her absence would crucially affect their marriage, she would never have gone. 'But I didn't. We were back together again and everything seemed fine.' Until, that was, her day of packing and flying. John was in a panic-stricken mood. 'He obviously knew something was going to happen while I was away and he was upset and frightened because he didn't know how it would turn out. Also he was probably worried about losing his son and he was already concerned that he'd spent a lot of time away from Julian when he was growing up.' But John was very distant as Les Anthony, their chauffeur, packed the Rolls-Royce that took them to Heathrow. 'We left with a cloud over the holiday,' says Cynthia. 'John was in a trance. He didn't even come to the door to say goodbye.'

John had decided to end his marriage to Cynthia but he didn't want to be the one to pass her the painful news. She thought it odd that, just before she left, he asked her if she had any affairs outside their marriage. 'No way. I've been totally faithful to you,' she answered. 'There have been mild flirtations but nothing serious that would jeopardize our marriage.' John seemed pleased, she says. His feeling for Yoko was now an obsession. As soon as Cynthia left, John saw as much of her as he could, despite a very busy work period.

An Italian newspaper brought home to Cynthia for the first time the fact that John and Yoko were now inseparable and her marriage irretrievable. Resting in bed with a sore throat, Cynthia was brought a newspaper by the hotel owner, Roberto Bassanini. It contained pictures of 'John Lennon, the Beatle, hand in hand with Japanese artist Yoko Ono', attending the opening night of a play, *In His Own Write*.

'I knew when I saw the picture that that was *it*,' says Cynthia. 'He'd obviously waited for me to go away to appear in the open with Yoko. He probably thought it would be easier for both of us. I knew it was the end because he would never flaunt something like an involvement with another woman if it were not very serious. It had been building up, I suppose, and was obvious to outsiders but not to me because John had kept up his same attitude, not hurting me.'

Next day John sent an unlikely emissary to give Cynthia a message – Magic Alex Mardas. Alex was to pass on his message to Cynthia and also to hire a private detective to monitor every move she made in Italy. After a tense breakfast with Cynthia, Roberto Bassanini, Julian, and Cynthia's mother he insisted on speaking to Cynthia alone. His message could not have been blunter: 'Well, John says he's going to divorce you. He's going to take Julian away from you and he's going to send you back to Hoylake.' His job done, he left immediately for London.

Cynthia's immediate reaction had been that John could not possibly do as he threatened and ignore her rights in this way. Her mother, vowing she would 'get to the bottom of this', also left immediately and headed for 34 Montagu Square, in London's West End, a flat which had been used alternately by rock star Jimi Hendrix and Ringo Starr, and to which she had moved after

An early public appearance with Yoko Ono. They were launching John's first art exhibition, 'You Are Here', at London's Robert Fraser Gallery in July 1968

Cynthia's first encounter with John and Yoko. On her arrival she found a bouquet of flowers from John at the door with the cryptic message: 'Beat you to it, Lil.' It was his caustic way of telling Cynthia's mother he knew she had got home quickly to try to play the role of amateur detective and to try to rock the boat between him and Yoko.

Back in London with Julian, Cynthia also went to Montagu Square. She had been shadowed by John's private detective, for within five minutes of her arrival there was a knock at the door and a solicitor handed her a writ for divorce on the grounds of her alleged adultery.

In the five months that followed before John and Cynthia's eventual divorce, rancour and mistrust ran alongside John's frenzied involvement with Yoko which he never sought to hide. His image with the Beatles' public changed dramatically as he openly courted the woman who was to change his life. The last six months of 1968 were electrifying for him: Yoko became pregnant; they began their artistic activities together; Apple was launched; he met Brigitte Bardot, his teenage idol, in a formally set-up meeting in London's Mayfair Hotel; he was arrested for possessing drugs; and he was divorced. John always loved fast action but this rapid turn of events, combined with the tensions surfacing within the Beatles, pushed him to the limits of his endurance. He leaned increasingly on L.S.D. and drink, usually Scotch.

The run-up to the divorce was complex and often ugly. Cynthia was angry at the speed with which her contact with John was severed. 'One minute I was with him at Weybridge, the next the whole fabric of my life and Julian's was destroyed.' After appointing her own solicitor, she phoned the Beatles' office and said she needed to talk to John.

She arrived at Weybridge with Julian and her mother in tow, probably a psychological blunder considering John's dislike of Mrs Powell. Yoko and John met her looking as one: both all in black, John extremely tense. Cynthia's mother waded in instantly by saying to Yoko: 'I think you should go in the other room and leave these two together.'

John interjected: 'No, Yoko, you stay here.'

Eventually Yoko left of her own volition: she could not stand the tension any longer as John and Cynthia lumbered into a battle neither could win. For fifteen minutes they argued about who had committed adultery. John insisted that Cynthia had done so; Cynthia denied this: 'You're totally unjust in putting me on the spot when you're the one breaking up the marriage.'

John said: 'We'd better get it in the hands of solicitors and get it all sorted out.' Cynthia said *she* was suing for divorce. Cynthia's mother fussed in and out saying her daughter should not be left on her own.

Finally John could stand her no longer: 'This is my house – you get out,' he roared.

In the end John and Cynthia agreed to disagree and to hand the divorce arrangements to their solicitors. Practicality was then re-established amid the thick cigarette smoke that filled the library. John said that as Cynthia was caring for Julian, it would be best if he and Yoko moved out to Montagu Square, and Cynthia, her mother, and Julian moved back into Kenwood. The house swap happened next day.

The lawyers began their work and there followed some attempts by Cynthia, by telephone, to agree the terms of the separation. Her personal savings amounted to a mere £2,500 and she clearly needed provision for her immediate future if she was to maintain Julian. She told John on the phone that it might be better if they agreed all the details privately because lawyers wanted her to 'screw him for hundreds of thousands of pounds'. An irate John roared: 'Look, my last offer to you is seventy-five thousand. What have you done to deserve it? Christ, it's like winning the bloody pools!'

A disastrous attempt at harmonious separation took place next on neutral territory: Paul McCartney's house at 7 Cavendish Avenue, St John's Wood, London. Against her solicitor's advice Cynthia went along to try to agree things with John. But Yoko was there, apologizing for not being able to make English tea, and John's demeanour was still aggressive. Cynthia left in tears, frustrated at her failure to break any ground in talking things over with him.

The lawyers set to work. In August Cynthia filed a counter petition against John, alleging his adultery with Yoko, which their solicitors said they denied. But by 25 October John and Yoko announced that they were expecting a baby the next February. That decided the legalities of the case: Cynthia was granted a decree nisi on 8 November 1968 and a settlement payment to her of £100,000 was agreed. She was granted custody of Julian and John was said in court to have made 'generous and proper provision for Julian'. Additionally she received £2,400 a year for Julian's school fees from a separate trust.

This trust was set up by John for Julian, providing him with £100,000 at the age of twenty-five. He would be the sole beneficiary unless any further children were born to John. When Yoko gave birth to Sean, Julian's entitlement from the trust became £50,000 plus the accrued interest, and Sean's the same.

Emotionally battered, Cynthia withdrew from John's life. Inevitably their paths would cross many times in the future, for John had said he wanted proper access to Julian who was five at the time of the divorce. Cynthia went on to marry Roberto Bassanini, the Italian hotelier from Pesaro. That marriage and another to Liverpool electrical engineer John Twist, ended in divorce. 'I'll always be in love with John Lennon,' says Cynthia. 'We went through some great times and bad times together, but whatever happened he made such an impression on everyone he touched.' The relationship between Cynthia and Yoko was tense. Cynthia was heart-broken in the early days of their break-up. Eventually, however, she accepted that John had met his match. 'It was a meeting of two minds and nobody could fight that,' Cynthia says candidly.

John had changed. Yoko, he said, took him back partly to how he was as a Liverpool rebel: fiercely independent, opinionated, an activist, a champion of causes. 'The Beatles had got rid of all that in me. The Beatles had turned me into a puppet. It was OK, but once we'd made it so big, the fun had gone and so had my own strength. The Beatles, if you must know, sapped me.'

In Yoko Ono he faced a formidable counterpart. 'But when I met her,' he told me later, 'I had to drop everything.' It was 'Goodbye to the boys in the band!' Jealous of her previous lovers, John questioned her closely and repeatedly about the men she had been with in addition to her husbands. And he wanted to know everything, quickly, about the art world from which she sprang into his life.

Her world was populated with dilettantes, artists with great inspiration but little notion of how to communicate. In the parlance of the art world, so few of them 'got it together'. Yoko was not among them. A shrewd communicator whose outlandish conceptual art exhibitions had gained her underground notoriety for originality, she believed firmly that if an artist produced a piece of work and then failed to get it through to the public, 'Then what's the point?' One of her greatest strengths lay in that simple truth: she was, and is, a gifted and thrusting sales person. She never believed that being described as avant-garde or underground meant she should lie fallow and hope the people would discover

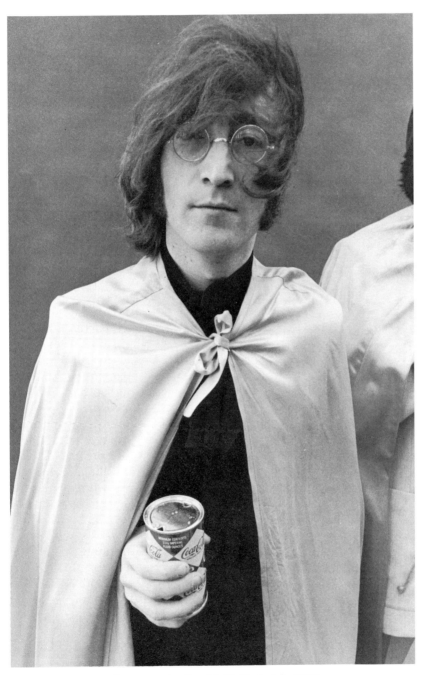

John as seen by Don McCullin in July 1968

her. She believed implicitly in packaging an original product and marketing it with a degree of humour. By 1968 the stage was set for the launch of a partnership that was a perfect foil for her sometimes fanciful ideas and a magic carpet ride for John's submerged personality. Amid the dying embers of the Beatles, the public had to understand just what Lennon meant when he repeatedly wrote of his new world as *JohnandYoko*.

A signing session in Selfridge's in July 1971 to promote Yoko's book, *Grapefruit*. John had written the foreword

2
BEATLES

'I'm breaking the group up'

Yoko Ono – her first name means Ocean Child – was born on 18 February 1933 in Tokyo. Her father Eisuke left Tokyo University with degrees in mathematics and economics. He was a pianist before taking up a banking career and quickly rising to head a Japanese bank in San Francisco. Because of his move from the East in pursuit of his career, he did not meet Yoko until she was two; she had stayed in Japan with her mother.

Yoko's aristocratic mother Isoko came from one of Japan's richest business families, specializing in property investment, insurance, and banking. Yoko grew up in an environment with maids and tutors and a strikingly attractive, slightly aloof, though caring, mother who enjoyed the material things of life like jewellery and good clothes. That may, Yoko believes, account partly for her own eventual adoption of art as her way of life: 'Inside me I could feel a certain rejection of my mother's show of her possessions but I got over that as I grew older,' she says. She coolly points out, however, that she was never the pauper seeking the millionaire pop star: in her life money had never been a problem. Yoko has a brother, Keisuke, three years younger, and a sister, Setsuko, eight years younger.

By the time Yoko was eighteen her father had been appointed president of the Bank of Tokyo in New York and the Ono family had moved from Japan to the high-class suburb of Scarsdale. Yoko attended the prestigious Sarah Lawrence College in New York but dropped out to elope with her first husband, Japanese-born Toshi Ichiyanagi. He proved to be her early partner in the discovery of the world of avant-garde artists. In her loft apartment at 112

Chambers Street, Greenwich Village, Yoko began her lifelong association with art, staging informal events, writing poetry and developing the conceptual theories which marked her out as an artistic radical. For years her work met either derision or a dull local response. 'I *do* know what it is like to be a frustrated artist,' she says with irony. One of her early liaisons was with American jazz musician–film producer Anthony Cox; he linked up with her to encourage her to stage exhibitions of art objects which demanded a response and some input from the observer rather than answering all the questions. Cox became Yoko's second husband and their only child, a daughter, Kyoko, was born on 8 August 1963, four months after John and Cynthia's Lennon's son Julian.

As an ambitious and highly organized partnership, Yoko and Tony Cox had a reputation in Europe in the underground art world for staging uncanny exhibitions. There was, as London art people recall, some kudos to be gained from staging a show planned by a talked-about Japanese woman who lived in New York; thus they arrived for their first trip to London in 1962 if not to rapturous acclaim, then certainly amid considerable curiosity. They came back frequently during the next four years.

London artist Adrian Morris, in whose flat Yoko stayed in 1967 soon after going to London from New York, recalls his first meeting with her at a party off the King's Road. He asked her what kind of artist she was, and she answered: 'I deal with music of the mind.' She had been heavily influenced by the 'extended and repeated image' work of Andy Warhol in New York. As their conversation flowed and Adrian Morris warmed to her, she said she was waiting to move into a flat but there was a complication. Adrian Morris said she and Tony Cox could stay the weekend with him and his wife Audrey at their home at 57 Tedworth Square, Chelsea. Yoko accepted with enthusiasm: the weekend lasted three months. The couples became friends and Adrian Morris attended several of her artistic events.

Yoko had arrived in London with a reputation for having made a film in New York about famous people's bottoms. She decided to repeat and extend the movie, called *Four Square*, in London, this time using 365 people's bottoms.

'I enjoyed their company and I was broadly sympathetic to what they were doing,' says Morris. He saw Yoko at London's Roundhouse, then a base for embryonic artists. She was performing a 'Word Piece', throwing a word into the audience and asking them to respond. Morris was intrigued by her determination and surrealist humour.

A day at London Zoo with the two couples joined by four-year-old Kyoko who was staying elsewhere with friends, turned into humour when Yoko asked someone to take her photograph alongside the bottoms of the baboons. 'Yoko,' Morris says tellingly, 'was always aware of what she was doing, observing and always profound. Once I came home to my house and, walking towards the kitchen from the back garden, I saw her listening to a clock with a stethoscope. She was running an exhibition at the time called *Time Piece*. Photographers were taking pictures of her and I then realized she was unique.' The kitchen was the scene of a favourite Yoko activity: cooking steamed mackerel on a bed of beanshoots, a dish that impressed everyone.

Yoko's marriage to Tony Cox was fraught with tension. Adrian and Audrey Morris were not surprised when Yoko told them privately that she was 'hung up on this guy', who later turned out to be John Lennon. Soon after Yoko had told her friends she was 'miserable out of this guy's company', the newspapers were full of their liaison and her split from Tony was inevitable.

Although the Morrises recognized her talent as an artist working in a difficult field, they were equally impressed by her business acumen. 'She was clearly an entrepreneur and absolutely brilliant at working things out,' says Adrian. 'One day in the kitchen, I playfully patted her on the head during a conversation and called her Little Yoko. I vividly remember her response: "You say *little* Yoko," she said. "But I have a *universe* in my head." '

While John's relationship with Yoko deepened, leading eventually to the break-up of his marriage, the Beatles loomed as a parallel crisis. With Brian Epstein dead and the meditation honeymoon over, the Beatles decided to grasp the business nettle. They launched the Apple organization, first as a boutique and then as a record label and management company. John was never quite as confident as Paul or George in the utopian hope that Apple would be a freewheeling 'umbrella for new talent'. But he accepted that there was an urgent and immediate need to do something about the management of their affairs. With Epstein gone, John felt that not even a tenuous link remained with NEMS Enterprises, now run by Brian's affable brother Clive. Apple, set up in London at 95 Wigmore Street, with a boutique at 94 Baker Street and later with offices at 3 Savile Row, was intended to be both philanthropic and efficient in handling the Beatles' business affairs. It was originally conceived to invest in new talent in music, electronics, films,

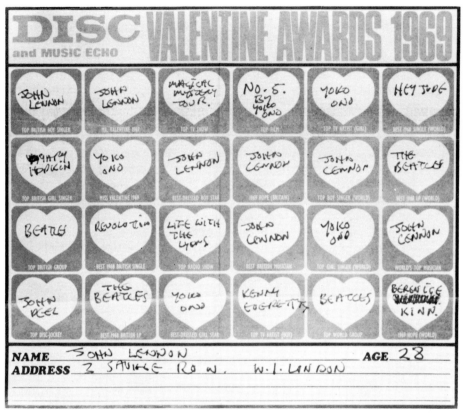

John was a compulsive filler-in of forms and sent this Yoko-laden handwritten voting coupon to *Disc and Music Echo* for its Valentine Day Awards in 1969: in the Top Radio Show section he votes for one of his favourite childhood programmes, *Life With The Lyons*; and in the '1969 Hope' category he names Berenice Kinn, wife of the founder of the *New Musical Express*

publishing, retailing, and records. 'Those were the days, my friend, I thought they'd never end,' sang sweet-voiced Mary Hopkin on her number one hit for Apple Records, produced by Paul McCartney. But they *did* end and quickly. Apple was doomed. And with John feverishly re-shaping his life and his attitude around Yoko and art, so were the Beatles.

Lifestyles and aspirations were at the root of the quarrel that erupted between John and Paul, eventually causing John, who had never been content with his achievements with the group, to inform the Beatles he was leaving. Despite the fact that he was high on drugs in 1967 and 1968, he characteristically remained, throughout his life, exceptionally clear-headed whenever business was called for and hard decisions were needed.

The rift with Paul dated back to McCartney's assumption of the leadership of the Beatles when Epstein died. It was Paul who concocted the ill-fated *Magical Mystery Tour* T.V. film. The Beatles' first real failure, it was never screened in America. It had a threadbare plot which consisted of a busload of Beatles and others travelling around the West Country as a kind of circus act. The songs were weak and decidedly McCartney-ish. John loathed the whole affair. He was angry at the cost – £75,000 for what he derisively called 'the most expensive home movie ever'. It came, also, right at the time when John was becoming intrigued with Yoko. The *Magical Mystery Tour* was McCartney's attempt to have the Beatles continue just as before, only under his aegis. With Epstein – who had considered Paul the most truculent Beatle – now dead, and with John's attention diverted, the stage was set for Paul to assert himself as king pin.

John, however, was not prepared to sit back and be ordered about. McCartney also underestimated John's dedication to Yoko and his boredom with the Beatles. The two of them had launched Apple in America, at a press conference at New York's Americana Hotel and on nationwide television on the *Tonight* show. John had fainted on the plane *en route* to New York, a victim of too many late nights, too much dope and not enough food. He arrived in New York with a plaster on his cut chin but he was in fine form, taking the chance to scorn the Maharishi publicly as well as to boost the Apple idea and prop up the Beatles' declining popularity in America.

It had taken a beating when they went to India and *Sgt Pepper*, released the previous summer, had made little impact with the millions of screaming fans in America: it was too far from 'She Loves You' and the Beatles most Americans loved. It was, however, a giant hit with the more discerning listeners, staying at number one for fifteen consecutive weeks and half a year in the top three.

When the job of publicizing Apple had to be done, John was semi-serious. 'We've decided to sell India and buy the Garden of Eden,' he said. As for the Maharishi, 'We thought he was God,' said John. 'I told him not to go on tour with the Beach Boys,' he jibed at the Maharishi's pretence to showmanship.

The entire American trip was an anathema to John. He was a lousy hypocrite. Privately he knew the Beatles were doomed. His polarization from Paul was accelerated by McCartney's acceptance of the show business embrace. However talented he was as a songwriter, Paul was, in John's view, content to continue churning out more of the same. The massive acclaim for 'Yesterday', the all-McCartney classic, had gone to Paul's head, John decided. The Beatles, Paul's bossiness, Apple – the whole package was stultifying to John, more than even he would admit. For the sake of unity he kept the peace for a few months to give himself time to develop his relationship with Yoko.

But soon that too became a vital issue. The other Beatles treated her shabbily and provocatively. In the Abbey Road studios during the summer of 1968, the Beatles were recording the 'White Album'. (The album was officially titled *The Beatles* but because of its all-white cover, and for easier identification, it became known colloquially around the world as the 'White Album'.) It consisted mainly of songs they had written in India including 'Yer Blues', 'Sexy Sadie' and 'The Continuing Story Of Bungalow Bill'. John broke a rigid, unwritten rule of the group: that their women would never be allowed in the studios. Getting inside a Beatles recording session was hard even for the accredited inner circle – Brian Epstein and song publisher Dick James were often invited to stay away and judge the *results* rather than see the group fiddling for hours with an embryonic song. John perversely attended every session for the 'White Album' with Yoko at his side. His message, unspoken, was obvious to all: they were inseparable. She sat on the speakers, offering suggestions and, incredibly, criticisms.

Their chauvinist pique apart, George, Paul, and Ringo were in a sticky situation in their resentment of Yoko's arrival. John, the leader and genius, was obviously changing even more tangibly than they had realized if he brought this peculiar Japanese artist so deeply into his life that she was even allowed to sing on one of his compositions ('Bungalow Bill') and help on another song, 'Revolution 9'. What flabbergasted them was John allowing Yoko to

comment on the Beatles' work. Only the four of them, plus George
Martin, had ever been allowed that privilege. But they might have
guessed his seriousness when he sang on 'Julia', the song about his
mother: 'Ocean child calls me', his first recorded reference to
Yoko's letters to him in India.

George Martin was unconvinced of the merits of enough of the
songs to justify putting it out as a double album but John loved the
record's individualism and persuaded him. The album remained
John's favourite Beatles work because it demonstrated the development of personalities rather than the Beatles as an entity, of
which by 1968 he had become tired.

With her thick, cascading black hair and unsmiling demeanour,
Yoko was also destined for a difficult time at the Apple offices,
where she and John held court in their own ground-floor office
overlooking Savile Row. At Apple, where she usually dressed in
white and exchanged ideas with a beleaguered staff coping with a
daily invasion of artists, wayfarers, and good causes wanting
money and the Beatle seal of approval, Yoko was treated with
disdain. George, Paul, and Ringo, particularly, did not give her the
warmth and fair reception she deserved, both as their leader's
new woman and as an artist. 'I'll never forgive them,' John
said later. 'They were bastards to Yoko and they knew it mattered
to me.

John naturally regarded the coolness towards Yoko as an insult
to himself. How, he reasoned, could people applaud him as a force
for good and as a fine artist while condemning his choice of
woman? He could not be great and dumb at the same time. When
Yoko's increased melodicism on *Double Fantasy* was noted by
reviewers in 1980, John was thrilled that at last she appeared to be
getting recognition. She had always been ahead of her time. 'I've
had two partners in my life, Paul McCartney and Yoko. That's not
a bad record, is it?' he once said to me.

In 1968 and 1969, the most important years of his life, John had
few friends, inside or outside the Beatles family. 'Yes, it was hard,'
recalls Yoko, 'but he and I had no doubt we would get through.
John's excitement at doing things together with me as an artist was
so obvious that he didn't have that much time to get upset about
what people were thinking, you know.'

The relationship was too important for both of them for any
opposition to dissuade them: 'We both think alike,' said John.
'We've both been alone. And we seem to have had the same kind
of dreams when we *were* alone. I can see now that I always
dreamed of a woman like this one coming into my life. You can't

go out *looking* for this kind of relationship. It's like somebody was planning it from above.'

While relationships with George, Paul, and Ringo simmered, with George as always the one with the best rapport with John in his new life, John and Yoko boldly stepped out in public to emphasize their togetherness, artistically and as man and woman. By now he was parting his hair in the centre to match Yoko's style and they both invariably dressed in all-white suits.

Their first 'event' in June 1968 fuelled the cynics' view that John had gone crazy. As part of the National Sculpture Exhibition John and Yoko decided to plant two acorns, one facing east, the other facing west, in the grounds of Coventry Cathedral. The idea, which was John's, was to symbolize the meeting of John and Yoko as two different cultures, and the phrase 'Plant an acorn for peace', coined by John, was to accompany the event.

The couple were driven from London in John's Rolls-Royce for the 100-mile trip to Coventry, where the event attracted only minor interest, considering it was an activity by a Beatle. The acorns were duly planted, the media scoffed and Beatles fans everywhere knew that whatever John Lennon was now up to, he meant it. The planting of acorns in the cathedral precincts – disallowed on consecrated ground lest the Church should be seen to condone the couple's liaison – was of great significance to John, more so than to Yoko. It marked his concentration on art and his first conscious proclamation of peace.

In contrast, John and Yoko's second public outing in the same month faced the full glare of national publicity. Word spread to a gleeful newspaper world that John's marriage was on the rocks and he was living with Yoko at 34 Montagu Square, London W.1. The couple were pursued by photographers twenty-four hours a day: a married Beatle escorting an unknown Japanese artist/actress had strong news value. But the couple faced the music, going hand in hand to the opening of the play *In His Own Write*. Photographers shouted: 'Where's your wife then, John?'

Angrily but firmly he retorted: 'I don't know.'

The play was directed by John's old friend from the films *A Hard Day's Night* and *Help!*, actor Victor Spinetti. When Victor phoned John with an idea from an American girl, Adrian Kennedy, that Lennon books be converted into a play, John burst into laughter. 'They must be fucking mad!' he screamed down the phone. But then he quickly added that he always thought that *he* was mad until he came across a word called surrealism and had thought: 'Oh, that's what I am, I'm a *surrealist*.' When Spinetti brought the conversation back to earth John readily agreed to grant him the theatrical rights.

They began working on the adaptation and John and Yoko attended a meeting with Sir Laurence Olivier, who ran the Old Vic, then the home of the National Theatre where the play was to be staged. During the meeting Sir Laurence told John that when the play went ahead, they might be faced with other business decisions, such as film and record rights. Lennon, sitting next to the white-hatted Yoko and looking like a bored hippie, suddenly stunned the assembled company. In a mildly peremptory manner he said slowly to Sir Laurence: 'Don't you have people that you pay to talk about these kind of things who can talk to the people that I pay to talk about these kind of things?'

Spinetti had immediate proof of the speed of Lennon's thought. He had asked John for a Queen's speech for one sequence in his adaptation. 'Without thinking,' says Victor, 'and instantly, he took hold of a piece of cardboard used to keep a new shirt firmly in place, and started writing:

One second's pause. . . .
'My housebound and eyeball take pressure in denouncing his ship. . . .'

Spinetti points out that although John often said he had no knowledge of Chaucer, his instinct was distinctly Chaucerian, and the word 'housebound' was a variant of 'husband' in Middle English. John, however, was adamant that the expression was his own.

John and Yoko's child was expected in February 1969, but in November 1968 Yoko was rushed to Queen Charlotte's Hospital, Hammersmith where she suffered a painful miscarriage. She was thirty-five, and the nursing staff said she might have expected problems. John insisted on staying in a spare bed alongside her and when that was no longer acceptable to the hospital he slept on the floor.

Although he had officially given up smoking during that period, Lennon persuaded Victor Spinetti to pop in at eight-thirty each morning 'before the crowds arrive' and sneak him a packet of twenty Players Gold Leaf. 'He looked truly awful,' recalls Spinetti. 'I said to him: "Which one of you had the miscarriage?" ' The loss of the child had a traumatic effect on John and, coming on top of

all the other dilemmas that clouded his love of Yoko, he became
nervous, edgy and less happy than ever with his role as a public
Beatle.

That autumn developed into a harrowing period for John. The
one problem he did not expect to face was a drugs charge. For
some five years various pop stars had been closely associated with
the use of cannabis but so far the 'Holy Beatles' had escaped the
law. Anyone talking to them was aware that they smoked pot and
in the pop world it was commonplace. But now the public view of
the Beatles, and particularly John Lennon, was not so cosy. To be
ensconced with a crazy Japanese actress who made a film about
bottoms was bad enough. To be *en route* to the divorce court,
having planted acorns for peace and having embraced and subsequently rejected the Maharishi and meditation, condemned John
to public scorn.

John and Yoko were in bed at the Montagu Square flat when
police with Alsatian sniffer dogs hammered on the door. John,
shocked and confused by this rough awakening, did not open the
door immediately. He phoned solicitor Nicholas Cowan, the
partner of David Jacobs, who was representing Brian Epstein's
estate and doing other work for the Beatles. 'John said there were
a number of people outside the flat who said they had a search
warrant and were threatening to break the door down,' says
Cowan. By the time Cowan arrived half a dozen police and a dog
were inside the flat. The police made a quick and thorough search
of the premises. 'The basement was full of recording equipment,'
says Cowan, 'all of which appeared to have been on for some time
and the temperature was extremely high. In one room there was a
large trunk full of clothes in which the dog was showing interest. A
search of the trunk revealed a small piece of hash. John and Yoko
were asked to go to Marylebone police station where they were
formally charged and fingerprinted in my presence.'

A cuddly Beatle no more, Lennon's anguish showed on his face
in the days that followed. A Beatle being busted for dope was big
news; journalists besieged the police station and John and Yoko
were given facilities to leave by the police headquarters back door.
They lay low for the night at Nicholas Cowan's home in Redcliffe
Road, Fulham. Next day their case was adjourned for six weeks.

When the court case finally came up, John pleaded guilty to a
charge of unauthorized possession of 219 grains of cannabis. He
was fined £150 with 20 guineas costs. John and Yoko were found
not guilty of obstructing the police in execution of a search
warrant. It was a terrifying episode, John confessed later. He was

always convinced that the bust was a 'set-up'. Don Short of the *Daily Mirror* had warned him three weeks previously that the police were on their way, so John said he had 'cleaned the place up, especially as I knew Jimi Hendrix had this flat before Ringo and me'. He maintained that the dope had been planted in the trunk, a spot in which he would never have tried to hide it. 'It was a frame-up. I guess they didn't like the way the image was looking. The Beatles thing was over. No reason to protect us for being soft and cuddly any more – so bust us! That's what happened.'

The drugs conviction in itself did not concern him but he was well aware of the problems it might cause if he wanted to visit America. Musicians lived in dread of being busted because American immigration authorities were so hot about it. But even John did not realize during that heady period, that the straight conviction for possession of pot would so painfully affect his future. At the time, however, there were enough pressures to divert him. He could handle his own change of identity perfectly well: his metamorphosis from hit-making pop star to thinking artist, and his publicly declared love for a ridiculed avant-garde artist, were things he revelled in. He loved taking on the public at the game of 'Who is Lennon?' What he found exhausting was the continuing problem of Apple and the Beatles.

By the summer of 1968 Apple Music, the Apple boutique, Apple Films, and Apple Electronics had not made a film, sold a single invention or opened shops outside London. When the Baker Street boutique closed, thousands of pounds' worth of clothes were given away to the public in an astonishing – and unbusinesslike – gesture of largesse. What Apple *had* done was spend £1 million of Beatles money, which had been frittered away on overstaffing, extravagant salaries, and an endless supply of alcohol for visitors.

Apple, beautifully described as 'the longest cocktail party' by one of its employees, Richard DiLello, in a hilarious book on the episode, was great fun. It was also cripplingly expensive and not functioning well. In its earliest days, with visitors like Peter Sellers, Harry Nilsson, Twiggy, and Kenny Everett, John enjoyed the fantasy of playing host to the world's artists. He also grew to believe more in Apple's philanthropy. But it surprised some who believed him to be the dopey Beatle, the druggy one, the one hopelessly diverted by Yokoism, that he became the first to say, effectively, 'enough is enough'. At the time John decided to sound the warning shots Apple was costing the Beatles £50,000 a week.

During an interview with me in January 1969 for the pop weekly *Disc and Music Echo* I asked John if he was happy with the

Top: In December 1968, a month after his divorce from Cynthia, John took Julian and Yoko to Wembley Television Studios for the filming of the Rolling Stones TV documentary *Rock And Roll Circus*. The show also featured Eric Clapton, the Rolling Stones and The Who, but it became entangled in legal and artistic problems and was never shown

Above: John shields Yoko, a week after her miscarriage, as they both leave Marylebone Magistrates Court in November 1968, surrounded by police. John's conviction for possession of cannabis was to cause him big problems four years later in the U.S.

way Apple was shaping. He answered: 'No, not really. I think it's a bit messy and it wants tightening up. We haven't got half the money people think we have. We have enough to live on but we can't let Apple go on like it is. We started off with loads of ideas of what we wanted to do – an umbrella for different activities. But like one or two Beatle things, it didn't work because we aren't practical and we weren't quick enough to realize that we need a businessman's brain to run the whole thing.

'You can't offer facilities to poets and charities and film makers unless you have money definitely coming in. It's been pie-in-the-sky from the start. . . . We did it all wrong – you know, Paul and me running to New York saying we'll do this and encourage this and that. It's got to be a business first; we realize that now.

'It needs a new broom and a lot of people there will have to go. . . . It doesn't need to make vast profits but if it carries on like this all of us will be broke in the next six months.' (Typically Lennon did show the accounts to someone right at the top – Lord Beeching. After studying the books he gave Lennon terse but sound advice: 'Go back to music!')

I asked whether he and the Beatles missed Brian Epstein's guidance. 'Sure we miss him,' John replied. 'His death was a loss. That's probably what's the matter with Apple or the Beatles at the moment – Brian's death left us on our own. He handled the business and we find it hard to.'

Lennon's outburst rocked Savile Row and reverberated around the world as international newspapers, television, and radio picked up on the confession by a Beatle that they had made a colossal mistake and might go broke. The Beatles had no more desire to be shopkeepers, John told me, than to become rock 'n' roll museum pieces and part of the showbiz Establishment. It was time for them to own up. The interview confirmed the unpleasant truth that nobody had wanted to face since the disastrous *Magical Mystery Tour* and optimistic founding of Apple: the Beatles, as an operating company, was in an appalling mess. While the fans were shocked, the media had a field day. It also brought the uneasy relationship between John and Paul to breaking-point.

A week after my interview with John I visited Apple to see him again. Coming out of John's office I met the heavily bearded McCartney. He was furious with my decision to publish John's comments. 'What did you want to go and use all that for?' he snapped. 'You know this is a small and young company, just trying to get along. And you know John always shoots his mouth off. It's not that bad. We've got a few problems but they'll be sorted out. I'm surprised it was you – we thought we had a few friends in the Press we could trust.'

Paul was suggesting that John's remarks should have been considered as 'off the record'. Like many writers who had been close to the Beatles from the start, I had used discretion when secrets were either unimportant to the public or impolitic to reveal for the sake of the Beatles or their families. But on this occasion Lennon talking about Apple's looming disaster for the first time was manifestly an on-the-record interview. John knew it would be used and that it would be big news: he was an avid media freak, he knew the value of a quote and always said what he wanted, on reflection, to be left out of any interview. The day he spoke he was as clear-minded as he had ever been. Thus began the long, bitter battle between John and Paul. A few weeks later I saw John again and he did not mention his explosive comments on Apple. Had he regretted them or their ramifications he would certainly have told me. For Apple, and the Beatles, the end was in sight.

The musical rapport between them had long gone as well as the accord. But before the end they had a commitment to fulfil: to complete their third film, *Let It Be*, which was to show their album being made. The four, with Yoko, shuffled desultorily into Twickenham Film Studios in early January 1969 to undertake the multi-media project. The internal bickering and antipathy can be seen in the finished film. Ironically it also shows them performing much of their early Hamburg/Liverpool repertoire, joyously together, and revelling in the therapeutic qualities of the music. It was a painful, if evocative affair, in particular the twenty-minute session on the roof at Apple. John's words to the crowd spoke the Beatles' epitaph as poetically as we had come to expect from him: 'I'd like to say thank you on behalf of the group and ourselves . . . and I hope we passed the audition.' It had been a long journey from Liverpool Cavern but for John, life was just beginning.

By now the Beatles were virtually dead as far as he was concerned. Paul, who had steadfastly been arriving at Apple each morning at ten o'clock (often travelling in from his home in St John's Wood by bus), did not realize how serious John was about quitting the Beatles. It wasn't simply a question of his utter absorption with Yoko. It was the growing mental distance between him and Paul. Apple Records' first number one hit, and one of the Beatles' greatest single successes, had been 'Hey Jude', a song which Paul wrote during John's separation from Cynthia and composed partly on his way to Weybridge to comfort Cynthia on the breakdown of the marriage. Paul later admitted that John had helped him decide on some lyrics for the song, particularly Paul's line which John loved best, 'The movement you need is on your shoulder.' John had reluctantly agreed to it being the major side of the record, rather than his own song, 'Revolution', which became the B-side.

Commercially there was no choice. But it emphasized finally to him the different directions he and Paul were taking. While Paul was still composing beautiful melodies and writing of love, John's words tilted at the student revolutions in Europe during 1968.

> But if you want money for people with minds that hate
> All I can tell you is brother, you have to wait.
> But if you go carrying pictures of Chairman Mao
> You ain't gonna make it with anyone, anyhow.

John simply believed that his new rock 'n' roll should have his mind and his message in the music. The old Chuck Berry and Little Richard rave-ups would always be his roots but mentally he was moving quickly and his profound new music had to accommodate the change in him. Paul, intimidated by Yoko's presence, felt that every time he was in John's company and making music, he ought to be producing something avant-garde. It was not in his nature. The split was inevitable and acrimonious.

John broke the news of the break-up of the Beatles in his usual rapier-like style. Paul remembers a meeting at Savile Row in which all the Beatles sat stonily discussing business. 'The group was getting very tense,' says Paul. 'It was looking like we were breaking up.

'One day we came in, had a meeting, all Apple business, and it was getting very hairy and nobody was really enjoying themselves. We had forgotten the music bit; it was just business. I said: "I think we should get back on the road, small band, go and do the clubs, sod it. Let's get back to square one and remember what we're all about." McCartney suggested several other projects which he thought would be the only thing to occupy the group's creativity to the full and hold them together: a concert – no ordinary show but the Beatles playing a Roman amphitheatre in North Africa; or the Beatles as a house band on a round-the-world cruise. John would have none of it.

'John's actual words were: "I think you're daft. I wasn't going to tell you but I'm breaking the group up. It feels good. It feels like a divorce." And he just sat there. And our jaws dropped. And that

John and Yoko outside their new home, Tittenhurst Park, Ascot, Berkshire, in September 1969, a month after moving in

was it. No one quite knew what to say. Then after that we thought we should give it a couple of months. It was a big act to break up just like that. We talked for a couple of months but it was never going to be on. Looking back, it was largely that John needed a new direction that he went into headlong, helter skelter. He went right in there and did all sorts of stuff he had never done before – with Yoko. And you can't blame him because he was that kind of guy. He wanted to live life, do stuff and there was no holding back with John. And it was what we all admired him for. So we couldn't really say: "Oh we don't want you to do that, John. Stay with us." You'd feel so wimpy. It *had* to happen.'

What was remarkable about John and Yoko's frenzied activities together is that they managed to do so much despite the business problems of 1968, 1969, and 1970. Between John's divorce, Yoko's miscarriage, the drugs bust and the bickering between the Beatles and worry over Apple, John and Yoko released their first album and continued their assault on a now punch-drunk public by appearing in a large white bag on stage at the Royal Albert Hall, London. This was an event called the Alchemical Wedding, the underground art movement's Christmas party.

The move that was to shake the foundations of John's most ardent supporters was the release of their début album. *Unfinished Music No.1: Two Virgins*, a collection of bizarre sounds and effects, the result of their first collaboration that night in Weybridge when Cynthia was away, was neither surprising nor important musically. It was their decision to have themselves photographed nude on the front and back of the album sleeve, however, that convinced Lennon's detractors – and many of his supporters – that he had now indeed gone insane.

The pictures were taken by John with an automatic camera. The *Two Virgins* concept was his: Yoko was 'terribly embarrassed' by it. Any theory that it was a continuation of her film theme of people's bottoms was absurd, she says. 'We were both very shy about it, really,' she recalls. 'But John had the original idea. He thought it suited what we were doing at the time.' In those days nudity on the London theatre stage in the show *Hair* was making front-page news. John, who told me eventually that he was 'testing people's reactions, and it was mostly bad', enjoyed extending his and Yoko's audacity as far as he dare.

The nude pictures caused an immediate censorship problem. Apple Records were distributed through the Beatles' original record company, E.M.I., whose chairman at the time was Sir Joseph Lockwood. He remembers the Beatles arriving for lunch at his official dining-room in Manchester Square, a few weeks before the problem with the nude pictures arose. 'When the four boys came they had with them this person all in white, surrounded by hair, and I couldn't see anything. I wasn't sure if it was a human being or an animal. John Lennon introduced her to me: "This is my secretary," he said. After the lunch, he told me she had tape-recorded everything we had said. It was a business meeting. John was pretty clued up on everything that was going on.'

Sir Joseph's meeting with John and Yoko a few weeks later was more pointed. They arrived at his office with the nude pictures which they wanted releasing by E.M.I./Apple for their *Two Virgins* sleeve. Paul McCartney went with them to act as diplomat. 'He didn't want any row,' says Sir Joseph. 'At that time he was very anxious to prevent a falling-out with E.M.I.'

As he looked at the picture Sir Joseph was asked by John: 'Well, aren't you shocked?'

The E.M.I. chief said: 'No, I've seen worse than this.'

John weighed in quickly: 'So it's all right then, is it?'

'No, it's not all right,' said Sir Joseph. 'I'm not worried about the rich people, the duchesses and those people who follow you. But your mums and dads and girl fans will object strongly. You will be damaged and what will you gain? What's the purpose of it?'

Yoko said: 'It's art.'

Sir Joseph answered sharply: 'Well, I should find some better bodies to put on the cover than your two. They're not very attractive. Paul McCartney would look better naked than you.'

Sir Joseph recalls: 'It didn't go down too badly, except that poor old Paul McCartney blushed. We went on and on for a long time. They wouldn't give way. They were pressing and pressing.

'Paul McCartney was not in favour of it, I'm sure. He just wanted to prevent me from blowing up with them, which I had no intention of doing.'

Finally Sir Joseph established a perfect British compromise. E.M.I. would press the album but Apple would have to distribute it themselves. E.M.I. would have nothing to do with the actual sale of *Two Virgins*. John reluctantly agreed and Paul, whose great commercial future was bound up with E.M.I., breathed a sigh of relief. Sir Joseph, who regarded John as the most talented Beatle, even if Paul was the most commercial, felt vindicated when thousands of exported copies of *Two Virgins* were impounded by customs men and eventually confiscated. The record was a critical and commercial failure both in Britain and America but John felt it was 'a statement'.

On 12 March 1969 Paul McCartney married New York photographer Linda Eastman in London. No other Beatle was invited to the wedding.

Paul's choice of bride had a marked effect on the cauldron that was by then the Beatles' business empire. John and Yoko, on the advice of Mick Jagger, had decided that a fast-talking American show business lawyer, Allen Klein, should be hired to weed out the chaos at Apple. George and Ringo went along with the Lennon line, eventually signing a business management contract with Klein, who convinced John that he could streamline Apple and negotiate better record deals for the Beatles. Paul flatly refused to become involved, but was outvoted at a board meeting by three to one. Klein was in. Paul had wanted his new father-in-law, widely respected American entertainment lawyer Lee Eastman, to handle his affairs, and he went ahead and appointed him to manage his personal business concerns. The stage was set for the rift to become even wider.

Klein, whose openly stated ambition was to manage the Beatles, had flown to London immediately he heard of John's interview with me in which he laid bare the Apple financial quandary. All his life, Klein, the New Jersey orphan who had clawed his way through the pop jungle, wanted the 'fabulous Beedles'. Once in Britain, through Jagger, he quickly met John Lennon who told him that he did not 'want to end up broke like Mickey Rooney'.

The American went about his work with savage determination, alienating Sir Joseph Lockwood at E.M.I. with his foul-mouthed demands – on one occasion Sir Joseph ordered him out of the building – and encountering stubborn resistance from McCartney. Paul's tactic was simply to stay away from the Apple he had so conscientiously nurtured. Len Wood, managing director of E.M.I., noticed that John had confidence in Klein during their meetings together; even when letters with major proposals for an Apple takeover came in and Klein wanted John's views, Lennon waved him away saying it was his job to deal with them. Allen was visibly thrilled at such a vote of confidence.

By mid-1969 the only question unanswered about the Beatles' future was how the group could split formally. John simply didn't care. He was off and running with Yoko. As far as he was concerned he'd served notice on Paul, George, and Ringo and Klein could hammer out the details with Lee Eastman.

The Plastic Ono Band had utterly eclipsed the Beatles in John's affections. Its appeal lay in its spontaneity: in September 1969 John and Yoko had been asked to appear at a rock concert in

Toronto and Lennon actually did what McCartney had urged the Beatles to do – get back on the road as a small band. Instead of talking about it, John got a band together, literally overnight. Eric Clapton recalls a phone call from John twenty-four hours before the show: 'He said: "We're doing this concert in Toronto. Why don't you come over with us?" ' Eric, thinking it would be fun, agreed and bass player Klaus Voormann, John's old friend from Hamburg, joined in. They rehearsed old rock 'n' roll songs on the plane on the way over. The music on stage, though scrappy, had a raw quality John liked. On the plane he had told Clapton and Voormann that the Beatles were finished.

On his return I asked John about the Plastic Ono Band, the Beatles and his current attitude to Paul. Was the Plastic Ono Band more crucial to him than the Beatles? 'Neither more important nor less,' he said. 'Sometimes the Plastic Ono Band sessions are a drag, sometimes great. Sessions with the Beatles likewise. Just meself and a tape recorder can be good, sometimes it's boring. I like *change*.' Were the Beatles split? I asked. 'We're going through changes, sure. The thing is – we change in public. It's a menopause or something like that.'

When had he last seen Paul? 'About two months ago. I keep meaning to go and see him. We write a lot – postcards to each other. I see Ringo and George every other day because they're here at Apple but Paul hasn't been here for ages. I want to ask him why.' It was an astonishing turnaround in the pair's behaviour: Paul had until this period been the determined executive, always keen on discovering and nurturing new talent like Mary Hopkin. John was not so keen on talent-hunting: he was too busy discovering himself.

Drastic change was affecting John, privately and professionally. With Allen Klein at the helm in Apple he was back in a buoyant mood, despite the rift with Paul. 'It's going to be great here at Apple,' he said as their record successes increased. He was trying to boost his confidence in Klein. But yet another business crisis hit him badly.

Dick James, the friendly, enthusiastic song publisher who was managing director of Northern Songs, which owned the copyright to nearly all the Lennon–McCartney songs, had been wooed for several months by Sir Lew Grade, then chairman of A.T.V., who wanted to take over the valuable Beatles song catalogue. With a vision that the songs would earn money for the copyright holders well into the twenty-first century and probably until the end of time, Grade repeatedly offered James a great deal of money but one man alone could not decide to sell about 200 songs that dated back to their earliest hits such as 'From Me To You', 'She Loves You' and 'I Want To Hold Your Hand' and went through to their now huge selling album titles. 'When Brian Epstein died and the Beatles were visibly torn asunder, Grade began romancing me,' recalls Dick James. 'In old money the shares for Northern were marketing at seven shillings and ninepence at the start and fourteen shillings and sixpence when Brian died. Lew's final offer was thirty-five shillings a share, so the financial gain to everyone, including John and Paul, was very considerable.' James put Grade's offer to the board of Northern Songs, who represented more than 3,000 outside shareholders. The decision was unanimous: accept the offer, which would bring in £10 million in cash.

Dick James' theory was that he was doing the Beatles, and John and Paul as the major songwriters, a favour. Northern Songs was, he believed, very vulnerable to all kinds of City takeovers and with the Beatles at loggerheads they would suffer badly if different factions in the City pulled it to pieces. Better, he thought, to sell to A.T.V. where at least it would be under the roof of a serious, stable music publishing house. 'The protection the Beatles' songs could have within the framework of a much larger company like A.T.V., as has been proven, was much safer. When A.T.V. took it over the wolves stopped baying. It would have been wrong to sell Northern Songs to John or Paul individually and with Allen Klein and Lee Eastman representing them each, they could hardly buy it jointly at that stage.'

John was furious at what he considered a betrayal of his interests without giving him any options. At a meeting at Paul's house, Lennon tore into James. 'I tried to point out to John that his capital gain was at the lowest rate of tax paid anywhere in the world, as opposed to his tax from record sales which were subject to ordinary income tax,' says James. But John was inconsolable. Paul was annoyed but John, says Dick James, was 'hurt and I was very sorry, and Yoko was annoyed'.

Finally, after a tense meeting James tried to win John over. He told Lennon about the huge lump sum coming his way from the sale: 'Well, John, at least this means you can put some money by for your children.'

John's cynical retort ended any cosiness: 'I have no desire to create another fucking aristocracy,' he said bitterly.

Relations between John and Paul began to decline swiftly after John left the group. And although it had been John who made the break, it was a public relations tactic by Paul that broke the news to the world. With his first solo album, called *McCartney*, he issued a press release with forty-one questions and answers which left the world's media in no doubt that Paul was out of the group. It contained barbed references to his non-association with the Beatles. Issued in question-and-answer form, part of the text ran:

Did you enjoy working as a solo?

Very much. I only had me to ask for a decision and I agreed with me.

Is this album a rest away from the Beatles or the start of a solo career?

Time will tell. . . .

Is your break with the Beatles, temporary or permanent, due to personal differences or musical ones?

Personal differences. Business differences. Musical differences. But most of all because I have a better time with my family. Temporary or permanent? I don't know.

Is it true that neither Allen Klein nor ABCKO (his company) have been or will be in any way involved in the production, manufacturing, distribution or promotion of this new album?

Not if I can help it.

Lennon was furious at what appeared a pre-emptive strike by McCartney to gain the momentum and wrest the decision-making role from him. Paul's dislike of Yoko was one thing: to upstage him by causing the world to surmise that Paul was the one taking the initiative was another. John reacted with a beautifully laconic piece of venom: by telephone he told me for an article I wrote: 'I received a phone call from Paul last Thursday afternoon. He said: "I'm going to leave the Beatles as well." I was happy to hear from Paul. It was nice to find that he was still alive.

'Anyway, Paul hasn't left. I sacked him.'

The sour relationship with Paul continued right up until John and Yoko left to settle in America in 1971. John and Yoko and their newly named Plastic Ono Band had taken flight in a surge of activity that camouflaged the McCartney situation, from the public at least. But when Paul usurped him by releasing the press statement, John was livid. The two men had little contact but newspaper conjecture carried on. McCartney again ended the world's speculation with a letter to the *Melody Maker* on 29 August 1970:

> In order to put out of its misery the limping dog of a news story which has been dragging itself across your pages for the past year, my answer to the question: 'Will the Beatles get together again?' is no.
>
>   Paul McCartney

By the end of 1970 Paul McCartney began proceedings in the High Court to wind up the Beatles partnership. Even against the background of bickering it was a difficult decision: he made it during a sojourn with Linda at his farm in Campbeltown, Argyllshire. 'It's not easy being in a top job one second and the next someone says: "Well, we're breaking the group up." And you haven't got a job. It screwed my head for years,' he says. As for the questions that persisted about a reunion: 'It's like asking a divorced couple: Are you getting back together? . . . when you can't stand to look at each other.' It was agony, 'suing my best mates and being *seen* to sue my best mates. That was the worst.' The Beatles were formally ended as a performing group in the High Court on 12 March 1971 and a receiver appointed to look after their business interests. The Beatles continued only as a business name.

On a personal level the wrangles continued and began to manifest themselves in Paul and John's music. Four months before John left for America in September 1971 Paul released a solo album made with Linda McCartney, *Ram*. Two songs in particular, 'Too Many People (Going Underground)' and 'Back Seat Of My Car' (ending with the chant, 'We believe we can't be wrong') were unsubtle jibes at John and Yoko. Quite why Paul, well known for his anodyne tendencies, chose to pick a fight on record, and in public, with such a master of invective as John, will always be a mystery. Lennon's reply was the vitriolic 'How Do You Sleep?', on his classic *Imagine* album. Unlike Paul's songs, John's tactics were not cloak-and-dagger but a full frontal assault:

> So Sgt Pepper took you by surprise
> You better see right through that mother's eyes
> Those freaks was right when they said you was dead
> The one mistake you made was in your head. . .
> You live with straights who tell you you was king
> Jump when your mama tell you anything

Dear mailbag.

In order to put out of its misery the limping dog of a news story which has been dragging itself across your pages for the past year, my answer to the question, "will the Beatles get together again?"...

is no.

Paul McCartney.

Paul McCartney's letter to *Melody Maker* in August 1970

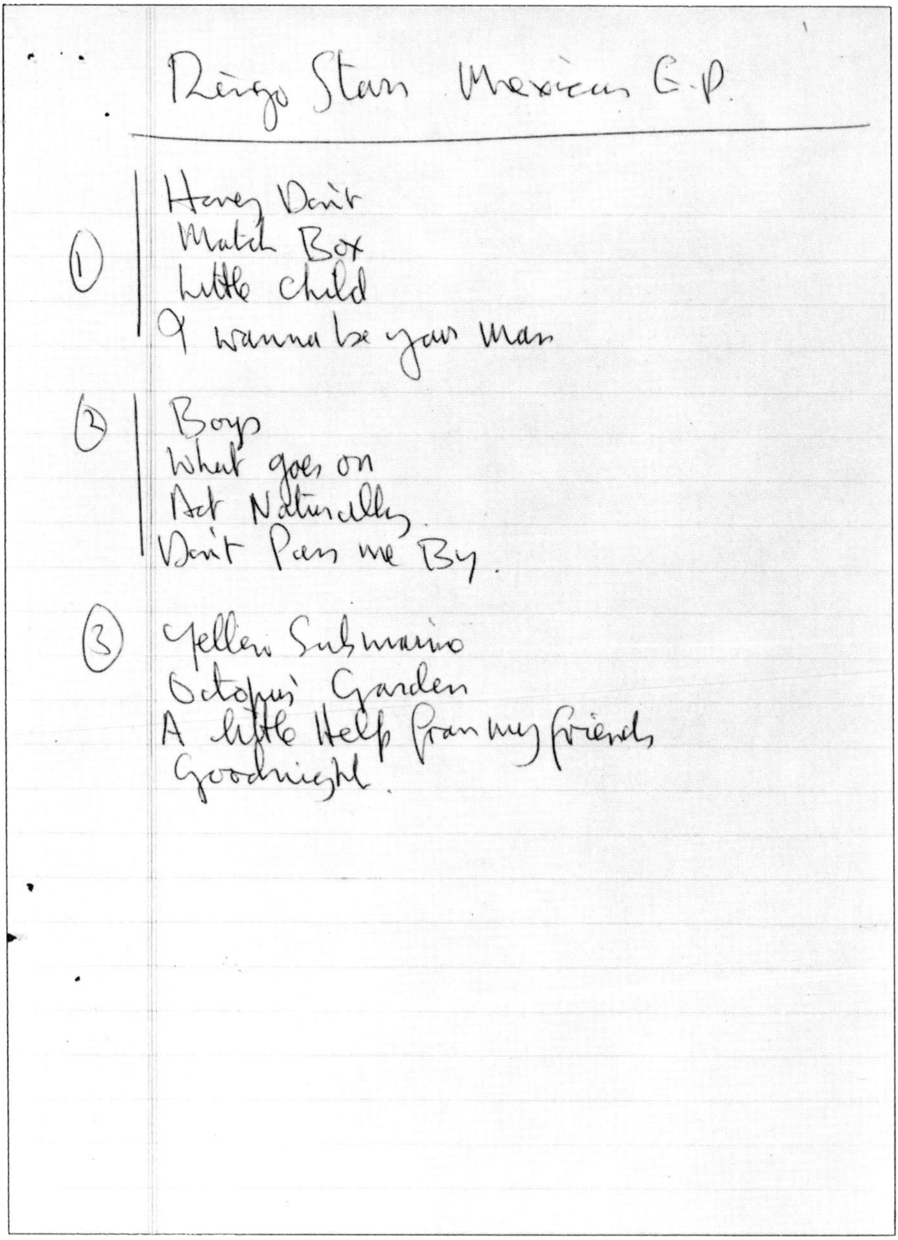

Ringo Starr Mexican E.P.

(1)
Honey Don't
Match Box
Little Child
I wanna be your man

(2)
Boys
What goes on
Act Naturally
Don't Pass me By.

(3)
Yellow Submarine
Octopus' Garden
A little Help from my friends
Goodnight.

In the summer of 1974 E.M.I. Records managing director Len Wood asked John to 'pair off' some Beatles songs for release as E.P.s in Mexico. John took the time to write these suggested lists of Ringo Starr and George Harrison tracks

three
~~the~~ spare songs (Roll over Beethoven, Something. Everybodies trying to be my baby). June 26 1971

George Harrisongs Mexican EPS

(1)
I'm happy just to Dance with you
Do you want to know a secret?
Chains
Devil in Heart

(2)
Don't Bother Me
Taxman
If I needed Someone
Think for Yourself.

(3)
I need you
You like me to much
~~Its only~~ Its only a Northern Song.
its all to much.

(4)
Savoy Truffle
Old Brown Shoe
Blue Jay Way
Long Long Long.

(5)
Within You Without you
The inner Light.
Love You too
I want to tell you.

(6).
Here Comes the Sun
For You Blue.
While My Guitar Gently Weeps.
Piggies.

The only thing you done was Yesterday
And since you've gone you're just Another Day
How do you sleep?. . .
A pretty face may last a year or two
But pretty soon they'll see what you can do
The sound you make is Muzak to my ears
You must have learned something in all those years

The rancour over Yoko, over Klein and Eastman and how best to end the Beatles had now turned bitterly personal. At the root of it lay the fundamental truth which millions of Beatles fans still find unpalatable: John and Paul never had much in common. They had different aspirations: Paul, with his gift for melody and musicianship, and love of popularity, headed securely for the world of entertainment where he will always be a giant figure. John was on a perpetual adventure, picking up and adopting, then quickly rejecting ideas and causes, writing poetry, and writing from within himself. He was an artist with a distinct anti-Establishment backbone. McCartney greatly admired John's mercurial, often whimsical, style, his originality, his arrogance, his wit. To a lesser extent Lennon acknowledged Paul's strengths as a songwriter. But John had little time for craftsmen, dismissing them as 'people who could write little ditties to order'. He sweated over his own work. His post-Beatles writing was inspired by personal relationships, observations and events. John could recognize Paul's commercial power but it was all too often vapid, mawkish, and sentimental in contrast with his hard edge. They were right for each other at a certain period of their lives. But put simply, where McCartney had great talent, Lennon was a genius. By 1971 they had irrevocably parted company, both personally and artistically, and John's feelings were further inflamed by Paul's digs at Yoko, whom John regarded as part of him.

The fight continued in public. Paul gave an interview to *Melody Maker* in November 1971, emphasizing that although the music had ended, business problems still faced them: 'I just want the four of us to get together somewhere and sign a piece of paper saying it's all over and we want to divide the money four ways.

'No one else would be there, not even Linda or Yoko or Allen Klein. We'd just sign the paper and hand it to the business people and let them sort it all out. That's all I want now. But John won't do it. Everybody thinks I am the aggressor. But I'm not, you know. I just want out.

'John and Yoko are not cool in what they are doing. I saw them on television the other night and thought that what they are saying about what they wanted to do together was basically the same as what Linda and I want to do.

'John's whole image now is very honest and open. He's all right, is John. I like his *Imagine* album but I didn't like the others. *Imagine* is what John is really like but there was too much political stuff on the other albums. You know, I only really listen to them to see if there is something I can pinch.' (He laughed.)

What did Paul think of 'How Do You Sleep?'? 'I think it's silly. so what if I live with straights? I like straights. I have straight babies. It doesn't affect *him*. He says the only thing I did was "Yesterday". He knows that's wrong. He knows and I know it's not true.'

Referring to the Beatles' album, *Let It Be*, Paul said: 'There was a little bit of hype on the back of the sleeve for the first time ever on a Beatles album. At the time the Beatles were very strained with each other and it wasn't a happy time. It said it was a new-phase Beatles album and there was nothing further from the truth. That was the last Beatles album and everybody knew it. . . . Klein had it re-produced because he said it didn't sound commercial enough.'

Talking of John's Toronto concert with Eric Clapton, Yoko, and Klaus Voormann, Paul said: 'John wanted to do a big thing in Toronto but I didn't dig that at all. I hear that before he went on stage he was sick and that's just what I didn't want. Like anybody else I have been nervous because of the Beatles thing.

'I wanted to get in a van and do an unadvertised concert at a Saturday night hop at Slough Town Hall or somewhere like that. We'd call ourselves Rikki and the Red Streaks or something and just get up and play. There'd be no Press and we'd tell nobody about it. John thought it was a daft idea.

'Before John said he was leaving the Beatles I was lying in bed at home one night and I thought I would like to get a band together like his Plastic Ono Band. I felt the urge because we had never played live for four years. We all wanted to appear on a stage but not with the Beatles. We couldn't do it as the Beatles because it would be so big. We'd have to find a million-seater hall or something.' And in a remark which made John smile, Paul said what he thought of New York: 'I went for a walk in Central Park and there was a layer of dirt on the grass everywhere.' The grass on his farm in Scotland, where he had 100 sheep on sixty acres of land, was so much better than American grass.

John's letter of reply which was published in the *Melody Maker* two weeks later, was accompanied by a request that it be published in full to give 'equal time' to his side of the story. Part of the letter referred to McCartney's claim that if he (Paul) had appeared at George Harrison's summer 1971 Bangladesh concert in New York, Allen Klein would have taken the credit for pulling the Beatles back together again. John's classic letter, positively dripping with invective, ran as follows:

Dear Paul, Linda *et all* the wee McCartneys,
Thanks for your letter.
1. We give *you money* for your bits of Apple.
2. We give *you more money* in the form of royalties which legally belong to Apple (I know we're Apple, but on the other hand we're *not*).
Maybe there's an answer there somewhere . . . but for the millionth time in these past few years I repeat, *What about the TAX*? It's all very well, playing 'simple, honest ole Paul' in the *Melody Maker* but you know damn well we can't just sign a bit of paper.
    You say, 'John won't do it.' I will if you'll *indemnify* us against the tax man! Anyway, you know that after we have *our* meeting, the fucking lawyers will have to implement whatever we agree on – right?
    If they have some form of agreement between *them* before *we* met, it might make it even easier. It's up to you; as we've said many times, we'll meet you whenever you like. Just make up your mind! E.g. two weeks ago I asked you on the phone, 'Please let's meet without advisers, etc. and decide what we want', and I emphasized especially Maclen [John and Paul's songwriting partnership company within Northern Songs] which is mainly our concern, but you refused – right?
    You said under *no condition* would you sell to us and if we didn't do what you wanted, you'd sue us again and that Ringo and George are going to break you John, etc. etc.
    Now I was quite straight with you that day, and you tried to shoot me down with your emotional 'logic'. If *you're not* the aggressor (as you claim) who the hell took us to court and shat all over us in public?
    As I've said before – have you ever thought that you might *possibly* be wrong about something? Your conceit about us and Klein is incredible – you say you 'made the mistake of trying to advise them against him [Klein] and that pissed them off' and we secretly feel that you're right! Good God! You must *know we're right about Eastman*. . . .

One other little lie in your 'It's only Paulie' *MM* bit: *Let It Be* was not the 'first bit of hype' on a Beatle album. Remember Tony Barrow? And his wonderful writing on 'Please Please Me' etc. etc. the early Beatle Xmas records!

And you gotta admit it was a 'new-phase Beatle album', incidentally written in the style of the great Barrow himself! By the way what happened to my idea of putting the parody of our first album cover on the *Let It Be* cover?

Also, we were intending to parody Barrow originally, so it was hype. But what was your *Life* article? Tony Barrow couldn't have done it better. (And your writing inside of the *Wings* album isn't exactly the realist is it?) Anyway, enough of this petty bourgeois fun.

You were right about New York! I do love it; it's the ONLY PLACE TO BE. (Apart from anything else, they leave you alone too!) I see you prefer Scotland. . . . I'll bet you YOUR piece of Apple you'll be living in New York by 1974 (two years is the usual time it takes you – right?).

Another thing, whadya mean *big thing* in Toronto? It was completely spontaneous, they rang on the *Friday* – we flew there and we played on the *Saturday*. I was sick because I was stone pissed. Listen to the album, with no rehearsal too. Come on Macka! Own up! (We'd never played together before!) Half a dozen live shows – with no big fuss – in fact we've been *doing* what you've said the Beatles should do, Yoko and I have been doing it for three years! (I said it was daft for the Beatles to do it. I still think it's daft.) So go on and do it! Do it! Do it! E.g. *Cambridge*, 1969, completely unadvertised! (A *very* small hall.) *Lyceum* Ballroom, (1969, no fuss, great show – thirty-piece rock band! 'Live Jam' out soon!) *Fillmore East* (1971) un-announced. Another good time had by all – out soon!!) We even played in the streets here in the Village (our spiritual home!?) with the great David Peel!! We were moved on by the cops even!! It's best just to DO IT.

I know you'll dig it, and they don't even expect the Beatles now anyway!

So *you* think *Imagine* ain't political, it's 'Working Class Hero' with sugar on it for conservatives like yourself!! You obviously didn't *dig the words*. Imagine! You took 'How Do You Sleep?' so literally (read my own review of the album in *Crawdaddy*). *Your* politics are very similar to Mary White-house's – saying *nothing* is as loud as saying *something*.

Listen, my obsessive old pal, it was George's press conference not dat old debbil Klein! *He* said what *you* said – 'I'd love to come but. . . .' Anyway, we did it for basically the same reasons – the Beatles bit. They still called it a Beatle show – with just two of them! [Ringo played drums in the superstar band George Harrison formed for the spectacular Bangladesh concert in New York.]

Join the Rock Liberation Front before it gets *you*.

Wanna put your photo on the label like uncool John and Yoko do ya? (Ain't ya got no shame!) If we're *not* cool, WHAT DOES THAT MAKE YOU?

No hard feelings to you either. I know basically we want the same, and as I said on the phone and in this letter, whenever you want to meet, all you have to do is call.

All you need is love
Power to the people
Free all prisoners
Jail the judges
Love and peace
Get it on and rip 'em off

John Lennon

P.S. The bit that really puzzled us was asking to meet WITHOUT LINDA AND YOKO. I thought you'd have understood BY NOW that I'm JOHNANDYOKO.
P.P.S. Even *your own* lawyers know you can't 'just sign a bit of paper' (or don't they tell you?).

The wounds were deep and lasting. Relations between John and Paul never fully recovered from the encounter. When John wrote that letter, two months after arriving in New York, he scarcely realized that he would never visit Britain again. And it would be four years before Paul finally visited him in New York, the Beatles dead and the business hatchet still not properly buried. At the time of their friction, George Martin said: 'I don't think Linda is a substitute for John Lennon any more than Yoko is a substitute for Paul McCartney.' The producer of the Beatles' records was judging each artist's new direction in music. He was also, unknowingly, echoing their desires. John had shed the Beatles, Paul, and Britain. And he was opening his mind.

The Beatles phenomenon, he said, was so enormous that he had

had to be a Beatle and nothing else. 'It was not a monster at the beginning. We communicated with people, in clubs and ball-rooms; we spoke to people and it was really great. But then it became a kind of machine. It's like a guy who makes millions, say Rockefeller or Getty. They become totally obsessed by money, how to make more. That's how the Beatles became, and that's what I could not accept. There wasn't a moment to think about anything else, so the Beatles was just a period in my life.' Before the Beatles, he had known nothing about world politics, but he had been aware of his position within Liverpool society – 'trying to get into university and all the silly things that go with that'.

But he accepted that the Beatles had a vital social influence. He always seized on anyone who denied the importance of the Beatles to the world. *He* was allowed to denigrate the group, but woe betide anyone else who did, particularly musicians. 'The Beatles had a social impact then became sterile like a government that has stayed in power too long. When that situation arises, you abdicate. So we abdicated.'

3
PEACE

'We are willing to be clowns if it helps spread the word'

Just before going to America in 1971, John told me: 'We'd like to be remembered as the Romeo and Juliet of the 1970s.'

Yoko continued: 'When people get cynical about love, they should look at us and see that it *is* possible.' They were holding hands, smiling and obviously meant every word. I had asked them what their real aims were, in the heat of the great controversy surrounding their union and demonstrations for peace.

'I'd like everyone to remember us with a smile,' said John. 'But, if possible, just as John and Yoko who created world peace for ever. The whole of life is a preparation for death. I'm not worried about dying. When we go, we'd like to leave behind a better place.'

In the wake of the limping Beatles and the *Two Virgins* album furore, three other major landmarks had just re-shaped John's life. The speed of events was breathtaking.

In February 1969 Yoko was divorced from her second husband, Anthony Cox. Seven weeks after that, John and Yoko had married. Five days after that they staged the renowned bed-in demonstration for peace in Amsterdam. And a month after their wedding John formally changed his middle name by deed poll from Winston to Ono. He was following his maxim to Paul, 'Do it!' with a speed that was not to let up for the next six years.

John's formal change of name from Winston to Ono was a mark of togetherness but it had a diplomatic motive too. Yoko had said to John, light-heartedly but with meaning: 'I don't like being known as Mrs Lennon. How would *you* like it if you had to change your name upon marriage to Mr John Ono? Why should that not be?' (Ono is Yoko's given surname which she does not

On the roof of the Apple building in April 1969, John formally changes his name by deed poll from John Winston Lennon to John Ono Lennon

drop upon marriage.) She was intent on asserting her independence and even wrote a song, 'Mrs Lennon', which, she says now, summed up her cynicism at the irony of the situation.

'My God, it really is unfair,' admitted John as they joked about it.

Then, Yoko recalls, John 'showed what an incredible politician he was'. He had repeatedly told Yoko that he disliked his middle name, Winston, with its wartime connotation and implication that he was somehow a subscriber to the spirit of the upper-class 'British empire and all that'. It made him feel hypocritical. 'I don't want that name. It's always following me around,' John told Yoko.

'He hated being compared in any way with Winston Churchill,' she says. 'His incredible idea of having his middle name changed to Ono, to accommodate my request, made me feel good and amazed me at the same time. He said I could carry on being known as Yoko Ono, and why not, and he had made a step towards me without dropping Lennon, which nobody wanted him to do, anyway.'

John decided to have the ceremony performed by the Commissioner of Oaths on the roof at Apple. But there was a technical problem: he was told that day that, while he could adopt the name Ono, he could not renounce the given name of Winston. What he decided to call himself was totally up to him and he was re-registered as John Winston Ono Lennon that day. John grumbled: 'Why am I paying all these lawyers if I'm not getting rid of Winston?'

The legalities of whether John still owned the name Winston dragged on for months. 'I don't feel patriotic enough to keep the name,' he said. 'I am John Ono Lennon.' In all the oaths which he swore during his statements on the winding-up of the Beatles in 1970 John was written down as John Ono Lennon and all his personal documents were named accordingly. He often signed himself with just his new initials: J.O.L. But when it came to his American immigration battle between 1972 and 1976, he diplomatically added back the name Winston and the Green Card was eventually made out to him in the name of John Winston Ono Lennon. 'Although he may never have technically lost the Winston, he disliked it and never used it,' says Yoko. Her own situation is exactly the same: the world knows her as Yoko Ono, the name she prefers, but technically she is Yoko Ono Lennon. John particularly liked to add extra 'o's to his name because he and Yoko said the letter was a sign of intuitiveness and was good on psychic grounds, too. 'Between us,' Yoko says, 'we were very psychic. We knew all the time what the other was thinking, what was going to be said by the other, our responses, everything. It was sometimes unnerving.'

Their wedding was unconventional but romantic. Based in Paris for a couple of weeks in March 1969, they decided to charter a plane and marry in Gibraltar. The bride and groom wore white tennis shoes and their clothes were also white. Yoko wore a white linen mini dress and coat, a huge brimmed white hat that contrasted vividly with her flowing black hair and white socks. John had a white jacket and off-white corduroy trousers. The man who had been cast as the waspish Beatle, hard and cynical, was old-fashioned about his marriage. 'We are two love birds,' he said. 'Intellectually we didn't believe in getting married. But one doesn't love someone just intellectually. For two people, marriage still has the edge over just living together.' At the ceremony he stood before the registrar in the British Consulate office with one hand in his pocket and the other holding a cigarette. 'Oh, that wasn't important at all,' he answered when asked if it was irreverent. 'The event was *ours*. If I can't stand and do what I like at my own wedding. . . .'

They had their honeymoon, he explained, before the wedding. 'Just eating, shopping and looking round Paris. In love in Paris in the spring was beautiful. We're both tremendous romantics!' They would have liked to have been married in church by the Archbishop of Canterbury but that was impossible because divorced people could not be married in church.

The scorn that had been directed at Yoko vanished immediately. People suddenly realized that she was human after all. 'I got so emotional at the wedding I broke down and John nearly did, too,' she said, 'This man, rabbiting on about "Do you take this woman for your wife?" — it was a tremendous experience.' Back in Paris after only a seventy-minute stay in Gibraltar, John and Yoko went to the Plaza Athénée Hotel. Yes, Yoko reflected, marriage was old-fashioned but both of them definitely respected it as an institution. John said that from then on they would do everything together, as artists and as husband and wife. Yoko said she would certainly not be the traditional wife, if that meant bringing him his slippers. She added that their marriage was one of their happenings, very important and indicative of the future. 'We're planning another one in the next seven days. You'll know soon enough when it is.'

The next stop, Amsterdam a few days later, was to be the pivotal event of their peace campaign. Since they had already appeared on stage at London's Royal Albert Hall in a large white bag in December 1968 and as Yoko had fast gained a reputation for leading John into the realms of fantasy, it should not have been so surprising. But John and Yoko were in a hurry to ram home some principles. The mid-1960s had educated the world into accepting that rock stars could have brains; some saw their role as messianic. John, encouraged by Yoko, sensed the power that being a Beatle had given him and believed it could be used intelligently to advocate peace. He had first been encouraged to launch a peace campaign in a letter from Peter Watkins, producer of the film *The War Game*, Watkins spoke of the obscenity of war and the power of artists like John; reflecting on his appearance in the anti-war film *How I Won The War*, John became totally committed to the idea.

For seven days in the presidential suite of the Amsterdam Hilton John and Yoko lay in bed together in white pyjamas. They were surrounded by flowers and two notices adorned their bedhead: 'Bed Peace' and 'Hair Peace'. They invited the Press, and during that week nearly 100 reporters from all around the world came to watch the event that became known as the Amsterdam bed-in for peace. What was *this*? Mad John and crazy Yoko having a public honeymoon? In the eyes of the conventional world they had now cooked up the most outrageous happening of all.

'Ha! They all thought John and Yoko were going to fuck in front of the world's Press for peace,' John laughed. 'That was never on, and anyway we're far too shy to do anything, *anything*, like that.' The idea was to stage a genuine demonstration when they knew that publicity would be guaranteed: 'The Press would have found us whatever we'd done for a honeymoon, so we decided to invite the Press along and get some publicity for something we both believe in,' John said later. Sporting a beard and with his hair at its longest, John urged others to grow their hair as a symbol of their peace campaign; strangely, John also seemed calmer during the week in Amsterdam. Fans besieged the hotel, listening patiently to the messages of peace that John and Yoko propounded. They kept the windows of their room open so they could hear the fans in the street outside. And the Press, at once bemused and amused by the whole episode, was cynically grateful. Good old John and Yoko had given them a decent story, at least. John saw it more profoundly: he believed the peace message had got across. Hundreds of newspapers and radio and

The famous Bed-in for Peace at Amsterdam's Hilton Hotel in March 1969:
John and Yoko, in their favourite colour, white, with their drawings and
slogans pinned to the wall of their suite, gave seven days of interviews to
propound their peace message

television programmes had sent out their message. It was better propaganda than any prime minister had yet achieved. As for the fans: well, he was óld now (twenty-eight at the time) and Yoko was thirty-six; he felt that his days as a pop idol had run out and that it was time to concentrate on more serious work.

At the time the Amsterdam bed-in was regarded by many as a stunt or a joke. A cynical British police chief described it as disgusting, adding: 'If wealth does this to people then I do not want it. Power corrupts.' But John and Yoko had optimism firmly on their side: if there was a wave of cynicism in 1969 then in the years since John and Yoko's palpable sincerity and the importance and urgency of their message and motive has rung true throughout the world.

There was never any let-up, either, in their proclamation of love for each other: signs proclaiming 'John loves Yoko' and 'Yoko loves John' hung next to them in bed for seven days. And when Yoko told John her £3 10s. wedding ring was too large and was slipping off her finger, John drew a temporary one in ink on Yoko's finger while the real one went for shrinking. A solid streak of conformity, convention, tradition, and romanticism bound them together while the world had exactly the opposite impression of them. They were much more demonstrative in their affection for each other than many 'normal' husbands and wives; and with John and Yoko, every facet of their partnership was played out in public. They quickly damped down any speculation that Yoko, because of her far-out stand in art, was an aggressive fighter for women's liberation who had hammereed her views into a chauvinistic Beatle. 'John is a very aggressive, masculine man and I enjoy being submissive,' said Yoko. But three years of observing Yoko had changed John's outlook. By the time they married he was re-thinking his whole attitude to women. Yoko's strength convinced him that to go on looking for merely physical attributes would never satisfy him. As he commented: 'I guess I was looking for a woman who would give me everything I got from a man, intellectually, as well as the fact that she was female.' He took a keen interest in women's emancipation partly because Yoko had demonstrated her equality and often superiority. John resented very strongly the middle-class snubs that Yoko had suffered: after she had appeared nude with him on the *Two Virgins* album cover she was called an 'ugly old cow', and he felt she should fight back. 'How dare they? I think she's beautiful,' he said. More importantly he knew something that was going to be much harder to get across: mentally, intellectually, and conceptually Yoko not only suffered racial prejudice and opposition from all women and, naturally, Lennon's girl fans from the Beatles days, but as an artist she was years ahead of her time and her work was constantly misunderstood. What Amsterdam convinced him of was that she should strike out even more, together with him, for feminism, and articulate it, while he should also shed the mental restrictions of being labelled a Beatle.

The fecundity of their partnership was nourished more in Amsterdam than anywhere. 'We are willing,' said John, 'to become the world's clowns if it helps spread the word for peace. Too many people talk about it but not enough do anything.' With his famous name and Yoko's ideas they would continue doing things for years that would force people to react, he said. After the previous year's acorns in Coventry Cathedral and the 'bagism' on a London stage, Bag Productions, John and Yoko's film and production company was formed, based at the Apple headquarters. John Lennon, man of peace, had been launched. As with everything he ever did, he was serious, intense, simple, hurried, and infectious. As he admitted in song, it wasn't easy, 'the way things are going, they're gonna crucify me'. The world had become used to the abrasive, opinionated Beatle. It had slowly realized he meant Yoko to be more than a passer by in his life when they married. For the next eleven years John Lennon was gradually to jump the biggest hurdle of all, the foundations of which had been set up in Amsterdam: the pop star idolized by millions was to become known as a spokesman and campaigner for goodwill and humantiarianism.

There was a double edge to John's adoption of the peace cause. It came at a perfect time in his life with the Beatles at a crossroads. And he had reflected that, for six years as a pop star he had reluctantly been conscious of his image, not getting too involved in politics or philosophy. It had always been against his nature: after he had tripped up over his remarks on Jesus Christ in 1966, Brian Epstein's rule that the Beatles should be non-controversial seemed to make sense. Lennon wanted to condemn publicly American aggression in Vietnam at the height of the Beatles' fame. Epstein warned him against it and John, who for a time did not want the roller-coaster of Beatlemania to wane, went along with the 'party line'. It was a bitter pill to swallow.

Now, with fame and wealth, he would pretend no more. He told the Amsterdam press conference: 'All I'm saying is peace. We're not pointing a finger at anybody. There are good guys and bad guys. The struggle is in the mind. We must bury our own monsters and stop condemning people. We're all Christ and we are all Hitler. We are trying to make Christ's message contemporary. We want Christ to win. What would He have done if He had advertisements, records, films, T.V. and newspapers? Well, the miracle today is communications. So let's use it!'

John and Yoko's method was expensive. Hotel suites and travelling expenses ran into thousands of pounds a week as they continued their European trip that spring. The critics tried another pin-prick: wouldn't it be better if John gave some money to the starving rather than indulging himself and his ego? He was ahead of them on that one: he regularly sent money to needy refugees, particularly in Biafra, that era's crisis point. All his life John was to give away thousands of pounds to charities and good causes. He did it quietly, not wanting the publicity of the rich, demonstrative pop star displaying his wealth.

Amsterdam was only the start. As a continuation of the Coventry Cathedral acorn plantation, John and Yoko sent a pair of acorns to prime ministers throughout the world, urging them to plant them symbolically for peace, as they had done.

Films had always intrigued John and he and Yoko decided they would make them another aspect of their work together. Their first two, shot at Weybridge, were *Smile* and *Two Virgins*. *Smile* was Yoko's idea and was typically spare in its conception: simply a shot of John's face, smiling, in different expressions which were multiplied by the camera to complete a film lasting nearly an hour. *Two Virgins* was similar in theme, using John's face superimposed on Yoko's. Made early in their relationship, they were not so important as films as in sealing the chemistry between John and Yoko. Yoko was John's launching pad and it was she who showed him the true dimensions of his talent as a communicator.

He loved, too, the sense of humour in her work. Their third film, *Rape*, virtually parodied the story of the Beatles' escalator to success. A girl's reaction during her pursuit by journalists reaches a desperate finale in which she struggles violently and attacks a television camera. The film's première on Austrian T.V. followed the Amsterdam bed-in in March 1969. John and Yoko flew to Vienna and petrified the staid community by announcing that their press conference would be held where they were staying – the dignified and historic Hotel Sacher. The press conference rocked the august foundations of the grand old hotel. John and Yoko, by now christened 'Joko' by some cynics, appeared sitting on a trestle table covered totally by a white sheet. 'Bagism', they explained, was part of their peace drive.

With Yoko at his feet covered in a white sheet, John is clearly having a ball onstage at London's Lyceum during the concert by the Plastic Ono Supergroup in December 1969

John desperately wanted his propaganda machine for peace to
have a big launch in America, then heavily involved in the Vietnam
war. Asked why he had not had a bed-in there he had answered:
'Because I don't want to get shot.' His honesty usually got him
through. The real reason, however, why they could not stage a
bed-in in New York, as they wanted, was because John was
refused a visa in May 1969: the London drugs conviction had
blocked his freedom of movement. Montreal proved a happy
alternative and John, by now an enthusiast of the telephone that
he used to hate, used the proximity with North America to do
literally hundreds of phone interviews with radio, television, and
newspaper people anxious to learn what lay behind the Amsterdam idea.

'One problem with what we're doing,' he said, 'is that we'll
never know how successful we are. With the Beatles, you put out a
record and either it's a hit or it's a miss. I don't expect the prime
ministers or kings and queens of the world to suddenly change
their policies just because John and Yoko have said "Peace,
brother". It would be nice! But it's *youth* we're addressing. Youth
is the future. If we can get inside their minds and tell them to think
in favour of non-violence, we'll be satisfied. What's the point of
getting fame as a Beatle and not using it?!' John's urgency, his
enthusiasm, and the still-glowing embers of Beatlemania in Canada and North America made for enormous press coverage. Since
John never made any bones about his hunger for publicity for the
peace cause, he viewed the seven-day Montreal bed-in as a winner.

He clinched it by making one of his strongest pieces of music.
For months he had been using the phrase 'Give it a *chance*', when
pleading with reporters to listen to the peace campaign fairly.
Amid the huge spread of carnations in his hotel room, he was
inspired to write the snappy little chant, 'Give Peace A Chance'. It
quickly became popular with the entourage and John decided to
order a portable eight-track tape recorder so that it could be
recorded. Among the people singing along on the chorus were
Timothy Leary, high priest of the drug culture, Montreal rabbi
Abraham Feinberg, and comedian Tommy Smothers. The spontaneity of the song and John's unmistakable conviction gave it a
sharp edge. The peace campaign now had an international
anthem.

Just as with 'Give Peace A Chance', so many of John's phrases,
inextricably linked with his humour and masterful word-play,
serve as soundtracks for his life. Once his world was rolling with
Yoko, John's one-liners and his song lyrics became even more

memorable. 'The sixties were all about learning to swim,' he said once. 'So when you've learned to swim – swim!' Another classic summing up of the Beatles was: 'The dream is over . . . nothing's changed. Just a few of us are walking around with longer hair.' And, with his 1975 album of rock'n' roll songs, John coined the phrase: 'You shoulda been there (signed) Dr Winston O'Boogie.' 'Imagine', his best-loved song, has a wealth of allegorical lines destined to enchant people for ever.

One of John's proudest word collaborations with Yoko came as the finale of their peace campaign in 1969. It had been a spine-tingling year. The simplicity of the slogan they invented gave it its power: 'WAR IS OVER! If you want it. Happy Christmas from John and Yoko.' Huge billboards went up in eleven cities around the world to display the poster and thousands of posters were distributed internationally. A full two years later, at Christmas 1971, John and Yoko joined together with the black children of the Harlem Community Choir in New York to make their classic Christmas song, 'Happy Xmas (War Is Over)'. The chorus, 'War Is Over, if you want it', lived on, which pleased John. 'And so this is Christmas,' he sang. 'And what have you done?/Another year over, a new one just begun.' By the end of 1969, though, John realized that the energy he had poured into the peace campaign needed one final boost. The answer, of course, lay in music.

To aid the United Nations Children's Emergency Fund he got together the Plastic Ono Band for a show at London's Lyceum ballroom. With the backdrop of the 'War Is Over!' billboard John assembled George Harrison, Eric Clapton, Klaus Voormann, the Who's Keith Moon, singer-pianist Billy Preston, and the Delaney and Bonnie Band. Yoko sat at John's feet on the stage, covered for much of the time by a white bag. Nobody was in any doubt, after a full year of propaganda, that they meant what they preached. On Christmas Eve they went to Rochester Cathedral, Kent, to join a sit-in and fast to spotlight world poverty. The cynics could not resist the temptation to take a negative view: Lennon was talking about poverty, they sneered, while arriving at the steps of the cathedral in a Rolls-Royce. John's retort was: 'Would they want me to walk here? The people who criticize us have cars. If they give up theirs, first, for peace, I'll give up my Rolls.'

It took Britain time to get used to John's antics. He was prepared for total rejection by Beatles fans because in his mind he had ceased to be a pop star. 'I've left all that to the Monkees,' he told me. But that summer, a heart-warming example of teenagers' support gave John and Yoko the feeling that the peace campaign, and their partnership, had succeeded.

In an opinion poll among readers of *Disc and Music Echo* John was voted the most popular Beatle and, the paper reported, his extrovert behaviour had 'made him a figure of respect rather than ridicule'. The paper asked: 'Some people think John Lennon's behaviour since he met his wife Yoko has been eccentric. What do you think?' The majority of young readers felt he was 'eccentric, but harmless and sincere.' A fifteen-year-old girl said: 'I thought he was very eccentric when he married Yoko but my opinions towards him are now changing because I can see some sense in what he's aiming at.' A nineteen-year-old Scotsman said: 'That John Lennon's behaviour pattern is tending towards the unorthodox cannot be denied, but Lennon is no orthodox character. He is an honest, sincere, Christ figure of a man in whom the passions of peace flow strongly and there are too many out to crucify him.' A Midlands teenager replied: 'I never used to take very much notice of the Beatles as individuals before but I do now. John isn't just a guitar stomper any more. He is . . . well, I suppose you could call him a saint.' And another said: 'He's doing more good than most politicians. At least he's taking action to try to get peace, which is better than sitting discussing it.' It was not all honey, however. One critical fan said: 'The Beatles would be better off without John Lennon. He's going downhill and unfortunately he has enough influence over the rest of the group that, unless he leaves, the Beatles could go down with him.'

John also emerged as the Beatle people would most like to meet. 'I'd like to talk to him about peace,' wrote a sixteen-year-old girl. 'I also admire the way he stands up in front of the public even though they treat him disgustingly.' And: 'I'd like to try to assess whether his endeavours on behalf of world peace are sincere or just the self-indulgent whims of a very rich, egotistical young man.' Among pop fans the news that John had overtaken Paul as Britain's favourite Beatle was big news. And the fact that John achieved it for his ideas, rather than his music or his good looks, made an even greater impact. Crucially, too, John and Yoko's peace efforts, while scoring a direct hit for them, had not, in the main, affected public love of the Beatles, even though traditional British bluntness put a sting in the tail of a poll that boosted John's morale: 'Going off with the Maharishi to do this meditating lark ruined them,' said one boy. 'They should have retired after *Sgt Pepper*,' said another. But John was ecstatic at the results. He sent

The launch of the 'War Is Over! (If You Want It)' campaign by John and
Yoko in their Apple office, December 1969. He is holding the poster that
was displayed on billboards in eleven cities

me, as the paper's editor, an enigmatic drawing 'as my way of saying thanks to all your readers who are with us'. He threw in a typical aside before the end of our phone conversation: 'Hey, why don't you ask the readers what they make of the drawing? We could have another poll on that!'

So we did. The response was enormous, the interpretations deep, patient, and understanding. 'The drawing is about peace, present and past,' said one reader. 'The two faces are reflected images of themselves, with John as a modern-day saviour. The scene is tranquillity – a pleasant day, sunshine, an animal in the foreground. . . . Peace. It could also represent the Nativity, with a stable on the horizon and an animal waiting for the birth.' And another went further: 'The Lennon cartoon is a visionary work showing John and Yoko after deification. The playing card symbolism in the representation of John and Yoko suggests that in the process they have lost their personal identity (as in the case of Henry VIII in a pack of cards) to be known only as 'God' or 'The Gods'. This interpretation is supported by the fact that Lennon has no eyes. The title ('ART') suggests John and Yoko have attained divine status on artistic merit rather than through their efforts for peace.'

At last John felt vindicated. So many readers of *Disc and Music Echo*, a large proportion of them teenagers, felt a rapport with his cause for peace that he plunged headlong into a long and exhausting schedule of press interviews. The paper had also canvassed opinion on John and Yoko's new music, asking for reactions to their *Life With The Lions* album. (The title was a wry piece of word-play by John, invoking the radio series of his childhood, *Life with the Lyons*.) Many young people sympathized with the new, avant-garde direction in which the chief Beatle was going with this far-out Japanese artist. 'They are sending out feelers to explore new areas of experimental music,' wrote one enthusiast. 'Instead of taking tentative steps, like many groups, John and Yoko have gone in head first and are courageous to have done this. Although we cannot yet understand much of their music, I am sure it will be accepted in ten years' time.' Others wrote of how much they enjoyed its sound, simplicity, and emotion. Long-time Lennon observer David Stark wrote: '*Life With The Lions* is a haunting, intriguing experience. Its pure concept is so refreshing and the sadness of the music – it *is* music – just makes me happy.' As always one fan put the knife in but with humour: 'This new music by John and Yoko certainly has something to offer. It makes me appreciate my other albums much

John's drawing for the readers of *Disc and Music Echo*, after they had named him Britain's Most Popular Beatle in 1969

more than I did before!' John loved that. 'Tell him avant-garde is French for bullshit,' he said, laughing.

Despite his involvement in the cause for peace, John decided he had to find time, in mid-1969, to find a new home for him and Yoko and also to take her on a short holiday. Weybridge held too many memories of his old life as a trapped Beatle. So Kenwood was sold and he settled on Tittenhurst Park. The vast, thirty-roomed Georgian mansion just outside Sunningdale, Berkshire, cost John £150,000. When he went for a look at the 300-year-old house John floored the estate agent by describing its sprawling grandeur as 'functional'. Included in the estate were seventy-two acres of parkland, featuring formal gardens, a farm, cottages, outhouses, and a lodge at the entrance gates. The two-storey house had seven main bedrooms, three reception rooms, three bath-rooms, a large kitchen area, and extensive staff quarters. The striking feature of Tittenhurst, which attracted John and Yoko, was its tranquillity. Only twenty-six miles from London, it offered an oasis of peace and space in which John could plan his recording studio so that no neighbours would be affected.

Just before moving in John and Yoko set off on a trip north. John had spent a year consistently telling Yoko about Aunt Mimi, his roots in Liverpool and his childhood holidays in Scotland with 'Mater', his Aunt Elizabeth.

The perfect holiday for them both would be by car. 'I took Yoko round the streets of my youth in Liverpool and to meet all my relatives,' John said later. He also mentioned to me a vague plan to return one day to Liverpool and stage an event with Yoko at his old art college.

John kept up occasional contact with Cynthia because he felt guilt at the loss of his son, Julian, from his regular company. When he moved into Ascot John asked for Julian to be a regular weekend visitor. One weekend Yoko's daughter Kyoko was visiting her too, and the four of them set off for Liverpool and Aunt Mimi, and Durness, where Aunt Mater and Uncle Bert ran the croft where John had holidayed as a lad.

Mater gave him a cool reception. She had loved her nephew as a child, was proud of him as a Beatle with his wife and son, but the new-look John, complete with bushy, unkempt beard, biblical-length hair, a strange reputation for displaying himself in bed, and the new wife he introduced, was not so acceptable. John told her that he wanted to secure custody of Julian, then six years old.

'You've ruined all chances of that,' said Mater curtly. 'You've made your bed, now lie on it.' An angry John left, with Yoko, Julian, and Kyoko, with John driving a hired Austin Maxi saloon for the Highlands.

He was an erratic driver and his attention tended to wander. On a narrow country road not far from Mater's house at Golspie, Sutherland, he missed a bend and the car rolled over, ending up in a ditch. John was the most badly hurt and blood poured from his face. Yoko, too, had facial injuries. A passer-by called an ambulance and they were taken, with Kyoko and Julian, to hospital. John's face had seventeen stitches and Yoko fourteen. Kyoko needed four stitches, while Julian, the least affected, suffered shock.

Cynthia was astonished to hear the news of the car accident on the television news. She had no idea that John and Yoko were taking Julian on a long car journey. She phoned Peter Brown, the Beatles' assistant, and asked to be taken to the hospital so that she could bring Julian home. Unfortunately they got on a plane going to Belfast, not Scotland. Eventually, another flight from Belfast and a four-hour taxi ride later, Cynthia arrived at the cottage hospital to be told that Julian had just been sent to stay with Aunt Mater. John and Yoko did not want to see her. She set off immediately to collect Julian from Mater's and they returned to London next day.

The whole strategy behind the 'peace offensive' called for constant action. Headline hunting was, by John's admission, a key part of his philosophy. He had always felt uneasy about the Beatles' acceptance of the M.B.E. in 1965, which he thought symbolized the Beatles selling-out to the Establishment. Four years later, with the Beatles in ruins, John felt it was a good time to have the courage of his earlier convictions. He would send his medal back to the Queen and do it as a gesture for peace.

John's chauffeur, Les Anthony, was despatched from Tittenhurst to Poole, Dorset, and Aunt Mimi. She proudly kept the medal on top of her television set. 'Mr Lennon said would you lend him the M.B.E. medal for a while,' said Les Anthony when he arrived.

Says Mimi: 'I said, "Yes, but tell him, don't forget it's mine and I want it back." ' The next day she was as aghast as the rest of Britain to read that John had returned it to the Queen at Buckingham Palace, accompanied by the following letter:

Your Majesty,
I am returning this M.B.E. in protest against Britain's involvement in the Nigeria–Biafra thing, against our support of America in Vietnam, and against 'Cold Turkey' slipping down the charts.

With love,
John Lennon of Bag

A copy was also sent to Prime Minister Harold Wilson. Reaction was immediate: it was a rare event for anyone, particularly a Beatle, to return an honour bestowed by the Queen. Cranky old Lennon hit the headlines again and achieved his purpose. He explained that he had always felt uncomfortable at receiving it; he believed the Beatles were part of the Esablishment and he had accepted it because he was a Beatle. Now he was rejecting it as his right. The reason behind its return was to draw attention to his peace campaign. The mention of 'Cold Turkey', his latest record, was 'humour to stop it from sounding like it was another stupid letter to the Queen from some boring colonel'.

Aunt Mimi, furious, was on the phone immediately. 'Over my dead body would I have given you the medal back to insult the Queen with. She's just a figurehead. Why did you go and embarrass her?' John told her he meant to keep up his long protest for peace and that this was a good way. 'John, you can't worry about the whole world,' she sighed. 'It's good that you do contribute and give money but this way was so ridiculous.' John was used to Mimi's condemnations, but this time she left him in no doubt: 'He broke my heart over that. And also, he didn't tell me first why that medal was being taken away.'

Predictably irate lords and ladies, not to mention retired colonels bellowed that what they feared all along had now been amply demonstrated by that young lout Lennon. He was a bad egg, a disgrace to the country, a mere pop idol, totally unworthy of receiving the honour in the first instance. (Although John had rejected the medal, the honour itself remained; he was still technically an M.B.E. Recipients can send back their medals but they cannot renounce an honour once it has been bestowed.)

Lord Wilson, who as prime minister had originally recommended the award to the Queen, remembers John fondly and now believes he was 'naïve' in sending his medal back. 'John Lennon lived his life from day to day,' Lord Wilson told me. 'He didn't have to look two, three, five years ahead and people in showbiz don't have to have a relationship with fifty to a hundred countries,

John telephones journalists around the world from his Apple office in
November 1969 to explain why he has returned his M.B.E. medal to the
Queen. A copy of his laconic letter lies on the desk in front of him

all of whom have different ideas. The Prime Minister has got to think in terms of long-term relationships.'

Lord Wilson had no regrets over having recommended the award. 'John's rejection of it was his personal right. The award at the time shocked a great many people because the Press was mainly hostile to me. They'd spent all their time trying to keep Labour out of government. Many of them had not come to realize what the role of the Beatles in young people's lives had come to be. The award was well earned. . . .' Many of John's critics at this time felt that he was setting a bad example to youth by his drug-taking. Lord Wilson takes a more understanding view: 'It's easy to condemn. He was living a very, very strange existence when on the platform, broadcasting, or doing music for a bit of fun. As a superb performer, he was under great strain and he would not at any cost want to fall below the performance standard he had set himself.

'It was tragic that he had to take something. I don't suppose it was necessary but a lot of people his age had a shot of it. But if he was going to do it it was a pity he didn't keep it to himself. People who worshipped the ground on which he walked would say that if he does it, it's all right, never mind what Dad and Mum say.' Resentment of John by the media, says Lord Wilson, stemmed partly from the fact that most journalists were of an older generation and 'resented the kids making all that money'. He adds: 'John Lennon used to put his hands very deep into his pockets if he heard of a good cause, and despite the lack of publicity, on which his trade sort of depends, most gifts were anonymous.'

Another aspect of John's past which reappeared in his life in that summer of 1969 was his father. Much as he often tried, John found it impossible to shake off his roots. He had never properly forgiven his father for deserting him in childhood. But his conscience and sentimentality won the day occasionally: he had for example invited Freddy Lennon to the party to launch the *Magical Mystery Tour* back in December 1967. The event, at London's Royal Lancaster Hotel, had ended with John and his father getting very drunk and dancing happily together. (John spent a lot of time chatting up women other than his wife. Singer Lulu was furious and remonstrated angrily with John for his bad behaviour.)

Relations with his father had always been strained, ever since he had reappeared in John's life during Beatlemania. In 1968 Fred had married student Pauline Jones and in the summer of 1969, John's first half-brother, David Henry Lennon, was born in Brighton. When Freddy phoned John at Tittenhurst Park to tell him his good news, John was delighted. He invited Freddy to his new home, with the child, so that he could meet Yoko too. But when Freddy arrived, John was in a black mood and he happened to be in the firing line. 'How dare you come back into my life whenever you think you can?' roared John to his baffled father. 'You weren't around when I needed you most. Get out.' John added the final, crushing blow when he said he didn't want to see him again. Freddy, who had after all been invited, left, hurt.

That proved to be their last meeting. Freddy Lennon died, aged sixty-three, from cancer of the stomach at Brighton General Hospital on 1 April 1976. From his New York home John phoned the hospital during Freddy's illness and spoke to him, thinking back to their last ugly encounter. Over several hours of conversation he tried to instil in him the will to live. He told him of his new-born son Sean – 'You can't die,' said John.

John told friends that he would have preferred to have totally resolved his relationship with his father but that obviously it was not possible. He always looked two ways at their division and his father's abdication of his responsibilities by going to sea when John was a toddler. 'Some parents,' said John, 'just can't take the responsibility of kids. I realize that now. I would like to have had a better relationship with him, but we didn't and that was OK, too. It's the way it was meant to be.' The loss of his ebullient mother, killed in a road accident, was different. He rarely spoke of her but when he thought of her tears were never far away.

The early 1970s found John and Yoko in complicated situations over Julian and Kyoko. Both their former partners were looking after their respective children but John and Yoko wanted regular contact. It proved harder to achieve than either expected.

Cynthia, with her second husband-to-be Roberto Bassanini, was so anxious to keep good relations with John and Yoko that she invited them to her housewarming party in Kensington, London. John and Yoko, Paul, George, Ringo and his wife Maureen, and Neil Aspinall all went. John had a good chat with Roberto, and Cynthia hoped she had staged a successful event. But suddenly tension developed as the Beatles recalled the factors that separated them, both professionally and as husband-and-wife teams. 'It wasn't successful,' agrees Cynthia. 'It taught me that you can't step back into the past. Too many dramatic things had happened to all of them and the break-up of the very first Beatle marriage came home to them. They were all shell-shocked after they'd been there a while. Tight, nervous, everybody watching everyone else.'

Shortly afterwards, John phoned Cynthia: 'I want to come round and see Julian.' Their son had started at a new school and John wanted to check on his progress. He spent two hours alone with Julian in his bedroom, talking and drawing with him on the six-year-old boy's blackboard. 'He was really bright, cheerful, and friendly,' says Cynthia. He gave her a book to read by an American psychologist, Dr Arthur Janov, saying it was proving a great eye-opener to him. 'Oh no,' said Cynthia to herself. 'Not another! Either it's Janov or the Maharishi or drugs and vegetarianism!' But John said he had been feeling guilty about his absence from Julian and that Janov had convinced him that he should see his son more often, alone.

Yoko's contact with Kyoko was much more complex. In December 1969 John and Yoko holidayed in Denmark with Anthony Cox, Yoko's second husband, together with his new wife, Belinda, and Kyoko. Anthony Cox pronounced John 'a great guy'. Everything looked set fair for harmonious access. But it was not to be so easy.

The issue of custody of Kyoko was never properly resolved when Yoko and Tony Cox were divorced, and Yoko expected free access to her daughter. But after an ugly experience in Majorca in 1971, when John and Yoko were detained by police for a day on suspicion of kidnapping her, Anthony Cox vanished with Kyoko. The search in Majorca had appalled John and Yoko. 'How can you kidnap your own daughter?' said Yoko. Anthony Cox's evasiveness with the eight-year-old girl was what decided John and Yoko to move to New York. They first visited there in June 1971, believing that Cox had taken the girl into the city. Courtroom appearances and visits to the Virgin Islands, plus private detectives and international publicity, never properly resolved Yoko's and John's desire for a peaceful relationship with Kyoko and Anthony Cox. But in September 1971, while they were living temporarily in Manhattan's St Regis Hotel in the hope of finding Kyoko, they decided to live permanently in America. Yoko, who knew every corner of the city in which she had grown up in the 1950s, took John walking round it, and he needed little urging to convince him that it was the right environment for an artist. John applied the same logic, and description, as he had when first seeing Tittenhurst Park. 'Yoko and I seemed to be forever coming to New

John's first meeting with Kyoko, daughter of Yoko by her first marriage to film producer Tony Cox, in May 1969. Kyoko, aged five, had just flown in to London's Heathrow Airport from New York

York,' he explained later. 'It seemed more *functional* to come and live here.'

Two critical events preceded the emigration. In early 1970, while workmen were still re-structuring Tittenhurst to John and Yoko's specifications, Mr and Mrs Lennon began bickering. It was not surprising. For three intense years since their first meeting they had not been out of each other's sight. There was no danger of a split but every conversation was edgy. Yoko was very weary of the Apple battle and the resentful atmosphere towards her. She missed her daughter. John was tense too but he could see no way out of the forest. He was desperate to solve the Beatles' business wrangle. He buried himself in endless television, concentrating on very little except the commercials, which had always fascinated him and given him occasional lines for songs. John in a foul mood was bad news for anyone near him: he would bark or scream at the slightest intrusion into his self-imposed silence. But both he and Yoko realized the reason for their tension: 'We were close friends, twenty-four hours a day, as well as artists,' recalls Yoko. 'No relationship survives without highs and lows. It's realization of the situation that's vital.'

Luck had been a central ingredient in John's life. His childhood was marred but once into his teens and his music lucky breaks had been his salvation. The greatest break in helping him through this particular psychological barrier came from the book by Janov that he had tried to persuade Cynthia to read. It was called *The Primal Scream (Primal Therapy: The Cure for Neurosis)*. John was hooked as quickly as he had been on drugs and meditation. Janov's cool logic regarding the treatment of neurosis made total sense to John. Like everything he touched, he had to plunge into it at full tilt – and he could never go into something like this alone. Yoko was a quick believer too. They phoned Janov in California and invited him to Ascot. Primal therapy might well have been designed exactly for John in his state of mind at that time.

Its theory was simple. It worked on the assumption that the patient had layers of defences which needed stripping down to reveal the real person. By owning up to fallibilities and frailties and confessing to oneself the struggle of childhood, particularly one's relationship with parents, the person who underwent ther-apy willingly would come face to face with his real self again, literally screaming away the pain. It was simple but in John's case, effective. Janov had his first sessions with John and Yoko over three weeks at Tittenhurst Park. Then he told them they would have to go to the Primal Institute in California to continue the

Yoko's first husband Tony
Cox, his second wife Belinda,
Yoko and John, the four of
them together in apparent
harmony for once. The picture
was taken in Majorca in April
1971

Yoko, almost unrecognizable
in her wig, and John waiting to
fly home from Majorca after
failing to retrieve Yoko's
daughter, Kyoko, from her
father, Tony Cox, during the
battle for custody

course. There was no choice for John: he was deriving an
enormous amount of personal strength from talking himself
through the agony of his childhood and his inhibitions about his
lost parents. He and Yoko stayed in California for four months,
renting a house in Bel Air and plunging into what he later
described to me as something 'much more important to my life
than the Beatles'. He went on: 'Janov showed me how to feel my
own fear and pain, therefore I can handle it better than I could
before, that's all. I'm the same, only there's a channel. It doesn't
just remain in me, it goes round and out.'

One of John's most endearing characteristics, honesty, was to
pour out of him as a result of primal therapy. The new John sang
of his childhood in heart-rending songs: in 'Mother', 'Mother you
had me/But I never had you. . . Father, you left me/But I never left
you.' In 'Working Class Hero' he sang of the pressures of his
school years, which partly explained his outlandish behaviour; in
'Isolation', he pinpointed the dilemma of being John and Yoko:
'Just a boy and a little girl/Trying to change the whole wide
world.' And in 'God' he therapeutically listed all the points of
reference which his mind wanted to offload: 'I don't believe in
magic . . . I don't believe in Jesus . . . I don't believe in Kennedy . . .
I don't believe in kings . . . I don't believe in Elvis . . . I don't
believe in Zimmerman [Bob Dylan] . . . I don't believe in Beatles/I
just believe in me/Yoko and me/And that's reality.' The starkness
of his confessional was searing, simple, and it made a staggering
impact on those who had written off the post-Beatle Lennon as a
freaky sideshow. A straight song, 'Love', demonstrated that he
could easily outshine McCartney in this chosen route of romance;
the poetic beauty of the song attracted Barbra Streisand who
recorded her own version as did many other artists. *John Lennon/
Plastic Ono Band*, with John often accompanying himself on the
piano, featured Yoko, with Klaus Voormann on bass and Ringo
on drums. It stands as an album many of John's contemporaries
feel is one of rock's greatest works. Only Bob Dylan, with less
introspective genius, can have his work compared with *Plastic
Ono Band* and its successor, *Imagine*, for soul-baring intensity
and such a forceful projection of intense emotions. And even
Dylan never wrote so personally. The two albums, appearing in
1970 and 1971 in the wake of Dr Janov's primal therapy, were
vital signposts for John's future psyche. He often described himself
as a chameleon. With these two albums, he stepped outside the
traditional rock 'n' roll formula to show his inner self and to prove
that at least two of his old images were inadequate. Hard old

Lennon, the Liverpool rocker, would no longer do. Nor would the image of the lunatic peacenik. John came of age in 1970 and 1971. A change of country, to accommodate his philosophy, seemed the natural next step.

On the eve of their final departure from British soil, John and Yoko appeared on B.B.C. television's Michael Parkinson chat show. Yoko read some excerpts from *Grapefruit*, which John praised; Parkinson described the book as incomprehensible. John retorted: 'It's so simple, it eludes you. A lot of people over here don't understand it but a lot of people in America understand it because there's a lot of avant-garde there, especially in New York, which is where she lived for ten years. A lot of people who read the book when it was published ten years ago in limited form are now professors in American universities and *Grapefruit* is part of the curriculum in film schools.'

Parkinson persisted: 'I think the creative phase that you're going through at present . . . you've got to accept, that it's alienated you, particularly John, from the people that originally loved you in this country.'

John replied, 'When I left Liverpool with the group, a lot of Liverpool people dropped us and said: "Now you've let us down." When we left England with the group to go to America, we lost a lot of fans who had begun to feel as if they owned us. Well, the Liverpool people did and they did until we decided to leave. The same in England, a lot of people dropped us because we went to America. But of course we got a whole pile more, a different audience. And it's the same now. I'm not going to sort of gear my life just to attract an audience. I started off playing music because that's what I wanted to do. And in front of an audience is how you do it. And now it's not very different. I mean, then I sang "All You Need Is Love", and now I might sing "Power To The People". And the message is basically the same. It's just sort of slogans. The alienation started when I met Yoko; people do not seem to like people getting a divorce, you know. It's all right to do it quietly but we can't do it quietly. So we fell in love and it's unfortunate! We fell in love and we married. A lot of people think that to be odd, but it happens all the time. Yoko just happened to be Japanese which didn't help much. And so everybody had this impression that John's gone crazy. All I did was fall in love like a lot of people do who are already married, who married somebody very young. and that's all we did. I know we did *Two Virgins* which didn't help much!'

Yoko added, 'I'd be a masochist if I loved this country, where

I'm constantly abused. It's a bit tough on me, you know.'

Parkinson responded: 'Another reason for people taking a dislike of you is because you've become known, again through the newspapers in this country, as the woman who broke up the Beatles. But that's not true?'

'That's not true,' John answered. 'Listen, I'll tell you. People on the street and kids do not dislike us. It's the media. We go on the street and lorry drivers wave and say, "Hello, Yoko, hello, John," and all that jazz. I judge it by that. . . . Nobody could break the Beatles up. We broke ourselves up. When Brian [Epstein] died we got a bit lost because we needed a manager, all of us are artists and we're nothing else. We can't manage ourselves or look after ourselves in that way. But it's a lot for four big heads like the Beatles to stay together for such a long time. In the early days there was the thing of "making it" big, or breaking into America and we had that goal together . . . but when we reached twenty-eight or twenty-nine . . . our personalities developed and they were a bit stifled with the Beatles. And between us now we sell ten times more records than the Beatles did.' This was not true and, typically, John said it to demonstrate a point rather than accept the facts. By the end of 1970 sales of Beatles records totalled approximately 500 million units worldwide. The *Guinness Book of Records* states that between February 1963 and January 1972 the Beatles sold 545 million records. In the period January 1963 to August 1966 when they ceased to tour, the estimated international attendance at Beatles concerts was 2,676,000. The four Beatles as soloists (taken either separately or together) did not fill anything like that number of seats, nor sell anything like that number of records.

Michael Parkinson asked John how deep the hurt was between him and Paul McCartney. 'It's fairly deep,' John replied. 'We're playing Monopoly now with real money and so it's pretty serious. But I can't see it lasting and I think it'll probably cool off. It'll take a year after the whole thing is settled, moneywise, probably for us to relax a bit.'

Getting immersed in the spirit of things, Parkinson got inside a bag in the studio while he questioned John and Yoko. 'Hey,' said John, 'imagine if a black guy went for a job at the B.B.C. and he had to wear a bag. They wouldn't know what coloured people were and there'd be no prejudice, for a kick-off!'

Staying on the theme of the bag and relating it to the Beatles, John continued: 'There's no conceivable reason why the Beatles should come back together again because we're all individuals and

Top: John, naturally horrified by the lingerie advertisements in a Spanish magazine bought in Majorca

Above: Happiness exudes from John and Yoko in this picture taken at the Cannes Film Festival in May 1971. They went to attend the world premiere of their films *Fly* and *Apotheosis*

in the Beatles we grew out of it. The bag was too small. I can't impose far-out music and far-out films on George and Paul if they don't want to do it. We have to live our lives separately. We've grown up now. We've left school. We never *left* school. We went straight into showbiz.'

Yoko interjected: 'Michael, this is a typical example. We are so nostalgic and we're talking about the past. But we have to live in the present. You can burn the past. That's why even in this book, *Grapefruit*, I'd like people to burn it after they've read it.'

John said finally: 'There's a beautiful story Yoko told me about a Japanese monk, which happened within the last ten years. He loved this fantastic golden temple so much that he didn't want to see it disintegrate. So he burned it . . . that is what I did with the Beatles. I never wanted them to slide down, making comebacks. I said when I was twenty in the Beatles: "I'm not going to be singing 'She Loves You' when I'm thirty." ' John had a fine memory for generalization but a terrible recollection of details. The interview he was referred to was with me for the *Melody Maker* on 24 October 1964. He had actually said: 'I don't want to be fiddling round the world singing "It's Been A Hard Day's Night" when I'm thirty, do I? I said during a conversation with Mick Jagger that I'd be out of it in a few years. I enjoy playing really but in America it was spoiled for me because of the crap there . . . meeting people we don't want to meet. I suppose I'm a bit intolerant. Well, I was thirty this year [sic]. I didn't force it to happen this year. It just happened naturally.

'I guessed that by the time I was thirty I would have grown out of it. And I have, you know. And the guy burned the temple. And most people still like the Beatles and have a pleasant memory of them . . . let's remember them like that and remember their music like we remember people from the past. That's fine.'

British singer George Melly, whose clash with John over his musical roots is discussed in the first volume of this biography, met a very different ex-Beatle in the television show. (Melly was on the same Parkinson programme.) 'We had a very nice talk this time,' says Melly. 'Not very productive because it was difficult to understand what they were getting at, exactly, except for peace and love. But their gentleness and affection for each other was very, very powerful. I really felt warm to them because I didn't expect to. They irritated me with their bagism and the fact that they were very rich and constantly making humble gestures. If only the acorns had done some good or the bagism had persuaded people to be peaceful. But it just irritated most people and I felt it wasn't very useful. Together, though, she with her dreamy beads and long hair, he with long hair and granny glasses, and both holding hands constantly, they were charming, childlike.' Contrasting vividly with the drunken John who had seven years earlier berated Melly at a publisher's party, he was warm and polite.

'There you are, you see, Yoko,' John said, when they came to leave Melly. 'There *are* nice people in England.'

4
CHANGE

'My function in society is to be an artist'

John firmly believed in the adage that the best method of defence is attack. In the late 1960s, when he had married Yoko and taken a battering from both the Press and public opinion about their liaison and 'stunts for peace', John countered with some of his most forceful interviews. He still loved talking, particularly about himself: one of his strongest lines of defence of his publicly declared love for Yoko was that they were doing the Establishment a favour by making marriage fashionable against all the odds.

Talking to the new, post-Beatle Lennon, one encountered the man as he had originally been in Liverpool: in a hurry, warm and generous, full of invective, incurably idealistic. Between his marriage to Yoko in 1969 and their move to New York in 1971 I had many interviews with him, covering a wide range of topics. He said to me in 1969: 'Go on – ask me some questions that will get on the front page of the dailies. I'm not a moptop any more. I can say what I like!'

His ego was always big, but he said that he would rather have a following that did not seek his autograph. 'If kids want my signature and I'm in the right mood and it's the right person, they can have it. But it depends on the person who asks.' Living with Yoko had changed his outlook: there was nothing he had, materially, that he could not do without, now that he had found inner peace. 'I'm glad to have got the pop star thing out of the way. It was good and it gave me this freedom. But we grew up, grew apart.' He always firmly declared that the Beatles did not set any trends. 'We never did start anything. We were just part of the whole sixties thing, the movement, the fashion, the change in attitude among a load of people. The Beatles were just in the middle of it.'

Because of his nudity on the *Two Virgins* album cover, John said people thought of him as 'a perverted crank. They think Yoko and I are ravers, only interested in sex and causing a stir. But really, we're the quietest pair of spinsters around.' He was a vegetarian, and Yoko usually baked their bread. He wanted a farm so that they could grow their own macrobiotic food. 'It works like Zen Buddhism or meditation – you eat what you think's best for you and it's commonsense to me that you shouldn't eat most of the chemically treated rubbish most people seem to stuff themselves with. The trouble is most vegetarians don't get enough protein. My diet's based on meal, bread which Yoko makes, rice and no sugar. We have honey if anything needs sweetening.' But he wore leather shoes, I pointed out. 'I still wear the shoes I had before I changed my views. I don't see the point of not using them. I won't buy any more leather ones, though. I'm always wearing sneakers. I don't think animals were meant to be eaten and worn. We have enough resources to do without them. But it's big business again, you see.' Did he feel better, I asked him, since giving up meat? 'Yeah, but a car can last a long time on the wrong petrol. One day it packs up. I feel better mentally but maybe my diet's not right for everyone.'

He told me the best thing to come out of the Beatles was the power it gave him to do other things from a platform people would notice. 'I'm using my power all the time by doing things like releasing an album called *Two Virgins*. There are generation gaps and other gaps, plenty of them, in this world and they all need closing. I'm trying to open people's minds. There's nothing horrible about nudity. People said the Rolling Stones, and Elvis, and long hair were all obscene but they accepted them in the end. I hope it's the same with my scene. A lot of narrow minds need expanding. People say I offend "normal" people. . . . Society's full of people who think of themselves as normal, who aren't. It's as wrong as judging me as a hippy because I happen to have long hair. It's more what a man's scene is in his mind than how he looks or what he wears. You can be a pretty cool bin man.'

He believed in religion and had not regarded the Maharishi as a substitute for it. 'The Maharishi was good for me, like anybody who has something to tell you that you don't know enough about. He was no substitute for anything, though. There's a lot of good in Christianity but you've got to learn the basics of it, and the basics from the Eastern beliefs, and work them together for yourself. . . . Yoko and I are fighting a bit of a fight to spread understanding and a kind of freedom. I don't expect everybody to understand us but I just wish they'd try to be a bit more open-minded, that's all. Beatles wives always had a hard time, probably because the fans resented us marrying. I got more stick because I was the loud-mouth – and then I went and got meself a new wife without asking permission. And a Japanese one at that! It's "How dare Lennon go off with this woman who's not a housewife.?" ' They were hurt by a lot of anti-Japanese mail.

He pointed out that he wanted to use power constructively. 'When we say, "War is over, if you want it", we mean that if everybody demanded peace instead of another television set, there'd be peace. If you like, we're the Tolpuddle Martyrs of our day. People said the first trade union leaders were fighting a losing battle, but when people realized what they could achieve by banding together and demanding their rights, they got it. It's a communal thing. Everybody has power, not just John and Yoko. We want to spread awareness.' In himself he was striving for perfection but doubted if he would achieve it. 'I'd like to be like Christ.' He described himself as a Christian communist, 'in a pure sense, not in the way Russia or Italy think of Christianity or communism'.

He consistently denied that he wanted to be seen as a leader. 'I'm not falling for that one. Like Pete Seeger said, we don't have a leader, but we have a song, "Give Peace A Chance". I refuse to be a leader. . . . Our whole mistake is having leaders and people we can rely on or point a finger at.'

Yoko often took up a point during the interviews. 'For inst-ance,' she said, 'many people say . . . don't do anything that is misleading, like showing your genitals. Always keep a clean image so that people can believe in your peace movement.

'But that's exactly what the Establishment is doing, ['And that's what the Beatles did, too,' said John.] taking their children to church on Sundays. This is showing that "I'm the President of the United States and I'm all right and I'm healthy and very moral et cetera." You don't get anywhere that way. You just become another hypocrite and you're playing the Establishment game. We don't want to do that. We try to be honest and the point is, if we are really honest, just to make it between us is really a lifetime thing. And if we can't make it together and endure each other the world is nowhere.

'If ordinary couples can make it together and make it with their children and so forth, love-wise ['She doesn't mean "make it" as in "lay",' interjected John.] then you can look after the world.'

John said: 'One thing we've found out is that love is a great gift, like a precious flower or something.' He often harkened back to romantic analogies. 'You have to feed it and look after it and it has storms to go through, and snow, but you have to protect it. . . . It's like a pet cat. You know, people get a cat and they don't want to feed it, or they get a dog and they won't want to walk it. But love has to be nurtured like a very sensitive animal because that's what it is. And you have to work at love. You don't just sit round with it and it doesn't just do it for you. You've got to be very careful with it. It's the most delicate thing you can be given.'

'People hide from each other all the time,' he continued. 'Everybody's frightened of saying something nice about somebody in case they don't say something nice back or in case they get hurt. . . . Everybody's uptight and they're always building these walls around themselves. All you can do is try and break down the walls and show that there's nothing there but *people*. It's just like looking in the mirror. . . . Of course we mustn't take ourselves too seriously. What we try and do is be non-serious about things but we are very serious about being not serious!'

Yoko said: 'We may be too serious, even. We try to have a sense of humour and to smile at everyone, a really genuine smile from the bottom of our hearts.'

John's laconic humour always permeated his work, even at a peak of his peace campaign with Yoko. To a circle of friends at Christmas in 1969, he sent a dry, hilarious item called 'The John Lennon London Diary 1969'. He had handwritten an entry for each day. Most were a very slight variation on the same words: 'Got up, went to work, came home, watched telly, went to bed.' It was a beautiful parody of the routine of life. But, like John, it was unpredictable: forgetfulness and boredom set in as he continued and one or two entries read: 'Got up, went to work, came home, watched telly, went to bed, fucked the wife,' for example. It was reassuring for some to know that Lennon's wit was still intact, come drugs, bagism or peace.

Demonstrative humour was more difficult for Yoko. Critics constantly jibed at her expressionless demeanour. In truth she has a cool, subterranean sense of humour. Her smiles are few because, as a child, her mother warned her against too much smiling lest it be construed by people as a sign of weakness.

The theory that Yoko's inscrutability had vanquished John's sense of fun was knocked firmly aside when they released a 1970 calendar which, month-by-month, captured in photographs their lives together. The calendar featured excerpts from his songs, his writings in *A Spaniard In The Works* and *In His Own Write*, plus quotations from *Grapefruit*. John set off the calendar with this original piece, demonstrating that his gobbledegook type of wit was still intact:

> wonsaapoatime therewas two Balloons called Jock and Yono. They were strictly in love-bound to happen in a million years. They werer together man. Unfortunatimetable they both seemed to have previous experience – which kept calling them one way oranother. (you know howitis). But they battled on against overwhelming oddities, includo some of there beast friends. . . . Being in love they cloong even the more together man – but some of the poisonessmonster of outrated bus-lodedshithrowers did stick slightly and they occasionally had to resort to the drycleaners. Luckily this did not kill them and they werent banned from the olympic games. They lived hopefully ever after, and who could blame them.

Paradoxically, it was John, rather than Yoko, who whole-heartedly publicly championed the cause of women's liberation once he had met her in the early seventies. Len Wood of E.M.I. Records, recalls a visit to the Apple office at Broadway, New York, which had to be cut short. 'Yoko was going to a rally for women's rights, but she was most insistent that John should be the only male there,' says Wood. She was on the phone for ages impressing on these women that if they banned her husband from attending the rally, that would be a kind of reverse bigotry; she won her case and John attended. And on her striking double album, called *Approximately Infinite Universe*, she satirized the women's liberation movement with a song called 'What A Bastard The World Is'. 'So they would scream and kick out all the men? *Then* what are they going to do?' asked Yoko. 'I told John, and he agreed, that feminism involves men too. John helped the movement towards equality more by *doing* something, like house-husbandry, than a million people demonstrating for it. . . . Initial-ly, feminists thought that the fact that I was married was a betrayal of the whole idea. As for the idea of really *loving* John, and saying so – *loving a man*, what was *this*? I wrote a song called "I Want My Man To Rest Tonight", which was addressed to my feminist sisters and said: let's not blame our men too much. They are doing their best. That was sniggered at. But I think in a male chauvinist society it was just as difficult for men too. They had to adjust. The reason I did not become an extreme feminist was a lot to do with living with John. He was a good influence.'

Reflecting on her early years in London, Yoko says: 'I was getting sick and tired of the pseudo-intellectual, elitist atmosphere of the circle I was in in London. I was thinking: Am I going to end up as the Queen Mother of the avant-garde world, always meeting these snobs talking about elitist kicks? I was starting to feel frightened.

'When I started to make the bottoms film I became very known in England in a strange sort of way – like to taxi drivers, that sort of thing – and my elite friends were so very upset about that. They were saying: "Well, she copped out, she went commercial."

'I said: "It's great to communicate your art with the working class. What *is* this?" But all the same they stopped inviting me to their tea party; just sort of inverted snobbery.

'Around this time I met John. The first song we recorded on *Approximately Infinitely Universe* was "Song for John". It was a song I made actually before I met him. I was hoping to find somebody who'd fly with me, or whatever, and I made a demo record. It's the first demo of mine that John listened to when he visited me and that's why, for sentimental reasons, I called it "Song for John". It's the same tune, same lyrics.'

The Lennons at home were much more traditional as husband and wife than their public face indicated. 'There's nothing I like more,' John told the *Melody Maker*, 'than to get home at the end of the day and sit next to Yoko and say, "Well, we're together at last." Although we may have been holding hands all day, it's not the same when we're working or talking to the Press. We feel a hundred miles apart by comparison.'

Yoko confessed that she was lonely before she met John. 'Most people in the world are very lonely. That's the biggest problem,' she said. 'Because of their loneliness, they become suspicious. When I met John I started to open up a little, through love, you know, and that's the greatest thing that happened to me yet. . . . I never met anybody else who could understand me. We understand each other so well and I'm not lonely any more. Through loneliness, I was starting to become a very firm and strong ego. That's melting away and that's nice.'

John described his pre-Yoko loneliness this way: 'I didn't have full communication with anybody and it took a bit of adjusting. She re-discovered or cultivated the thing that existed in me before I left Liverpool, maybe, and re-cultivated the natural John Lennon

John and Yoko in carefree mood
outside their home, Tittenhurst
Park, in January 1970

that had been lost in the Beatles thing and the world-wide thing. She encouraged me to be myself because it was me she fell in love with, not the Beatles or whatever I was.

'When you get sidetracked you believe it, and when you're in the dark you believe it. She came and reminded me that there was light and when you remember there's light you don't want to get back in the dark again.'

Yoko continued: 'It's the falling in love bit. You start to see all sorts of things that you don't see if you're not in love. I found that he has all these qualities that he was hiding away. Music-wise, he was doing all sorts of freaky things at home, just recording it on a cassette, but not really showing it publicly.

'Publicly he was doing the Beatles things. But he showed me all these cassettes and things and I said: "Why don't you produce these as records?" I performed the role of a mirror in a way. He was doing all those things anyway. I didn't suggest them. It was there and that goes for his drawing, paintings, and poetry too, especially his drawings. I think he's better than Picasso.'

John stopped her: 'She's biased!'

On another visit to Ascot, John particularly wanted to talk to me about his rationale behind the peace crusade. How exactly, did they seek to make the world more peaceful? I wanted to know. What would John do, for instance, if he was elected prime minister?

'I'd stop selling arms to Nigeria and all that. I'd get rid of the army and the air force and become a Sweden. I'm not a practical guy, I only know peace can exist, and the first thing is for the world to disarm.

'But would I have enough power, as a prime minister to do this? How much control does Wilson have? What chance would a peacenik prime minister have? I don't know. I just know things are not very good now and it must be worth a try.'

Life with the Lennons down at Ascot was a communal affair: members of the Krishna Consciousness Society hung around and John and Yoko would join them in their chanting. The Lennons liked this scene: it appealed to John's ideas of 'mixing with the people'. He was philosophical and decisive in his attitude to his wealth.

'You don't have to be poor to be a communist,' he said, laughing. 'My money that was earned as a Beatle, it's almost a by-product. I'm not just going to give it all away to some people, just so that I can starve like a lot of others. What's *that* going to achieve?

'But the money doesn't give me any hang-ups. . . . Both Yoko and I have this dream of living in a small cottage in the country, eventually. But we ended up with this big Georgian house. Now we're going through this big house scene before moving on.'

'But for the moment we enjoy it,' said Yoko passively.

John said that he got more pleasure from old 78 records than from revelling in the size and glory of his home. 'It means nothing to me,' he declared. 'A little bit of ivory I bought in Japan, that's my grossest material possession which I like as much as anything.'

'Material pleasures are all right as long as they don't clog your mind,' observed Yoko.

'I wouldn't worry,' John said, 'if I never had a thing. If it took too much to carry on living in this big house I wouldn't want to stay and live here . . . but I'm hoping to farm some of the land. The Krishna people are helping me do this. . . . We're hoping to grow non-chemical food – maybe we can sell it to Harrods.'

He reflected on the Beatles' touring days like this: 'Those old tours were OK at the time but once we had taken over from Helen Shapiro, there was nothing else to do, except for us to go around and other people to see us standing there, doing the same songs and not hearing a note.

'The Stones seemed to get a good thing in Hyde Park but it's different for us. We're not that type. Jagger is the Charlie Chaplin of rock and roll – it's OK for Mick because he's dancing around like a puppet and putting on a show. We don't. We couldn't stand the shell of unreality, standing there like four dolls in the middle of Shea Stadium. It killed our music.

'But when I see a group like The Band playing, I think we should have got going again before now.'

'Did he, I asked, think the Plastic Ono Band would survive as long as or longer than the Beatles? He dodged the answer with some facts: 'I think it will survive – you know my records with Yoko and the Plastic Ono have sold well. We sold twenty-five thousand copies of *Two Virgins* in the States and sixty thousand of *Life With the Lions*. That's good going in the States.

'Our new album, *John and Yoko's Wedding Album* is going to sell as well. But in Britain we only sold about five thousand of each of those albums. I can understand that though.

'See, Americans like our albums because if you land in New York, it's like *Life With The Lions* anyway. If you play it in Britain, it doesn't have the same urgency, because of the environment. It'll be a few years before they turn on to that sort of thing properly here.'

Left and overleaf: Informal shots taken in July 1971 at Tittenhurst Park, the £150,000 house John described as 'functional': the cluttered spare room, the bathroom, and the bedroom

'But we are patient,' said Yoko, 'because we are doing something worthwhile.'

John summarized the division between himself and the Beatles: 'I am an artist and my art is peace and I happen to be a musician. My music is done with the Beatles – that's where I get my wages from. The peace thing isn't a gimmick. Other people make it a gimmick. Yoko and I are serious.'

He clearly believed passionately in the peace campaign. 'It's the goodies and the baddies, the Blue Meanies, and the rest. I think I'll win because I believe in what Jesus said.'

Drawing on his Gauloise cigarettes in the Apple office, John devoured newspapers with an intensity that floored those who worked with him. He surprised the Apple team by his contradiction of his own image. The tough-talking Beatle was replaced, with Yoko at his side, by a man who was funny, gentle, and kind but nobody's fool. He strutted down the corridors, hands on hips. Gradually it was conceded that their partnership was impregnable, their message pure and sincere. It took time though and probably only sank in when Apple turned sour, the Beatles were officially pronounced dead, and John and Yoko had moved on to the next phase of their lives.

But for three years, for every success John counted there were people with trip wires, testing him. John enjoyed the challenge; some of his finest eloquence came during self-justification.

The 'Smile' box was a favourite way of getting the conversation going. It was a box which you had to open and inside it was a mirror which told the truth about your expression. The box, concocted by John and Yoko, kept many baffled and bemused because it had no message other than how the 'viewer' reacted. This, John would repeat to anyone, was Art with a capital A. Yoko described it as 'con art', which was short for conceptual art; meaning that the idea behind the piece was more important than the exhibit. John described Yoko as 'straight from Duchamp and Dada, but she's Now'. As a book he said, *Grapefruit* stood alongside the Bible.

As a film maker he was definitely interested in the avant-garde and art. Two films took up his time in 1970: *Apotheosis* followed on from *Self Portrait*, and *Erection* followed on from *Rape*. *Apotheosis* featured a balloon taking off from a snowy field in an English village and climbing into the clouds. The soundtrack is the fading noise of barking dogs, a hunting horn, and a gun being fired. When the balloon reaches the clouds, silence reigns for five minutes. The onus is on the viewer to interpret. The same is true of *Erection*: this film, made over nine months, depicts a hotel being erected in London's West Cromwell Road. The bizarre touch is the inactivity and slow progress made by the builders.

Art possessed John by the time he and Yoko made plans to go to live in America. He reflected on what they had achieved since 'going public'. The Amsterdam bed-in, he considered, was one of the greatest happenings of the century. Not because of what they had done but because of people's reactions: it was illogical, *marvellous*, that they hit the headlines just by getting married and going to bed to ask for peace. It was an Event. Communication, he intoned, was everything. 'The English are eccentrics. I'm just another one from a long line of eccentrics.'

He thought advertising their art was not reprehensible, rather a clear duty. People who believed they were stunts were naïve. 'Andy Warhol – the biggest publicity man in the world! Salvador Dali! Or Duchamp!' All artists struggled for publicity if they knew what they had to do, he said.

He was a revolutionary artist and he'd been consistent, right from 'All You Need Is Love' to 'Power To The People'. He was dedicated to change and to revolution in forcing people to think and react positively. Art for art's sake was decadent; he was writing songs for people to express themselves with. For example, at concerts in America, 30,000 people had sung 'Give Peace A Chance', and 20,000 were singing 'Power To The People' on the streets. Use of art for propaganda was totally right. To deny that was 'like saying, don't make knives in case you kill with them'.

He wrote songs for himself, primarily. 'You can't blame me or the song. I'm not here to provide power to the people: I'm *singin'* about it. I'm the songwriter who sang the song about it that the people sang at the meetings they held. That's all. That's my job. Like, if we're a community on an island, I'd be the singer. Somebody would be the carpenter, somebody else would be the cook. My function in society is to be an artist.

'You see,' he went on, 'society is under the delusion that art is something you have extra, like crème de menthe or something. But societies don't exist with no artist. Art is a functional part of society: if you don't have artists you don't have society. We're not some kind of decadent strip show that appears on the side. We're as important as prime ministers or policemen. So "Power To The People" isn't expected to make a revolution. It's for the people to sing, like the Christians sing hymns.'

John with a blindfolded Yoko behind him appears on BBC television's *Top Of The Pops* in February 1970 to sing 'Instant Karma!'. It was the first appearance by a Beatle on *Top Of The Pops* for four years; they recorded two shows, and the next week showed Yoko knitting behind John

He likes slogans, he continued. 'I like advertising. I love the telly.' He hated classical music; it was too slow. 'It's "then" music. It really is a load of crap. I think I write much more relevant music for today than the classical composers. . . . And where's today's classical music? There isn't any.'

His song 'Instant Karma!' was much more important than most of the classical music he had heard. 'It's about human beings, which is more than can be said for the classics. "Instant Karma!" is about action and reaction. Whenever you do something, whatever it is, there's a reaction to it. Even if you cough, you cough germs out all over the place. If you cough love out, out goes love. That's what "Instant Karma!" is – it's a great step forward. The greatest artists always come round to simplicity. It took Picasso sixty years to go through the whole bit and learn to paint like a child. I hope to record and write songs like an adult child.'

He was always at his most vociferous on the subject of peace. 'I'm not under any illusion. My contribution will be small in the light of the universe. Compared with the size of the earth, what John and Yoko achieve will be small, but it's the best we can manage. It takes time to be taken seriously. It took the Beatles time and then they were taken too seriously sometimes.' Yes, he agreed, the peace campaign was costing him a fortune, 'but you reap what you sow. Whatever you do, you get something back for it.'

I asked him why he equated himself with Christ so frequently during this period of self-revelation. 'I was brought up a Christian, Sunday School and all that. It's OK, I have nothing against it except that it organizes itself as a business, the Church. What I do like about it is that Christians talk about being perfect; so was Christ and I was taught that as a child. Christ is the one who most people in the West refer to when they speak of good people. . . . If I could do what Christ did, be as Christ was, that's what being a Christian is all about. I try to live as Christ lived. It's tough, I can tell you.'

Did he believe in God? 'I don't know that anyone like me, who questions everything down to the colour of his socks, can believe in an old man in the sky.' He was very thoughtful and silent for several minutes. 'I believe in something, definitely. I believe there is a force at work that you can't physically account for.'

During talks like these John would often stop himself from getting carried away or sounding portentous. 'Hey,' he would say. 'My Auntie Mimi says I sound too serious when I go on like this. She also reckons that having my hair cut short like this has turned me into a skinhead. Mimi – I'm happier now that I've ever been!'

An unkempt-looking John photographed during October 1969, the month of Yoko's second miscarriage

John and Yoko's unique partnership derived partly from the great difference in their backgrounds. 'She had hardly heard of the music that turned me on, like Elvis and "Heartbreak Hotel". I had all that to get through to her,' he explained. She gave John new insights into art. What constantly surprised them both was how, almost five years after first meeting, on the eve of their departure from London to New York, they could not get enough of each other's company. 'Her and Elvis, they both turned me on most in my life. They're the greatest influences. It's a miracle. We're more in love than ever,' he said. By then Yoko had suffered three miscarriages. John worried that they were his fault, that his heavy use of drugs had made him either infertile or had a bad effect on Yoko's body. 'John needs to rest,' said Yoko just before they left for America. 'No drugs except tobacco, and I've been off that for a year too.'

Their togetherness was precisely what alienated many people who considered them 'over the top' in mawkish sentimentality. 'People say that if we're together twenty-four hours a day, we must get sick and tired of each other but it's the contrary,' said Yoko. 'We got so addicted to that situation that we miss each other more. It's a very strange scene.'

John weighed in: 'Somebody said: "Won't you get so reliant on each other that you can't manage without each other?" and we said yes! The only thing that could split us is death and we have to face that . . . and we don't even believe we'll be split then, if we work on it.

'Our only worry in the world is that we die together, otherwise even if it's three minutes later it's going to be hell. . . . Most marriages have a little pretence going on and we thought: are we going to have to pretend that we're happy together because we daren't say that we want to be apart? But that doesn't happen. When two of you are together, man and wife, there's nothing that can touch you. You have the power of two people, the power of two minds, which is a pretty powerful thing.'

5
THE MUSIC:
1966–1971

'Let me take you down 'cos I'm going to ...'

From 'Strawberry Fields Forever' through to 'Imagine', John Lennon's work, in and out of the Beatles, was distinct and highly personalized. While Paul McCartney's gift lay in composing love songs, John was incapable of songwriting as a craftsman, 'for other people'. None the less, he admired some less syrupy McCartney compositions, particularly 'Here There And Everywhere' and 'For No One.' Conversely, the extrovert McCartney found it hard to write about himself. In that, John Lennon excelled. For although he loved the speed of rock 'n' roll, he thought the golden oldies of that genre were unbeatable; his own writing would have to act as a mirror of his personality, particularly as he grew older and more observant, and wanted more from life than teenagers screaming his name. At twenty-six, John wanted his music to express the important things in his life: his childhood memories; his assiduous reading of newspapers and magazines; his love of words and sharp observation of the unexpected phrase; his own frailties and rejection of the tough-guy Beatle image; and an increasing interest in humanitarianism.

During his life Lennon had demystified rock 'n' roll, which he believed was conceptually the best form of communication through music. As an artist he had been vulnerable, idealistic, and a worrier, lapsing into a frequent insecure dissection of who-wrote-what in the Lennon–McCartney songs. He was never totally able to stand back sufficiently from his own songs and accept their social impact. What he did, inside the Beatles, long after they split, and even when he was dead, was to inject his unique personal experiences into popular music.

115

Often described as the best-ever pop single, 'Strawberry Fields Forever' released in 1967, marked the start of the vital change in John's music. It was attributable to several factors: his meeting with Yoko at the end of 1966; his disillusionment with the Beatles myth; his use of drugs; and the important influence of Bob Dylan who led the way in putting *himself* into his songs.

Strawberry Field was a real place, a Salvation Army home just down the road from Aunt Mimi's in Woolton. It was a special place where she sometimes took him for ice-cream cornets and garden fetes. John enjoyed his childhood memories: 'Nothing is real/And nothing to get hungabout. . . .' It was Lennon in wonderland, re-creating the era of childhood simplicity when he knew he was happy.

Musically it invoked the very spirit of psychedelia raging that year. To get the required dreamy effect of trees, fields, and escapism, Lennon and producer George Martin spliced together two quite different versions of the song. It was a superb piece of technical editing by Martin and conjured up perfectly the ethereal feeling of the lyrics. From 'Strawberry Fields' onwards it was a one-way ticket for John: his music would be more incisive, more personal, more reflective, and more adventurous.

John's public persona became more intimidating from 1967. His droopy moustache gave him a sombre, almost sinister look, and sometimes, when he was under the influence of drugs, he wore a manic leer. With his hair cut short, his confidence was now apparent: so much so that he now wore his glasses in public.

The genius of John's writing was first captured on *Sgt Pepper's Lonely Hearts Club Band* with the songs 'A Day In The Life' and 'Lucy In The Sky With Diamonds'. *Sgt Pepper* marked rock music's coming of age, its scope and intention resulting a critical respectability. John's input on it showed that rock 'n' roll had come a long way since Elvis Presley's first recording sessions thirteen years before. It was prime 'pop art', seminal psychedelia. It also marked the apogee of studio technology at the time: four-track machines, Mellotrons, and forty-one-piece orchestras. Six months in the making, the cost was enormous – £25,000. Just to have the album was to be part of a special world, with the jokes on the run-out grooves, the note for the family dog, the badges and cut-outs, the coloured inner sleeve, the pretty pictures, and lyrics printed for the first time on a rock album.

The original idea behind the album was that it should be a concept L.P.: a memory of a day in the life of Liverpool children (which was to have included both 'Penny Lane' and 'Strawberry

Fields'). A double album, evoking lost innocence, adolescence, and maturity. But *Sgt Pepper* grew and grew and the original plan disappeared (although vestiges were retained with 'A Day In The Life' and 'When I'm Sixty-Four'). In its place came an album that broke new ground with the segueing of tracks, the lyrical obtuseness, the rich production, and lavish instrumentation.

The material on the album was culled from various sources: 'When I'm Sixty-Four' even went back to Liverpool in the late fifties. Lennon collaborated with McCartney on this song, adding the memorable names 'Vera, Chuck and Dave'. He also threw in the caustic: 'What do you see when you turn out the light/I can't tell you but I know it's mine', to Paul's 'With A Little Help From My Friends'.

In 'Lucy In The Sky With Diamonds' Lennon immersed himself in the fantasy world of Lewis Carroll. It is a vivid, colourful world. Just 'Climb in the back with your head in the clouds/And you're gone!' The girl 'with kaleidoscope eyes' represents some sort of salvation but it is transitory and you're back, forever caught in that marshmallow world of dreams and fantasy.

'Getting Better' was John continuing to obviate his guilt about the women in his life, coming to terms with it directly, following on from the oblique inferences in 'Norwegian Wood'. Although 'Getting Better' is generally considered a McCartney song, and Paul certainly had the germ of the idea in the studio, John contributed some crucial, highly personal words. It was a classic example of how they helped each other in their writing.

> I used to be cruel to my woman
> I beat her and kept her apart from the things she loved
> Man I was mean but I'm changing my scene
> And I'm doing the best that I can

It was an indication of how he had mellowed; the guilt was apparent and made public. 'I was a hitter,' John explained later. 'I couldn't express myself and I hit. I fought men and I hit women. That is why I am always on about peace. It is the most violent people who go for love and peace. I am a violent man who has learned not to be violent and regret his violence. I will have to be a lot older before I can face in public how I treated women as a youngster,' he told David Sheff in *Playboy* magazine in 1980.

'Being For The Benefit Of Mr Kite!' was taken straight from an antique circus poster, which John transposed – in conjunction with George Martin's imaginative tape loops and cut-ups – into a beguiling cameo. 'Good Morning Good Morning' was a throw-away, inspired by a Kellogg's cornflakes television advert, which was on in the background while Lennon was in a vaguely 'writing' mood. John's songs for *Sgt Pepper*, while technically superior to anything he had yet attempted, were pillaged from the usual random sources: circus posters, advertisements, and newspaper cuttings.

The album's supreme achievement is still the massive 'A Day In The Life'. Again Lennon culled the song from disparate sources – newspaper headlines, his filming of *How I Won The War* in Spain in 1966, and snatches of conversation. Paul's middle eight slotted neatly into the scenario. After hearing the words 'went upstairs and had a smoke', the B.B.C. screamed 'drugs' and promptly banned the song. Lennon's jaundiced vocal is perfectly suited to the distanced picture of a man seated, 'reading the news today', and from that preface the song unfolds. The seemingly random flow ends with the enigmatic line which was inspired by a friend: 'Now you know how many holes it takes to fill the Albert Hall.' 'A Day In The Life' marked the pinnacle of the Beatles' recorded output. It tested George Martin's abilities to breaking-point, in having to encourage a classical orchestra to 'freak out', and to come up with an arrangement that sounded like 'the end of the world', sustaining the final note for forty-two seconds.

George Martin translated the impossible into sensational reality. The cumulative effect of the album was devastating. After playing it for the first time there was no choice but go right back to the beginning again, rather than – as had been the way with previous Beatle records – searching out individual tracks. The depth and variety of the album led to acts as diverse as Joe Brown and Joe Cocker covering songs from it.

At the time the scope and flair of *Sgt Pepper* ensured that it stood alone, the very zenith of rock 'n' roll. It ushered in the prime era of English psychedelia, which others were still trying to equal well into the eighties.

The scope and triumph of the album gave John even greater impetus. Barely had the dust settled than the Beatles were back within a month with a new single. John's composition 'All You Need Is Love' was premièred on the global *Our World* T.V. show. (It was a mark of the Beatles' position by then that they were chosen as Britain's representatives for this prestigious satellite link-up.) Four hundred million people saw the group première the anthem of the Love Generation; it took the Beatles to set the seal of acceptability on the hippy movement – although in truth it had already begun to burn itself out in Haight Ashbury, San Francisco by the time the single was released. Hearing it now is like activating a museum piece, but then, all those years ago, there were enough people who believed that all you needed *was* love and that entry into Shangri La was gained simply by wearing flowers in your hair.

On the finished single, just as it is fading, Lennon can be heard singing a cheerfully distorted 'She Loves You', as though publicly burying the Beatles legacy. The single's B-side was 'Baby, You're A Rich Man', a question-and-answer song, which Lennon originally, viciously 'dedicated' to Brian Epstein as 'Baby, You're A Rich Fag Jew'. 'How does it feel to be one of the beautiful people?' asked Lennon, a question millions asked of him. Like many other songs of the period it was a combination of two quite different songs: McCartney had the title and some odd lines in his head while Lennon supplied the questions.

And there was still more to come. 'Hello, Goodbye' was the final Beatles single of 1967. It was Paul's all the way through, another question-and-answer song, which perfectly captured the querulous atmosphere of the time. The B-side was 'I Am The Walrus', a Lennon *tour de force*, a psychedelic maelstrom. Here was John tripping into wonderland again, with the lyrics inspired by Lewis Carroll's poem 'The Walrus and the Carpenter' from *Alice in Wonderland*: 'To me, it was a beautiful poem. It never occurred to me that Lewis Carroll was commenting on the capitalist and social system. I never went into that bit about what it really meant, like people are doing with Beatles work. Later I went back and looked at it and realized that the walrus was the bad guy in the story and the carpenter was the good guy. I thought, Oh shit, I picked the wrong guy!'

The riff came about when John was going through one of his 'Nowhere Man' periods, and was actually 'Sitting in an English garden waiting for the sun'. He heard a police siren in the distance and the first three lines of the song flashed through his head. The lyrical obscurity left the song wide open to interpretation and to the end even Lennon admitted that *he* never really knew what the song was actually *about*. Much of it was obviously devious Lennon word-play. He was absorbing acid like milk, which must be where lines like 'Semolina pilchards climbing up the Eiffel Tower' come from. 'I am he as you are he as you are me and we are all together' was very much the feeling of the period. The song was also Lennon's sole contribution to the *Magical Mystery Tour* film, which the B.B.C. premièred on Boxing Day 1967 (he also had a co-writing credit on the throwaway instrumental 'Flying'). *Magical Mystery Tour* was a scrappy project, conceived in the wake of Brian Epstein's death. But there were occasional highlights, including the surreal walrus sequence, with eggmen and walruses floating dreamily past the camera.

The Beatles psychedelia persisted. At one time the group's extraordinary and still unreleased 'What's The News Maryjane' was scheduled by John as an official Plastic Ono Band single. 'Maryjane' is a euphemism for marijuana and the song features Lennon dreamily intoning such lyrics as: 'She like to be married to Yeti/Be grooving such cooky spaghetti!'

The Beatles first single of 1968, 'Lady Madonna', was another solo McCartney effort, which saw the group return to their rock 'n' roll roots, a decisive move away from the lyrical and musical complexities of *Sgt Pepper*. In August they inaugurated the Apple label, which was launched with the marathon 'Hey Jude' single, another solo McCartney work. The B-side, though, was pure Lennon: 'Revolution' was his explicit comment on the student riots which had split Europe and America in the summer of 1968. In France radical students came close to overthrowing the government and in America there were massive protests at the country's growing involvement in South-East Asia.

With Bob Dylan in seclusion the demonstrators looked to the Beatles and the Rolling Stones for guidance and leadership. The Stones offered the swaggering *Beggar's Banquet* album which included the call-to-the-barricades rock of 'Street Fighting Man'. John was much more cautious and when the Beatles' 'message' came through him it was almost pessimistic. 'Revolution' acknowledged that 'we all want to change the world' but sagely counselled: 'But when you talk about destruction/Don't you know that you can count me out?' For the first time the Beatles sounded like another generation advising their young: 'You say you got a real solution/Well, you know, we'd all love to see the plan.' John sat firmly on the fence. He recorded two versions of the song, one in which he asked to be included 'in', and another in which he asks to be left out. It was to be a further three years before he would advocate 'Power To The People'. The radical element in him would take some years to develop, but, typically, when it did Lennon opted for it whole-heartedly. In 1968 'Revolution' still showed the Beatles adhering to 'flowerpower' values, 'love is all you need'. There was never any justification for violence, said John in his music. The ends could not justify the means.

Yoko's growing influence on John began to manifest itself in his music. The first real evidence of this came in November 1968 with the release of the controversial *Two Virgins* album. It was the third album issued on Apple (George Harrison's *Wonderwall* can claim the distinction of being the first Beatle solo album). *Two Virgins* was recorded at Weybridge, utilizing tape loops and splices. Most Beatles fans found it completely unacceptable, consisting as it did of random electronic gurglings and burps.

The Beatles' first real musical punch of the year, in addition to the 'Hey Jude' single, came with *The Beatles* (or 'White Album'), their first double album, released exactly five years after *With The Beatles* on 22 November 1968. Here was the first real proof that the Fab Four weren't the happy beat quartet of fond memory and there was a clear distinction between Lennon and McCartney songs. It took them away from the production complexities of *Sgt Pepper*, and even allowed for the inclusion of outside musicians (Eric Clapton, Nicky Hopkins, Dave Mason, and, of course, Yoko Ono). It was, again, very much an album of its period. 'Jamming' was a recent development in rock; Jimi Hendrix's *Electric Ladyland* of the same year included star guests; and 'supergroups' were developing as musicians broke away from the strictures that they felt record companies imposed on them.

Even the more orthodox rock 'n' roll of the 'White Album' showed Yoko's influence. John's prolificness is reflected in his total of thirteen songs on the album. The only real concession to the avant-garde was 'Revolution 9'; Lennon's other songs reflect his love for good, old-fashioned, rock 'n' roll. Even from a visual angle the album is a reflection of the Beatles' desire to shake off their past – the plain white cover is a deliberate reaction against the colourful layers of *Sgt Pepper*.

The variety of Lennon's styles on the finished album are encouraging, from the beguiling 'Dear Prudence' to the nursery-rhyme charms of 'Cry Baby Cry'. Lennon's writing focused almost exclusively on Yoko: even 'Julia', his heartfelt tribute to his mother, was as much about Yoko. He told *Playboy*: 'She inspired *all* this creation in me. It wasn't that she inspired the songs, she inspired *me*!' The fans were not alone in thinking that Yoko was the one person responsible for John's barely veiled hostility towards the group. Paul, George, and Ringo saw her influence on John and their music as pernicious. Yoko herself commented in 1980: 'I went to bed with this guy I liked and suddenly the next morning I see these three in-laws standing there!'

Of the songs on the 'White Album', 'Dear Prudence' was conceived while meditating in India and was written to coax Mia

Farrow's sister Prudence out into the sun. 'Glass Onion' was a song designed to bemuse Beatle freaks ('The Walrus was Paul' was Lennon's concession to McCartney in the light of his obsession with his new partner). Lennon later described the song as 'just a throwaway', but his reference to former glories – 'Strawberry Fields', 'Lady Madonna', 'The Fool On The Hill' – gave fans a field day in exercising their own interpretations.

The most tragic case of misinterpretation of Beatle lyrics came when Charles Manson convinced himself that on the 'White Album' the Beatles were exhorting him and his 'family' to rise and destroy. It was, according to Manson's warped mind, the Beatles giving him the go-ahead for a bloody revolution. He tragically misinterpreted Paul's 'Helter Skelter' as a prelude to Armageddon, unaware that it was simply an English expression for a fairground slide. Manson also convinced himself that Harrison's 'Piggies' was a licence to kill pigs and that somewhere in the electronic mayhem of John's 'Revolution 9' there was a call to arms; this subsequently resulted in his bloody murder of Sharon Tate in California.

'The Continuing Story of Bungalow Bill' was 'a sort of teenage social comment song', which marked the first orthodox Lennon/ Ono collaboration. She can be clearly heard singing the line 'Not when he looked so fierce. . . .' It is populated by characters from comic books. 'So Captain Marvel zapped in right between the eyes' is straight from the territory of Stan 'The Man' Lee. It is a fragmentary, haunting song with echoes of Lennon's 'On Safairy With Whide Hunter' from his first book.

'Happiness Is A Warm Gun' was inspired by a caption in an American magazine, which George Martin showed John in the studio. The cruel irony of the phrase inspired the song and provided its title. The acid fragments are still there in sections such as 'Like a lizard on a window pane . . . the man in the crowd with the multicoloured mirrors on his hobnail boots. . . .' But a line like 'A soap impression of his wife which he ate and donated to the National Trust' is pure Spike Milligan, whose Goonish word-play John loved so much.

'I'm So Tired' is both Lennon's greatest song on the album and one of his finest ever. Recorded very late one night at Abbey Road, it perfectly captures that weary resignation, that three o'clock in the morning feeling, with the bizarre couplet: 'Although I'm so tired, I'll have another cigarette/And curse Sir Walter Raleigh, he was such a stupid get!' Still at the centre of the song is that plea for calm, 'a little peace of mind', which was John's cry for help – except that now there was someone to answer that cry.

Top: A masterpiece of music in the making: Paul and John in Number 2 studio at Abbey Road in May 1967, writing and recording *Sgt Pepper's Lonely Hearts Club Band*

Above: John in his small recording studio at Tittenhurst Park immediately after recording 'Imagine' in 1971

'Julia' is a haunting, wistful fragment, for the mother Lennon never had enough time to know and for the companion he so desperately needed. The song managed to reconcile past and present and found Lennon recognizing his own frailty in the first line: 'Half of what I say is meaningless. . . .' The impression of all the songs on the album is that they are fragments which developed into finished songs at the last moment. One feels that Lennon is pouring his heart out, for the past, the present, and the future. The songs are scraps of paper, riddled with ambiguity and tragedy, dry and lacerating humour, sometimes touching and affecting, sometimes throwaway and disposable.

'Yer Blues' was a tongue-in-cheek dig at the late sixties British blues boom, which boasted groups like Fleetwood Mac, Ten Years After, and Chicken Shack. It is none the less still a bleak and bitter song, which took shape in India – 'trying to reach God and feeling suicidal'. 'Yer Blues' conjures up an inconoclastic, nihilistic world: 'Blue mist around my soul/feel so suicidal/even hate my rock 'n' roll.'

'Everybody's Got Something To Hide Except Me And My Monkey' prefaces later songs like 'I Want You' and 'Come Together', repetitive lyrics written in gratitude to Yoko. 'Your inside is out when your outside is in,' Lennon sang. And who knew it better than he?

'Sexy Sadie' was directed at the Maharishi, who 'made a fool of everyone', promising the Beatles peace on earth and spiritual enlightenment but ending up as someone they distrusted. Lennon admitted that he 'copped out' by not naming the Maharishi in the song but everyone knew who the bitter put-down was aimed at. The whimsy of 'Cry Baby Cry' took Lennon back to Alice's magic garden: for the King and Queen of Hearts read 'The King of Marigold' and 'The Duchess of Kirkcaldy'. The song is cruel and spiteful – 'Make your mother cry, she's old enough to know better' – as only children can be.

Following the cacophony of 'Revolution 9' comes the syrupy 'Good Night'. It is hard to believe that Lennon was responsible for two such different songs. 'Good Night' was written for Julian Lennon and given to Ringo to croon. It was a George Martin *tour de force*, Busby Berkeley colliding head on with a radio favourite of John's childhood, Uncle Mac: 'Good night, children . . . everywhere.' As Lennon later laconically admitted: 'It was possibly overlush!'

The *Yellow Submarine* soundtrack surfaced in January 1969. The film was a contractual obligation for the group and United

Artists. Only four new songs were required for the finished animated film, which duly appeared on the album (an example of the Beatles giving less than full value for money). It bore all the hallmarks of having been hastily finished, with John's 'Hey Bulldog' and George Harrison's 'Only A Northern Song' knocked off as fillers. 'Hey Bulldog' was an unusually bitter Lennon song of the period – 'What makes you think you're something special when you smile?. . ./You think you know me, but you haven't got a clue!'

At the beginning of 1969 the Beatles were beginning to crumble. The making of the film *Let It Be*, which began in January, was, in the main, not a happy affair and tensions soon re-surfaced. On 2 March John and Yoko appeared at an avant-garde jazz concert in Cambridge (part of their set would appear on the *Life With The Lions* album a few months later). Significantly it marked the first time a Beatle had ever appeared solo on stage. 'Get Back' was the first Beatles single of 1969, a McCartney rocker. The other side was Lennon pouring his heart out to Yoko in 'Don't Let Me Down', a strong and persuasive riff with a stirring Lennon vocal.

As the *Let It Be* project sprawled on into an indefinite future and moved further and further away from its intended naturalism, the Beatles began recording what ended up as the *Abbey Road* album. John, meanwhile, launched his Plastic Ono Band project. Plastic Ono was never intended as a full-time group. The nucleus was always to be John and Yoko, and it involved whoever happened to be around. In the case of Lennon's anthem 'Give Peace A Chance' it was a cast of hundreds! While the flippancy of the verses recalled Lennon's *In His Own Write* and his love of word-association, the message of the chorus was imperative and sincere.

The Lennons' paranoia about the public's scorn was apparent on the next 'Beatles' single, 'The Ballad of John and Yoko' (only Paul and John actually appear on it). It was markedly autobiographical, a narrative account of John and Yoko's recent activities: 'Christ you know it ain't easy, you know how hard it can be/The way things are going, they're gonna crucify me.' Set to an infectious, shuffling, old-time rock 'n' roll rhythm, it was naïvely effective.

Plastic Ono gave Lennon the opportunity to escape from the Beatles' mantle; the band's product could be recorded and released as quickly as possible and need not have the same care and attention lavished on it that the world had come to expect from the Beatles. It was a safety valve and one of which Lennon grew increasingly fond. Lennon talked about its inception to B.B.C. Radio's Andy Peebles: 'Plastic Ono Band was a concept of Yoko's, which is an imaginary band. The first advert was a photograph . . . of some pieces of plastic with a tape recorder and a T.V. in it. . . . And her idea was a completely robot pop group. . . . There was supposed to be a party for the release of the "Give Peace A Chance" record but we'd had a car crash or something so we couldn't come; so at the dance hall where they had the party for the Plastic Ono Band, all the Press came to meet the band, and the band was onstage, which was just a machine with a camera pointing at them, showing them onstage themselves. So the Plastic Ono Band is a conceptual band that never was. There never had been any members of it, and the advert said "You are the Plastic Ono Band". So I just want to clear that, it wasn't the re-forming of a new band like Wings or a Hollies, or whatever, where you have a name and you belong to it. There's never been anybody in that band. There are no members.'

The album *Live Peace in Toronto 1969*, which resulted from Plastic Ono's appearance at the rock 'n' roll festival in September is something of a potted history of John Lennon's life at the end of the 1960s. Songs drawn from the early Hamburg days ('Blue Suede Shoes' and 'Money') nestled next to current Beatles hits like 'Yer Blues', which was included as Lennon had enjoyed performing it on the never completed TV show, *Rolling Stones' Rock and Roll Circus*. Lennon's dependence on drugs ('Cold Turkey') jostled with his desire for peace ('Give Peace A Chance'). The other side of the album comprised potent songs by Yoko with 'Don't Worry Kyoko' and 'John John (Let's Hope for Peace)'.

Meanwhile the Beatles limped on. Chronologically the set that ended up as *Abbey Road* was recorded *after* their final album *Let It Be* but because of the concomitant problems surrounding that album, *Abbey Road* was released first in September 1969. There was no need for a title or a name on the album cover, despite the fact that the four figures diligently trooping over the zebra crossing were virtually unrecognizable as the quartet the world knew as the Beatles. Side one of *Abbey Road* consisted of separate songs – almost like the old days. Lennon's syncopated 'Come Together', which opened the album, was based around a line from Chuck Berry's 'You Can't Catch Me'. Lennon cited it as one of his favourite Beatle tracks, describing it as 'funky . . . bluesy'. The competition was strong on that album. George Harrison's two best-remembered Beatle songs were there, ('Something' and 'Here Comes The Sun') as well as a clutch of McCartney classics. 'I Want

An invitation to the launch of the Unique Plastic Ono Band; the party took place in the absence of John and Yoko, who were in hospital after a car crash in Scotland

Apple Peace
POST 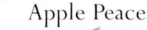 CARD

Communication

For Address Only

John and Yoko and Apple Records
invite you to join them on Thursday
this week, July 3rd to meet the Plastic
Ono Band in Chelsea Town Hall,
Kings Road.

The Band's first release "Give Peace
A Chance" (on the other side
"Remember Love") recorded in
Montreal, will be performed by the
Band and a splendid time is guaranteed
for all.

"Give Peace A Chance" is to be
released on Friday, July 4th and it
couldn't happen at a better time to a
nicer record.

The time: 5.30 p.m.
The place: Chelsea Town Hall,
          169/183 Kings Road
The date: Thursday, July 3rd
RSVP: Derek Taylor, Apple,
          Regent 8232

Plastic Ono Band

— This is a Real Photograph —

Ray Coleman,
Disc,
161 – 166 Fleet St,
E.C 4

You (She's So Heavy)' could well be John's definitive song of the period. Lennon pours out remorseless lyrics, pleading with Yoko: 'I want you so bad/It's driving me mad.' 'Because' came about from some Beethoven chords Yoko was playing on the piano, which were re-shaped by John, who then added some touchingly devoted lyrics: 'Love is old, love is new/Love is all, love is you.'

The second side of the album was made up of fragments from India and from Weybridge. Songs that were started, alone and together, but never finished. Somehow they produce a seamless suite. After 'Because', Lennon's contributions were characters who flickered across his imagination, 'Mean Mr Mustard', 'Polythene Pam', and 'Sun King' sung in cod Spanish. All were rooted in reality but distorted by drugs and his tendency to leave projects incomplete. Following on the heels of the 'White Album', *Abbey Road* displayed the Beatles as four individuals, who were none the less somehow bound together by some strange, tenacious loyalty.

Before the end of 1969 Lennon released the second Plastic Ono Band single, the harrowing 'Cold Turkey', which came out at the end of October just before the Beatles 'new' single, 'Something'. The single was pulled off *Abbey Road* at the insistence of Allen Klein to bring in some immediate cash. It was the first time a Beatles single had been released *solely* to make money and it reached only number four in the charts.

'Cold Turkey' seemed only to emphasize the disparate musical directions in which the Beatles were going. It was raw and powerful with the terse message 'Play Loud' printed on the label. It was strong rock 'n' roll, with thunderous drumming from Alan White and the lyrics drew on Lennon's harrowing experiences with heroin, graphically depicting the pain and suffering of addiction and withdrawal symptoms. It only reached number fourteen in the British charts, possibly because the subject was too spine-chilling for public taste. 'When I wrote it, I went to the other three Beatles and said, "Hey kids I think I've just written a new single!" But they all said, "Umm . . . aeee . . . well", because it was going to be my project and so I thought, bugger it, I'll put it out myself!'

Let It Be had by this time, in contrast to the free-and-easy Plastic Ono releases, developed into a monster with three separate producers, – George Martin, Glyn Johns, and Phil Spector – all trying to salvage something from the sessions at Twickenham and Apple studios.

By the middle of November 1969 the Lennons issued *The Wedding Album*, a verbal collage of their lives together during the year. Along with *Two Virgins* and *Life With The Lions* it stands on the shelf of those collectors determined to possess everything of the Beatles.

At the beginning of a new decade the Beatles were still together as a group but the ties which bound them were thin and close to snapping. The last rites had to be administered and the *Let It Be* album and film effectively did just that. Before the album's release a profusion of Beatle solo projects helped to fuel rumours of the eventual split – Ringo's *Sentimental Journey* and Paul's *McCartney* albums were released. John chipped in with another Plastic Ono single, the breezy 'Instant Karma!'. It was produced by Phil Spector because Lennon was one of the few people involved with *Let It Be* who felt that Spector had earned his salary for his work on the finished album. 'Instant Karma!' was written and recorded in one day, emphasizing Lennon's belief that records (particularly singles) should have the immediacy of newspapers. Lyrically, it marked Lennon's 'We all shine on' mood and his belief that togetherness and love could still save the world. 'It just came to me. Everybody was going on about karma, especially in the sixties. But it occurred to me that karma is instant as well as it influences your past life or your future life. . . . Also, I'm fascinated by commercials and promotions as an art form. I enjoy them. So the idea of instant karma was like the idea of instant coffee, presenting something in a new form.'

Prior to the release of the *Let It Be* album, the eponymous single was released in March 1970. It was a Paul McCartney epic, although he publicly voiced his dissatisfaction with Spector's doctoring of the finished tapes. The B-side was a rarity – 'You Know My Name (Look Up The Number)'. A throwaway number, written and recorded by Lennon in 1967, it features McCartney, the Beatles' road manager Mal Evans and saxophonist Brian Jones (not the late Brian Jones of the Rolling Stones but a session musician of the same name). It is an enchanting, sleazy cabaret number, set in a mythical night club – 'Slaggers' – with Lennon acting as M.C. and showman and McCartney crooning in his best put-on Vic Damone style.

The *Let It Be* album was finally released in May 1970. What had originally been intended as spontaneous proof of the Beatles' very existence and vitality comes across as a doctored valediction. 'It was hell,' recalled Lennon bitterly. 'Even the biggest Beatles fan couldn't have sat through those six weeks of misery.' The whole saga surrounding the 'finished' album was a sad reflection of how disillusioned the Beatles had become about their recording, their

future, themselves and, tragically, their music. The original intention was to show the group 'warts and all', deliberately stripping
away all the lavish production of their albums of the previous four
years, to capture their spontaneity in the studio. The world was to
eavesdrop on the Beatles in rehearsal and see them shape their
songs for their next album. Over thirty hours of music are on tape
somewhere; much has surfaced on sporadic bootlegs. You can
listen to the undoctored versions of 'The Long And Winding
Road', 'Let It Be', 'Across The Universe', the full version of 'Dig
It', and great original material like the rockabilly 'Suzy Parker'.
You can also hear the Beatles work out on songs of their youth,
Hank Williams' 'You Win Again', Cliff Richard's 'Move It', Elvis'
'Good Rockin' Tonight', Chuck Berry's 'Memphis, Tennessee',
Lennon's ripe parody of 'House Of The Rising Sun', and workouts
on Dylan's 'Blowin' In The Wind', and 'All Along The Watchtow-
er'. Ironically John Lennon began collecting Beatles bootleg
albums in 1974 when he could begin to enjoy re-living his
past.

By the end of the film and recording sessions of January 1969
neither the Beatles nor George Martin could face wading through
the miles of tapes. Given the original 'natural' idea of the project,
Phil Spector was called in to edit and polish up the material and
give the world the Beatles album it expected. Spector was a legend.
He had virtually invented the idea of the record producer with his
mini teen epics of the mid-sixties: 'Then He Kissed Me', 'River
Deep, Mountain High', and 'You've Lost That Lovin' Feeling'. All
were conceived and executed on a Wagnerian scale with Spector
inventing the 'wall of sound', utilizing multi-tracking, massed
instrumentation, and laborious overdubbing. He was a genius, but
like all geniuses, he could be difficult and unpredictable. Lennon
recalled the *Let It Be* débâcle: 'It just was a dreadful, dreadful
feeling. . . . We were going to let it out in really shitty condition. I
didn't care. I had thought it would be good to let the shitty version
out because it would break the Beatles myth. It would just be us,
with no trousers on and no glossy paint over the cover, and no
hype. "This is what we are like with our trousers off – would you
please end the game now?" '

But the old magic did surface, even during those acrimonious
final days. The album's opening track, 'Two Of Us', was a
McCartney song for Linda but (in context) it becomes a moving
requiem to two Liverpool kids, burning with ambition and talent:
'Two of us sending postcards, writing letters on my wall/You and
me burning matches, lifting latches, on our way back home.' It is a

Bob Dylan was one of John's inspirations as a songwriter, and he took
Yoko to see his giant open-air Isle of Wight concert in September 1969;
folk singer Tom Paxton is on John's right

memory of Liverpool as it was, when the world was open and bright for conquest, not shrouded in the acid connotations of 'Strawberry Fields'. At the dismal end, 'Two Of Us' serves as a moving reminder of that bright beginning.

'Dig A Pony' celebrated Lennon's omniscience – 'You can celebrate anything you want . . . You can penetrate any place you go . . . You can radiate everything you are. . . .' But as the refrain runs, 'I told you so, all I want is you.' That was definitely meant for Yoko. 'Across The Universe' was a song which infuriated Lennon at the time. He woke up one morning with the line 'Pools of sorrow, waves of joy' running through his head and proceeded to construct the song from it. The version on the album was 'subconscious sabotage' on his part, in the name of experimentation. One version ended up on a World Wildlife Fund charity album with two Beatles fans singing the 'Nothing's gonna change my world' chorus. 'The original track was a real piece of shit,' he recalled with some bitterness, 'I was singing out of tune and instead of getting a decent choir, we got fans from outside . . . Apple Scruffs or whatever you call them. They came in and were singing all off-key. Nobody was interested in doing the tune originally. . . . Phil slowed the tape down, added the strings. . . . He did a really special job.' The 'Jai Guru Deva OM' refrain harkens back to the days of gurus and avatars who could save the world. The song caught Lennon at a time when all his creativity and sexuality were being devoted to Yoko but when: 'Words are flowing out like endless rain into a paper cup . . . Thoughts meander like a restless wind.' Restless, the artist in him was beset by relentless images and a burning desire to create, while he wilfully stripped everything down for Yoko. 'Nothing's gonna change my world,' he sang. But it had.

'Dig It' was an example of the 'new-phase Beatles album' which the *Let It Be* album sleeve boasted. Distilled from a five-minute stream of consciousness rap, the existing forty-eight-second track finds Lennon invoking Manchester United boss Matt Busby, Doris Day, and a series of acronyms, ending with the emphatic 'Whatever it is, whoever you are – just dig it!' Lennon's sardonic comments pepper the finished album – opening the album with 'I dig a pygmy by Charles Hawtrey. . . ', prefacing the beautiful 'Let It Be' with the iconoclastic 'Now we'd like to do 'ark the Angels come. . .', digging up the traditional 'Maggie Mae', disembowelling 'Danny Boy', and pre-empting 'Get Back' with an improvised chorus of 'Sweet Loretta Fart/Thought she was a cleaner, but she was a frying pan'. It is only the tip of the iceberg, though, and unfortunately it is the poor-quality bootlegs which give a greater indication of the album's original concept.

'I've Got A Feeling' was a Lennon/McCartney collaboration of sorts. The first half of the song is all Paul, while the 'Everybody had a hard year' section onwards is John. 'One After 909' was a genuine collaboration, written in 1959 in those dim and distant Liverpool days and disinterred for their last album together. Here was a joyous slice of Eddie Cochran-style rock, written by two teenagers with no real idea of that so-distant America, culled instead from images of contemporary rock 'n' roll songs, with John and Paul singing enthusiastically together on the chorus. Sharply evocative of those earlier, sunnier and simpler days, it seems now a glorious finale to the partnership of Lennon and McCartney; as the years passed and the acrimony between the two men subsided, their preferred memory was, indeed, of 'sagging off school' as Liverpool boys and writing songs in the back of the Beatles' van.

All of John Lennon's subsequent musical activities would, inevitably, be measured alongside his achievement in creating the Beatles. They were the single most influential pop group ever. Their sounds and personalities had irrevocably altered not only the music but the social fabric of the western world. They were synonymous with youth culture and pop art. At the onset of a new decade, Lennon – perhaps more than anyone – was aware of his responsibilities and of the legacy he was condemned to carry.

The public had been warned of the 'new' Lennon by 'Cold Turkey'. Released in October 1969, it was John's harrowing confession of withdrawal from heroin. As the third single from the Plastic Ono Band, it went into the charts both in Britain and America, although not high enough to please John, who cited its poor performance in his letter to the Queen returning his M.B.E.

To Beatles fans, the record was astonishing, even from John. Yet it was perhaps his most honest moment in making his music a catalogue of his life. He sang

> Temperature's rising, fever is high
> Can't see no future, can't see no sky
> My feet are so heavy, so is my head
> I wish I was a baby, I wish I was dead.

The urgency of his voice, the nature of the record as a clear reference to his drug habits, the strength of Eric Clapton's guitar work on it and the dramatic departure from anything previously heard from John and the Beatles, mark it as a milestone in his life. 'Cold Turkey', uncomfortable at the time, now defines precisely the open heart of Lennon.

The Plastic Ono Band helped John to expunge the Beatles myth and the catharsis engendered by Janov's primal therapy manifested itself on the *John Lennon/Plastic Ono Band* album, which reached the shops a fortnight before Christmas 1970. It still stands as one of the bleakest, most compellingly honest albums ever released by a major rock artist. On it Lennon exorcized his past and offered precious little hope for his future. Its bleakness took root in his childhood, particularly on 'Mother' and 'My Mummy's Dead', a plaintive cry from a spiritual orphan. 'Mother' was harrowing; Lennon's hair-raising vocal, the sparse instrumentation and chilling lyrics were a public mourning of his dead mother and castigation of his absent father. There was no cosiness, no imagery, nothing to hide behind here. 'Working Class Hero' was bitterly dismissive of the system which bred Lennon, which 'gave you no time instead of it all'. It is a twentieth-century folk song, for Everyman; a withering, scornful attack on a society which 'Keeps you doped with religion and sex and T.V./But you're still fucking peasants as far as I can see.'

For many the album's most despairing track is 'God', Lennon's litany of rejection of his past which concludes with the withering 'I don't believe in Beatles.' The dream was finally over. As he commented: ' "God" was put together from three songs. I had the idea that God is the concept by which we measure pain, so that when you have a word like that, you just sit down and sing the first tune that comes into your head. . . . I don't know when I realized that I was putting down all these things I didn't believe in. So I could have gone on, it was like a Christmas card list: where do I end: Churchill? Hoover? I thought I had to stop. I was going to leave a gap and just fill in your own words; whoever you don't believe in. It had just got out of hand. And Beatles was the final thing because I no longer believe in myth and Beatles is another myth.'

Lennon's writing was as sparse as the instrumentation. The album, in fact, must be the sparsest Phil Spector has ever given his name to. Lennon admitted later: 'I started from "Mother" onwards, trying to shave off all imagery, pretensions of poetry, illusions of grandeur, what I call à la Dylan, Dylanesque. . . . As they say, Northern people are blunt, right, so I was trying to write like I am.'

That very bluntness shook many people on what amounted to Lennon's first solo album. There were no walruses or glass onions, no more masks to hide behind – here was the soul of John Ono Lennon. That 'Northern bluntness' was apparent on 'Working Class Hero', with its two 'fucks' that E.M.I. cut out on the inner sleeve. (The censorship was applied only in Britain; Capitol, who released the album in America, printed the words.) By then Lennon didn't care. He'd been performing to order for too long. If the public wanted John Lennon, they would have to take him on his own terms. He wasn't John Beatle any more.

There *were* moments of softness on the album: the beautiful ballad 'Love' which spoke of 'needing to be loved'; 'Hold On' was Yoko's plea: 'Hold on John, it's gonna be alright.' But the overwhelming feeling of the album is one of sadness, sadness for a past he never had, for the mother he missed, for the growing up in public. For all the fake gurus. For Yoko. For himself. It was from the heart.

Lennon's deliberate denunciation of his past was a brutal beginning to a new decade. With the Beatles gone, there seemed nothing to replace them musically or as a full-time occupation. Coupled with the long, confessional interview he did with *Rolling Stone* editor Jann Wenner in 1970, *Plastic Ono Band* renounced the past with all the accumulated bitterness and rancour of John's thirty years.

By early 1971 John and Yoko had thrown their hats firmly into the political arena. 'Power To The People' was a slogan echoing round the world at the time. The civil disturbances in Northern Ireland were erupting into civil war. The Nixon administration had taken the gloves off when they murdered four students at Kent State University during a demonstration in 1970. The Lennons became more and more active in radical politics. They donated money to Michael X's Black House, recorded a single, 'Do The Oz', for the defendants in the infamous 'Schoolkids Oz' trial, and Lennon gave an interview to Tariq Ali's left-wing paper *Red Mole*: 'I think we must make the workers aware of the really unhappy position they are in, break the dream they are surrounded by. They think they are in a wonderful, free-speaking country, they've all got cars and tellies and they don't want to think there's anything more to life. They are prepared to let the bosses run them, to see their children fucked up in school. They're dreaming someone else's dream, it's not even their own.' Lennon was expanding the resentment which had fuelled 'Working Class Hero'. Many found Lennon's avowed socialism at odds with his personal wealth but John was quick to counter his critics and always managed to equate it with his rapidly changing beliefs.

'Power To The People' was the most obvious musical indication of the Lennons' growing political involvement, even if it was only a type of catchy sloganeering which was to manifest itself more fully on the album *Some Time In New York City*. It recalled an earlier Lennon statement – 'Revolution' but this time he committed himself: 'Say we want a revolution/We better get it on right away/Well you get on your feet/And out on the street.' Now he was advocating direct involvement and action. His fence-sitting days were over.

He could not have produced a greater contrast with his next album and in no way did he see it as ironic that he was following his most politically motivated single with his lushest and most romantic album to date.

Imagine was released in October 1971 and is probably the album most associated with John Lennon with the haunting title track, the poignant 'Oh My Love', the vitriolic 'How Do You Sleep?' and the resonant 'Jealous Guy'. *Imagine* revealed a mellower Lennon. Although the basic themes of pain and suffering were still there its lavish instrumentation was light years away from the primal starkness of *Plastic Ono Band*. Virtually all the songs speak of his devotion to Yoko. Only 'I Don't Want To Be A Soldier' and the resounding 'Give Me Some Truth' strayed from the theme . . . as of course did 'How Do You Sleep?', his attack on Paul McCartney. In case any listener missed the object of his scorn, a postcard was included with *Imagine* that showed Lennon in a delicious parody of McCartney's *Ram* album cover. 'Those freaks was right when they said you was dead' sang Lennon in a vicious put-down. He was referring to bizarre rumours, particularly in America, that McCartney was, in fact, dead.

Imagine was classic Lennon. The album's title track was a beautifully melodic song which he had written in a plane, on a hotel bill. He always took trouble to tell people that Yoko had helped him with it, particularly its original inspiration on the theme of Utopia. Such was the intrinsic beauty of the song and the sincerity with which Lennon sang it that it will stand for ever as an international anthem. All Lennon was asking was that we should *imagine* a world without possessions or religion.

The world was by now so used to an abrasive, hard-faced Lennon, that a song like 'Jealous Guy', which actually apologized

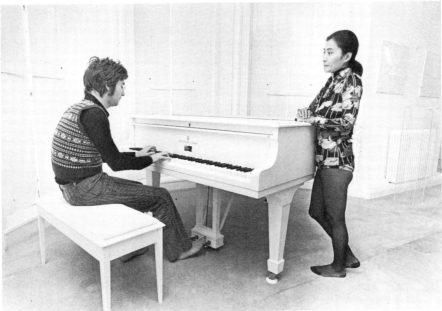

Top: John and Yoko during rehearsals for the 'One To One' concert at Madison Square Garden in August 1972

Above: At the piano on which John wrote his best loved song, 'Imagine', at Tittenhurst Park in July 1971; the piano is now in Yoko's lounge at the Dakota apartment in New York

for causing hurt and pain and recognized his emotional vulnerability, seemed uncharacteristic. On 'Crippled Inside' he sang once again of pain but without sounding self-pitying. 'One thing you can't hide/Is when you're crippled inside' – that was something John Lennon never did and he was respected for his honesty in conveying that pain by a world he viewed with an artist's eye.

Lennon recognized the difficulties of sustaining a relationship, of shedding his hard-man image and becoming a fully rounded person. On *Imagine* he finally reconciled his efforts with his craft. The album makes comfortable listening, thanks in no small part to Spector's co-production and the lavish arrangements, although lyrically Lennon was still speaking as directly as ever.

The reason, of course, was Yoko who had helped round John off as a person and had given him a perspective on his life. She had taken him into whole new areas, which initially proved to be dead ends (the avant-garde of *Two Virgins* and Side Two of *Live Peace In Toronto*). Latterly, however, she had steered him in the more fruitful directions signposted by *Imagine*. John's devotion to her manifested itself particularly on the beautiful 'Oh My Love' and the ebullient 'Oh Yoko!'. It was hard to reconcile the man who could write such sensitive love songs with the juvenile tough guy who could also sharpen his knife for the malice of 'How Do You Sleep?' But then, John Lennon always was paradoxical.

The cumbersome 'I Don't Want To Be A Soldier' was a clumsy intrusion, a laborious protest song, railing against the 'straights' who let themselves be hoodwinked into the army or other Establishment professions. 'Give Me Some Truth', though, was a blisteringly effective and sustained attack on the falsity of Nixon's America.

Musically *Imagine* packed real punch with legendary saxophonist King Curtis, Nicky Hopkins, Badfinger's Tom Evans and Joey Molland, George Harrison, and Phil Spector all contributing. Lennon spoke fondly of the finished album and pinpointed its strengths:, "Imagine", both the song itself and the album, is the same thing as "Working Class Hero" and "Mother" and "God" on the first disc. But the first record was too real for people, so nobody bought it. . . . You see "Imagine" was exactly the same message but sugar-coated. Now "Imagine" is a big hit almost everywhere – anti-religious, anti-nationalistic, anti-conventional, anti-capitalistic but because it is sugar-coated it is accepted. Now I understand what you have to do. Put your political message across with a little honey.'

But the honey was to stay in the jar during 1972. By the time *Imagine* was in the shops, John and Yoko had left England and settled in New York.

6
AMERICA

'New York is the Rome of today'

With the Beatles written out of his mind and the thrust of the peace campaign over, John by 1971 was a curious amalgam of superstar, artist, and mercenary. He reiterated that he could no longer be a 'slave to gold records', but he was too much of a realist to be dragged too deeply into the esoteric world of art. He imposed his own limits on everything.

He had lived his thirty-one years on a cliff, consistently pushing himself and his abilities to the edge. He often remarked on the 'nearly' situations which punctuated his life: how he nearly got kicked out of school; how he nearly got expelled from art college but escaped to Hamburg just in time; how he was nearly lulled into a safe, rich, bourgeois existence at Weybridge when Yoko entered his life; how the Beatles broke up at exactly the right time for him. What had anchored him to the wide world, whatever was happening in his life, was his obsession with looking outside, rather than inside, himself.

Yoko's battle for custody of her daughter Kyoko took her and John to New York in the autumn of 1971. John's attraction for the country had already been whetted by a visit that summer. He and Yoko had staggered fans by playing at a jam session with Frank Zappa and his Mothers of Invention at Fillmore East; in a show that ended at dawn, John had surprised even himself by announcing: 'This is a song I used to sing when I was in the Cavern in Liverpool.' It was called 'Well (Baby Please Don't Go)'. He had a neat line in self-deprecation: 'I did rhythm and booze, and Yoko sang on stage with what she calls voice modulation, which to the layman is screaming!'

In Britain John had explained why he felt so drawn to America, both on a personal and on an artistic level. 'It's Yoko's old stamping ground,' he explained, 'and she felt the country would be more receptive to what we're up to . . . in the States we're treated like artists. Which we are! Or anywhere else for that matter. But here [in Britain] I'm like the lad who knew Paul, got a lucky break, won the pools and married the actress.

'It's like 1940 here,' he said, warming to the theme. 'It's like coming back to Denmark or somewhere. It's really the sticks, you know. While in New York there's these fantastic twenty or thirty artists who all understand what I'm doing and have the same kind of mind as me. It's just like heaven after being here. Oh, it's terrible. You've seen how they treat me in the Press. There is an avant-garde here, but it's small.'

Political and other events had also depressed him in London: he was unhappy with the persecution of the editors of *Oz*, the Northern Ireland crisis infuriated him and when internment without trial began there, he declared that Britain should pull out and let Northern Ireland sort out its own problems; he didn't like the adoption by Britain of the decimal currency system that year. The only thing that made him smile was a record by Dave Edmunds, 'I Hear You Knocking', which Lennon rated as one of the finest sounds he'd heard in years. He played it endlessly, together with a single by B.B. King, 'The Thrill Is Gone'.

On 3 September 1971 John and Yoko left London to settle in New York. For nine years it was to prove an artistic and spiritual haven for him. 'It's the Rome of today, a bit like a together Liverpool,' he said to me shortly after the move. 'I'd always like to be where the action is. In olden times I'd like to have lived in Rome or Paris or the East. The seventies are gonna be America's.'

When they arrived John and Yoko made for Greenwich Village, which Yoko knew well from her days as a loft artist. They took a two-roomed apartment there at 105 Bank Street. A piano was quickly moved in, but mostly they shunned possessions. The apartment was spartan; the bed was a mattress covered with an American flag as a bedspread. They lived and dressed frugally, John in jeans, denim jacket and T-shirt and Yoko in jeans, black turtle-neck sweater and boots.

An early visitor was Bob Dylan, re-acquainting himself with his musical roots. He took John on a sightseeing tour of the Village, pointing out all the clubs and explaining the diversity of artistic activities that went on. John was immediately captivated by the freewheeling atmosphere.

May 1972. John and Yoko became enthusiastically involved in the street life of Greenwich Village shortly after arriving in New York. They bought bicycles, did their own shopping, and rented an apartment in Bank Street where they met some of the city's controversial personalities

As well as buying the Bank Street apartment they rented another nearby from ex-Lovin' Spoonful drummer, Joe Butler. They also bought push-bikes, 'the best way to get around the Village,' Dylan advised them. John's was a conservative, English, sit-up-and-beg handlebar model, Yoko's Japenese – pure coincidence, she said.

Yet even in those heady first few months John kept in touch with what was happening at home. He phoned Apple in New York and London regularly; he telephoned Aunt Mimi in Dorset to be warned against living in bad old America for too long; and he often went with Yoko to the Apple office at 1700 Broadway.

One day, amid the mountain of mail waiting him, was a copy of the *Melody Maker* containing a reader's letter. Headlined 'Dear JohnandYoko', it read:

> We love you very much and if all rock stars save one were to be lined up against a wall tomorrow and shot, you would be the one we'd save.
>
> But we're finding it more and more difficult to understand your simultaneous espousal of Rock Liberation and Mr Pete 'the President's friend' Bennett, promo man extraordinary (do you like being a 'product'?).
>
> Allen Klein may be a beautiful person but as far as we simple record buyers are concerned he's just another shrewd capitalist taking his cut wherever he can. Apple may be a wonderful company but all we notice is that its records get steadily more expensive and shorter (*vide* the new Mary Hopkin album with five short songs a side. Once upon a time *With the Beatles* had fourteen solid tracks on it.). If we want some Yoko music we have to fork out over four quid. Can you remember the time when you were lucky to afford an album a month? That's our upper limit.
>
> Power to the people, yeah – but which people? We were the Beatles' people all right but we still don't know if we're yours. We're T. Rex's, and Slade's – there they are on *Top of the Pops* (it might be rubbish but it's all we've got) and at St George's Hall, Bradford (at sixty pence a bit cheaper than a super album of your Fillmore gig). Are you one of us?
>
> So please, dear JohnandYoko, give us a break from your public nasties on Paul (we're not very interested in your tax situation) and start explaining what rock liberation can mean when art and money are so mixed up. There aren't many people

who can explain it. Peter Townshend has had a go; now it's your turn. Happy Christmas. Love,

Simon and Gill Frith,
Keighley, Yorkshire

Lennon's reply was instantaneous and revealing. On Apple headed notepaper he personally typed the reply which is reproduced as he typed it on page 147.

John's postscript about John Sinclair indicated his affinities during those early months in New York. As Lennon comments, Sinclair, a left-wing writer, had been jailed for possessing two joints of marijuana and John and Yoko attended a benefit rally at Ann Arbor, Michigan which resulted in Sinclair being freed within three days after serving two years of his sentence. The breakthrough thrilled John.

Left-wing personalities and political activists began to infiltrate his life. They, for their part, saw John as their Pied Piper. An early cohort in the Village was David Peel, an underground personality who amused John with his songs 'The Pope Smokes Dope' and 'Have A Marijuana'. Recalling that period, John said: 'I'd just arrived in New York and all these people, Jerry Rubin, Abbie Hoffman, David Peel, they were right on the corner when I was going out for a walk in the Village. It was that kind of community. I loved it. As usual, Lennon falls in the deep end, goes overboard, no half measures. At the time, though, it was a good scene and they meant no harm.'

Yoko felt safe in the Village; she was particularly keen on Jerry Rubin's philosophical book *Do It*, which had been in the Japanese bestseller list. John's first confrontation with the Village scene came when he dropped in, alone, to a clothes shop, the Limbo Shop, on St Mark's Place, only two weeks after arriving in New York. The best-known hippie in the Village ran up to him to shake hands and say: 'Hello, my name is David Peel, I work for Elektra Records.' They chatted for some time and a couple of nights later Peel was astonished when John and Yoko turned up at his concert in Washington Square Park. They enjoyed the irreverence of it all, and left the show chanting 'The Pope Smokes Dope.' It was the first of several encounters with Peel, who could scarcely believe that a Beatle was drawn to his scene, for whatever reason.

Shortly afterwards, Jerry Rubin told Lennon that Peel was going to do a 'walkabout', singing on the streets. John, with guitar, called on Peel and with Yoko went along Second Avenue singing

'The Pope Smokes Dope'. Fifty people joined the sidewalk minstrels. 'It was totally natural, spontaneous, and great.' Unfortunately the police thought a wandering Beatle was a security risk and broke it up.

Lennon loved street people as long as they were not phonies. What irritated him was when hangers-on bothered him, asking for money, drugs, or started to talk of the Beatles. He wanted to communicate with people on an ordinary level. New York, and particularly the crowd he was introduced to by Jerry Rubin, seemed to offer that; coupled with the radical politics preached by Rubin and his friends, it was John's automatic haven for the early months in the Village. Rubin effectively screened most of the people who wanted to get near John.

Peel's memory of those days with John is of a superstar who intuitively grasped the Village vibrations but could not become totally involved because he was a 'millionaire trendy'. Says Peel: 'John and Yoko were brilliant. They knew how to ad lib quicker than anybody I've ever met. What they liked doing best was getting things done quickly. They hated wasting time. John was open-minded, learned a lot, he had access to a lot of people, and he always *listened*. He wasn't as committed to the radical thing as a lot of us but because he was a Beatle he could make a call and get things done.'

Life for John and Yoko in the Village was a series of moments. John was so high on his freedom there that he even produced an album by David Peel and his band, the Lower East Side. 'John was an excellent producer,' says Peel. 'He had that Phil Spector Wall of Sound down pat, with everything exaggerated. He was heavily into *action* in the studio. . . . We had six guitars and ten congas and Yoko even played congas a little. "All right, let's go, *next*," he'd shout. . . . He was deadly serious but knew how to have fun. I never saw Lennon so happy as he was doing my album. John said: "Go in and play like you play on the street" – but how could I with that fantastic sound behind me?' The album, out on the Apple label, was instantly banned all over the world because it included 'The Pope Smokes Dope'.

Peel and his band played several times with John and Yoko. He was at the benefit rally for John Sinclair and on the David Frost T.V. show, and he jammed many times in their Bank Street apartment with John often playing washboard. Peel also played on their Dick Cavett T.V. appearance and at a Madison Square Garden charity concert for retarded children and adults. Peel was moved to write a song, 'Lennon for President'.

Apple

To: Simonandgill   and M.M. Readers   December 13 '71

From: JohnandYoko   the People

Dear Simonandgill   and M.M. Readers

Apple was/is a capitalist concern. We brought in a capitalist to prevent it sinking.
(with the Beatles on board). The whole problem the ex-Beatles have is concerned with
their committment to Apple. I referred to tax in answer to Paul's article in M.M.
and other British Weeklies, i.e. 'let's just sign a bit of paper'. You may not worry
about our tax-scene, but if we don't, your fab four will end up like Mickey Rooney,
Joe Louis, etc. - performing for the rest of their lives to pay back the tax man.

We, John and Yoko, have asked them, Apple, to reduce the cost of Yoko's album FLY,
they told us they had.

I personally have had enough of Apple/Ascot and all other properties which tie me
down, mentally and physically. - I intend to cash in my chips as soon as I can - and
be FREE.

John/Yoko intend to do all performances around the world FREE and/or whatever
we've earned will go e.g. to prisons to release people who can't afford bail, etc.
- and many other ways of getting money back to the people.

This is one way of paying the people back.

Until we find an alternative, the Pete Bennetes and the Apples, EMIs, etc., are
the only way of getting our product to the people. (Not to mention the contractual
angle) - if you know of any other way - don't keep it a secret!

                              Power to the People

                                          JohnandYoko

P.S. The number of tracks per album is irrelevant - it''s the amount of time per
side that counts. Anything over - say 25 minutes at most results in less power-volume,
bass/drums, etc. But 'Live Jam' Plastic Ono Band - out soon - has about at least 30
minutes a side!
P.P.S. Dear ███████ - who wants to sound like the Beatles?
P.P.P.S. We like Raggae, too! Paul likes Rock!
P.P.P.P.S. I personally have had enough of Apple/Ascot long before John has and
I'm very happy that John's coming around - and not only "Imagine no posessions"
but wanting to get rid of it - the things that interfere with our work and our life. (y.o.)
P.P.P.P.P.S. If you'd like to know where my earnings go - every cent of it goet
to various 'causes'. (y.o.)
P.P.P.P.P.S. Please stop attacking John for "How Do You Sleep", It happens to be
a good song (very powerful and full of pathos) and also, it happens to be an answer
to Paul's "Ram". Listen to "Ram" carefully and you'll see. (y.o.)
this is the last word on that subject! J.L.
P.P.P.P.P.P.S. Rally on Friday for John Sinclair. Released on Monday
after 2 years of a 10 year sentence for possession of 2 joints.

From New York, John's erratic typing carries his usual pungent words in
reply to a reader's letter in *Melody Maker*

'I used to go over to Bank Street a lot to jam, especially to eat dinner,' he says. 'I knew a good free meal when I saw one. Yoko was a terrific cook of macrobiotic food.' Only one thing irritated Peel: that John maintained his bodyguards while he was in the Village. 'Nobody would bother him when he was with us. Allen Klein said to Lennon that the reason he liked hanging around me was because Peel does everything Lennon was afraid to do himself: That's what I did. I brought out the side of John that just wanted to go crazy, party all night. But the bodyguards . . . he was cynical and mistrustful. A lot of people wanted handouts. He was paranoid about it.

'When you are close to John Lennon, the guy's so powerful and aware of the world events that you start losing your own identity. Being so close to him for a year or so was good and bad, you know. Look . . . as soon as the carriage turned back to a pumpkin, Cinderella was a housemaid. When you're with John Lennon you're a prince. When his trendy thing is over, you go home a pumpkin. Twelve midnight, you're back in your rags doing what you did before. Like me.'

Life among the Greenwich Village hippies was a natural diversion of fun and freedom for John. But President Nixon's American government viewed it as something almost sinister. From the start of 1972, only a few months after setting foot on American soil, John was faced with an immigration battle that proved almost stranger than fiction.

John was in America on a temporary visa which expired on 29 February 1972. As early as January he and Yoko realized that staying in America permanently might not be easy and that the government could use John's 1968 drugs conviction to refuse them a visa, known as a Green Card. Lawyer Leon Wildes was among those interviewed by them that month in their Bank Street apartment before the real problems began. 'John was quieter than Yoko,' recalls the urbane Wildes. 'While she asked us questions, he was making us tea.' At that time there was no interest expressed in permanent residence in the U.S.A. 'The interest was only in staying a couple of months so they could continue their efforts to find Kyoko; they were in the middle of some complicated custody proceedings.'

Wildes told them that if all they wanted was an extension of another month or even three, 'You don't really need my help. The Apple solicitor can handle it as the custody problem is one of the strongest reasons you can give for the extension of a temporary stay.'

But Yoko answered: 'Yes, we really *do* need your help.' A puzzled Wildes was appointed as their immigration lawyer; he was, frankly, too much of a heavyweight lawyer to be dealing with a simple extension of John's visa. He had no idea, initially, that John was being harassed.

One of the Beatles' classic songs, 'We Can Work It Out', had been written by Paul. But John had injected the middle lines which made the song special: 'Life is very short and there's no time/For fussing and fighting my friend.' But as his initial foray into the relaxed New York lifestyle gave way to tension and worry, he began to realize that fussing and fighting was precisely what he would have to do to clear his sullied name and stay in the country he wanted to adopt.

The source of the government's hounding lay in the little-known Senate Internal Security Sub-Committee. Many politicians were surprised that the committee still existed; it had originated in the 1950s during the scares of communist infiltration. Even in 1972 it apparently operated on the same philosophy: anyone with a view different from the government's was subject to investigation.

The committee received a memorandum suggesting that Lennon might be bankrolling or otherwise supporting the group that had disturbed the 1968 Democratic Convention and, it was feared, might do the same at the Republican Convention due to be held in 1972. Says Leon Wildes: 'Lennon, of course, always denied that he had anything to do with, or had any knowledge of, this plan, if it existed. Nor was he really interested, he said. I always believed this, because he was a principled kind of guy and he wasn't interested in disturbing, rather in stating his piece, explaining his position.' (John's denials were underlined by David Peel's opinion that Lennon was never a believing radical and by John's statements throughout his life that his true role was to write songs and make music. His liaison with Jerry Rubin and others had, however, left him exposed to the charge. When he deviated from the role of writer-musician, he always ran into problems.)

The committee chairman sent the memorandum to John Mitchell, who was Attorney-General, with jurisdiction over the entire immigration process and also chairman of CREEP, the 'Committee to Re-elect the President'. A note at the foot of a covering letter said that a copy had been sent to the White House. 'There was obviously an interest by the Nixon administration, at the highest levels, in what John was doing,' says Wildes.

Evidence of a government campaign mounted. The *New York Times* summed it up:

> According to the government documents which Mr Lennon's lawyer Leon Wildes obtained from the government under court orders, Senator Strom Thurmond, Republican, of South Carolina, wrote a personal and confidential letter to the then Attorney General, John N. Mitchell, on 4 February 1972 suggesting that action against Mr Lennon could avoid 'many headaches'. Attached to the Thurmond letter was a memorandum from the files of the Senate Internal Security Sub-Committee, asserting that a commune group was preparing to go to California to disrupt the 1972 Republican National Convention, and that a confidential source had learned 'that the activities of this group are being financed by John Lennon.' A second memo from the same files contended that 'radical New Left leaders plan to use Mr Lennon as a drawing card to promote the success of rock festivals, to obtain funds for a "dump Nixon" programme.'

The Thurmond letter discovered by Wildes had a handwritten footnote: 'Can we keep him [Lennon] out?' And the New York District Director of Immigration acknowledged that he had been specifically told from 'on high' what action to take on Lennon and exactly when to start deportation proceedings.

Initially, in March 1972, John was ordered to leave America within two months, which allowed some breathing space. John became extremely tense. Winning the right to stay in America was a matter of principle and other worries were adding to his jitters. There was the complex lawsuit with Northern Songs and Maclen Music in London dating back to the rights to his songs written since 1965, with Yoko. There was a simmering battle with Allen Klein. John was a confused, angry man during the early days in America. He drank too much and smoked too many Kool cigarettes.

He suspected that his immigration problem might have been part of a wider plan to split the unity of youth which, in the early seventies, was such a potent force. With Paul McCartney marooned in Britain because of his own drugs bust, John afraid to leave the U.S. because he wouldn't get back in, Jimi Hendrix and Jim Morrison, two catalysts of the youth culture, dead, and the Rolling Stones being carefully watched, Lennon thought that it was perhaps a plot. 'They're chopping off the "revolution" at its source,' he said. 'So there'll be no more mass gatherings like the

Woodstock peace festival. These things inspire change. Politicians don't want change, so it's in their interests to split us all up.

'I'm not the only rock star who's harassed, but nobody else tried to stay here in America. And nobody else hung out with the baddies like I did. Maybe I'm dumb but I'm interested in people. I wanted to find out what they had to say about everything. I didn't want to read a book on them, so I met them all to find out where it it's at, y'know. Now in 1968, the cops beat up some people at a Chicago convention. I'm discussing with Jerry Rubin, Allen Ginsberg and everybody what they're talking about – and they're saying, "Shall we go to San Francisco to have an anti-war rally?" Next thing it's in the papers that John and Yoko are going to lead a vast rally in San Diego with all these people!'

In April 1972, John and Yoko addressed a crowd in New York which was protesting against America's bombing of North Vietnam. Clearly John would not be hounded or compromised by any threat of deportation. At the same time he wanted the freedom to stay in New York. The pulse of the city was right for him.

Once the machine was rolling on checking Lennon out, it was unstoppable. Agents from the F.B.I. (Federal Bureau of Investigation) attended his concerts, studied his song lyrics – particularly those on the heavily political *Some Time In New York City* album – and C.I.A. (Central Intelligence Agency) men shadowed him in his private life. John's phone conversations were tapped so much that he rarely bothered to use it; instead Yoko did most of the talking. The F.B.I. strongly suggested at one point that John 'be arrested, if at all possible, on possession of narcotics charges' so that he might be 'immediately deportable'. Why this was not followed through is unknown; John was smoking marijuana in Bank Street quite often and it would have been easy for police to arrest him.

Leon Wildes now set to work with a counter plan of meticulous detail and careful strategy. 'The government wanted to be able to prove that Lennon was an undesirable because of his 1968 marijuana conviction,' he says. 'They planned to ease him out by bringing proceedings against him as an "overstay" on his temporary visa, telling him that unless he accepted this deal and got out voluntarily, they could always charge him with being deportable as a person with a drugs conviction. That way, he would be seen to be not leaving voluntarily but forcibly. They thought he would not want that and they believed that with a carrot-and-stick routine they could force him out within a month or two in mid-1972.'

While accumulating his proof of the government vendetta,

Wildes managed to secure a 'waiver', a six-month extension for John and Yoko, which changed their status from Non-Immigrant Visa to that of Visitor of Distinguished Merit and Ability. John Lindsay, Mayor of New York and one of Lennon's main pro-tagonists had in former years helped to write and reform America's immigration laws: 'There's a thing called Suspension of Deportation by which, if a good character is proved, and there are sound and equitable reasons not to execute a technical deportation, the Attorney-General can suspend it. John Lennon was not the first by any means to be the beneficiary of a waiver of the technicality.'

This enabled John to appear on the influential Dick Cavett T.V. show. Typically he didn't shrink from confronting the situation head-on, telling millions of viewers that he was being followed by government detectives and that his phones and Wildes' were being tapped.

Although he was nervous about it, John's friend, the black comedian Dick Gregory, who had also been the victim of phone tapping, had convinced him he should tell the world about it.

John described his feelings at the time: 'I'm not saying they had plans other than just keeping tabs on me, to see what I was up to, who I was seeing. But I felt followed everywhere by government agents. Every time I picked up my phone there was a lot of noise. Somebody gave me a number that if you call it, you get this feedback sound that confirms your phone is being tapped. And I did it and it did. Suddenly I realized this was serious, they were coming for me, one way or another. They were harassing me. I'd open the door and there'd be guys standing on the other side of the street. I'd get in the car and they'd be following me and not hiding. That's what got me paranoid. They wanted me to see I was being followed. Anyway, after I said it out on the air, on T.V., the next day there was nobody there. Was I dreaming? No, I wasn't. Look, my lawyer, who's as square as the next one, started to agree. He found his phones were being tapped and he didn't know how to prove it either.'

What the Nixon government had not considered was the enormous groundswell of public opinion in John's favour. During several lawsuits, which included Leon Wildes suing the government at one stage over a technicality in the irregularity of a temporary visa, he pleaded humantiarianism under the Freedom of Information Act. 'There were people in the United States completely deportable, who nevertheless were allowed to remain here; I claimed that Lennon would probably fit within those standards, but since the standards had never been published we were entitled to the benefit of any doubt.' Further, Wildes claimed that Lennon was suffering Selective Prosecution for political rather than legal reasons.

The battle to get a Green Card took four agonizing, exhausting years. It was a long, dark tunnel, but during nerve-wracking days when Leon Wildes would call once or twice daily with news of an advance or a setback, John received heartening support from some of the most influential people in the U.S.A.

Mayor John Lindsay was one. 'This town,' he told me, 'always had a very important history of welcoming contributing talent. I could see no over-compelling reason to get rid of this kind of artist. John Lennon was a major force as we saw it, far more good than bad. Some people just didn't understand the nature of the beast. They didn't really know what Lennon stood for, didn't understand his world, his music, his behaviour, his whole theory of life. A lot of middle-aged politicians, and people who didn't want to stick their neck out, sometimes through fear, took the "pull up the drawbridge" attitude. I was interested in the cause and in this city, and anxious that this country demonstrated to John Lennon that he was welcome here. It seemed unthinkable that a major artist should be shown the door. This city has good Philharmonic, and good opera, and good Carnegie Hall, but it also has the John Lennons.

'Unless there's vigilance, civil liberties suffer. Governments start poking about and letting you know they're using police tactics. My colleagues in city government could sense that this was no hula-hoop thing, here today and gone tomorrow. We sensed that John Lennon's threatened deportation was affecting young people very deeply. It was in the tradition of New York that there remained a mixture of talent in the city.' He also stressed that his role in the Lennon battle, writing to the Commissioner of Immigration in Washington pleading for the deportation order to be dropped, was not to condone John's use of drugs. He did not consider that Lennon was damaging the community by his drug-taking.

John was particularly grateful also for the interest and campaign of Jack Anderson, the highly-rated writer with the *Washington Post*. Anderson, who has a reputation for tenacity and exposé reporting, had written about the 'Watergate tactics' being used to hound Lennon. 'When Jack Anderson started writing about what was happening,' Lennon told me, 'I knew I had to go on fighting until I won.' When John was murdered, Anderson recalled the immigration battle in a column in the *New York Daily News*:

> The immigration service reserves a special bureaucratic hell for aliens who have the slightest taint of narcotics in their past. Thieves, rapists, and even murderers have less trouble gaining admission to the United States than someone convicted of even the most minor drug charge. Six years ago, John Lennon . . . came close to being deported because of a 1968 marijuana charge in England. I took up his case in 1974. I reported that the deportation move was really a political vendetta against Lennon who had been outspoken in his opposition to the Vietnam war. Lennon was able to beat the trumped-up deportation order partly because of official embarrassment over my columns and partly because of the superb legal work of his attorney, Leon Wildes. Since that time the public attitude has changed towards both the Vietnam war and the drug habits it spawned. Most Americans now agree with Lennon that the war was a tragic mistake and his arrest for possessing a small amount of marijuana for personal use is no longer considered a horrendous crime.

Another ally was the Washington lawyer, Steve Martindale. Visiting New York, he met the Lennons at a party also attended by Mayor Lindsay and his wife Mary. 'John and Yoko were extremely shy,' says Martindale. 'Yoko took the lead in explaining the problems they were having with the U.S. government. I suggested they come and spend some time in Washington and we would get to the bottom of it.

'When they came I had a dinner for them. Henry Kissinger was there, so was Senator Alan Cranston. John and Yoko were awed by it all. . . . As I remember it, Henry [Kissinger] put in a call to John Mitchell [the Attorney-General] and we succeeded in softening the government up somewhat.'

The political and diplomatic ramifications of the case were lost on John. He reacted strongly, though, to one twist to Leon Wildes' reports to him. When Yoko was granted permission to remain a permanent resident he erupted. Wildes told him to cool it; the government was playing into their hands, he argued, by putting itself in a position of attempting to split up a married couple. 'That was why I applied separately for Yoko's permit,' says Wildes. 'I got her acknowledged to be an outstanding artist.'

Wildes' ace lay, ironically, in tracing with Yoko the circumstances of John's 1968 drugs bust. John had told Wildes that at the time he had been forced to plead guilty because of Yoko. That was the only action he could take: 'If I pleaded innocent, I would still have been convicted. Yoko at that time in England was an alien, and unless I took the rap they would have charged her and she would have been deported.' Wildes surmised that, having been legally advised by the best opinions in London, what John said could be true. After all, the police pounced on him in a flat which he didn't own, where John had been tipped off by a *Daily Mirror* reporter in advance about their coming and had even cleaned up the flat. He *could* have been framed. And pleading guilty might well have been the best way out. Wildes decided to pursue this, and hoped to win the point in the U.S. Court of Appeals.

Chief Judge Kaufman, with two other judges, provided a positive answer. By a two-to-one vote, they ruled that John's conviction could not be recognized as a conviction for the '*illicit*' possession of marijuana. He had been convicted purely on the discovery of the marijuana on his premises – under British law at the time guilty *knowledge* was not something that needed proving before a conviction could be made. 'In the U.S.,' says Wildes, emphasizing the legal difference, 'there's no such thing as a crime where the government doesn't have the burden of proving that the man had a guilty intent.' The Court of Appeals remanded Lennon's case until the immigration service could re-consider the discretionary aspects of the case. They also admonished the government.

News of this triumph, a major hurdle in the case which virtually broke the government's back, came to Leon Wildes unofficially. A clerk at the Court of Appeals phoned: 'Mr Wildes, I shouldn't be doing this because it's still not in final form, but I'm a long-time Lennon fan . . . there is a decision here which will be in final form in an hour or two, and if you want to send someone down I'll give them a copy of it, in which you win the case two to one.'

Under the headline 'Deportation of Lennon barred by Court of Appeals', the *New York Times* reported the case on 8 October 1975:

In the twenty-four-page decision Judge Irving R. Kaufman issued a strong warning that the courts will not condone selective deportation based upon secret political grounds. This alluded to government documents that were submitted to the court, indications that the Nixon administration started deportation proceedings against Lennon in 1972 for fear that the

Within months of settling in America, John and Yoko were heavily involved in radical politics. In February 1972, in temperatures well below freezing, they were out demonstrating their support for an airline union leaders' boycott of British exports as a protest against British policy in Northern Ireland

July 1973: John followed the Watergate hearing in New York, which indicted the government of President Richard Nixon, with keen interest, and attended them regularly with Yoko

former Beatle would make appearances in the United States promoting opposition to the then President.

In his summing-up and ruling in John's favour, Judge Kaufman said the court did not take lightly Lennon's claim that he was the victim of a move to oust him on political grounds. 'If in our two hundred years of independence we have in some measure realized our ideals, it is in large part because we have always found a place for those committed to the spirit of liberty, and willing to help implement it. Lennon's four-year battle to remain in our country is testimony to his faith in the American dream.'

Says Wildes: 'I can't describe how my feelings were after four years of courtroom appearances, with and without John.' He called Lennon immediately.

'What do you *mean*? We've won?' John asked.

The cautious Wildes said he must remember they agreed they would never claim victory. 'But John, what I thought couldn't happen has happened. The court is remanding the case back to the immigration service, saying they may not consider your conviction. I think the government is now wiped out and they're not going to get into all the other political things they've been threatening, your writing and your songs and all the nonsense they were going to scrape together.'

The following morning John had double cause for jubilation. His son Sean Ono Lennon had been born safely at 2 a.m. and the precious Green Card was on the horizon.

It was nearly a year before John actually received the Green Card (which is actually blue.) On the day John, dressed in suit and black tie (slightly askew) went to court. Paradoxically, the effect of the immigration battle had been to transform lawyer Wildes' dress style from suits into jeans and long hair, while John began veering towards the formal every time there was immigration business to discuss. In court John ritualistically answered the questions put to him by Wildes:

Have you ever been convicted of any crime anywhere in the U.S.?

No.

Have you ever been a member of the Communist Party or any other organization that may seek to overthrow the U.S. government by force?

No.

Do you intend to make the U.S. your home?

I do.

Will you continue your work here?

Yes. I wish to continue to live here with my family and continue making music.

The speeches in John's favour were eloquent and forceful. Sam Trust, president of A.T.V. Music which owned the rights to John's compositions told the court: 'There are two very positive reasons why Mr Lennon should be allowed to remain in the U.S. The music scene in the U.S. is in the doldrums right now and the current resurgence of interest in the Beatles and their material proves that they are the most powerful source of music in the last thirty years. I believe we can look forward to many new innovations in music if Mr Lennon is allowed to remain in this country.'

Trust's second point was that Lennon was a tremendous revenue generator. 'The U.S. will be the scene for the reception of that revenue if he is allowed to remain here,' he said.

Writer Norman Mailer was next to take the stand. He described John as 'a great artist who has made an enormous contribution to popular culture. He is one of the great artists of the Western world. We lost T.S. Eliot to England and only got Auden back.'

Leon Wildes read out a letter from the Bishop of New York, the Rt Rev Paul Moore. Emphasizing John's contribution to the culture of New York, the bishop praised him as a 'gentleman of integrity'.

Gloria Swanson told the court that for years she had been actively interested in the physical fitness of New York's youth. 'My husband met John Lennon in a health food store in this city and we found we had feelings in common on this subject. Good food is essential to physical well-being and we are anti-junk-food. I hope very much that he will help us in this sphere. We must educate the country and the Lennons will help do something about it.'

Among the other witnesses who had given evidence to support John's claim to stay in the U.S. were the noted sculptor, Noguchi and T.V. personality Geraldo Rivera. Also in the courtroom were composer John Cage and actor Peter Boyle, both close friends of John and Yoko.

As Judge Ira Fieldsteel announced his verdict John embraced Yoko, dressed radiantly in white, and the packed courtroom burst into spontaneous cheering.

Outside the courtroom John was buoyant but he spoke quietly. 'The Immigration Service has finally seen the light of day. It's been a long and slow road but I am not bitter. On the contrary, I can now go and see my relations in Japan and elsewhere. I can travel now! Until today my attorney wouldn't even let me go to Hawaii for a vacation in case I couldn't get back. Whenever I flew to Los Angeles I was paranoid in case the plane was diverted to Tokyo on the way!'

Leon Wildes' celebratory gift to John to mark the success was a leather passport case, bearing the bald eagle and the seal of the United States.

The emotional stress on John during the four-year campaign had been enormous. 'I didn't know him before it, but he'd obviously been a light, airy, *up* person,' says Leon Wildes. 'The psychological strain showed. It had a big effect on him, putting him down.'

John's dry humour did, however, surface on a television show discussion about the case. He went with Leon Wildes. John said to his announcer: 'I want you to interview *Leon*.' The announcer diplomatically said he wanted more time with John. Lennon pleaded for his lawyer: 'Look, let Leon go on. His mother's watching!'

John always remained both puzzled and angry at the immigration hassle. He summed up his feelings in a typically incisive sentence: 'I can't understand it. I always thought the Statue of Liberty said "*Come*". . . . Now I'm going home to crack open a tea-bag and start looking at some travel catalogues.'

John felt completely at home in New York where he had battled for so long to stay. 'My life here is not dissimilar to what it was in England, actually. One's life revolves around family or friends or the work you do. My life for the past ten years since I became "famous" has changed, but basically it's a bedroom, a studio, a T.V., a night out, back home! And they talk an American version of English on T.V. and it goes on a bit longer, all night. But beyond that there's not much difference.

'I imagine New York is like London must have been in the Victorian days when Britain was at the height of its power or on the decline. The American Empire is now what the British Empire

In July 1976, after a four-year battle, John wins his vital Green Card from the U.S. Immigration Department. It gave him freedom to leave and re-enter the country

used to be. The French had their empire – Paris was cooking. And America now has the empire of the world even though they're losing bits of it. It has that quality about it. And although Washington's the capital, a lot of the action is in New York because that's where the monied people are and it's an old place that's been built up, so that although it's not physically big it's big in the amount of power and the number of people here. I reckon it must have been like this in Queen Victoria's day in London, when everybody wanted to be there. Or even when that Bloomsbury group, Virginia Woolf and all those people were writing their books and poetry. This is like that: it's where a lot of people come to and I became enamoured of it.'

He also liked the fact that there was no language problem. 'Fortunately or unfortunately they speak English so I just fitted in. It's pretty hard to pinpoint what an American is: they're all Italian-Americans or Irish-Americans or African-Americans or Afro-Americans. It's *nice* here.'

During the period of worry over the Green Card his mind had travelled back to his English roots. He particularly enjoyed an invitation from the *New York Times* to review scripts of *The Goon Show* which he and his Uncle George had chortled over back in Liverpool when John was fourteen. The Goons, especially Spike Milligan, inspired the Beatles, he often said, as much as Elvis Presley and Chuck Berry had. They were to the Beatles' generation what the Beatles were to the next.

When Princess Anne married Captain Mark Phillips John stayed up all night in Los Angeles to watch the royal wedding on television. 'It was the right and proper thing for an Englishman abroad to do such a thing,' he explained, tongue in cheek. 'It was a good excuse to have a few drinks to toast the royal family.'

He took special pleasure in teasing the public about a Beatles reunion, rumours of which continued to simmer in the early seventies.

'Beatles to re-form?' screamed the writers excitedly in 1973 when John, George, and Ringo got together in Los Angeles for a Ringo Starr solo album session. In a parody of the Paul McCartney press release which still irritated him, John released this statement under the headline of 'Newswecanalldowithout':

Although John and Yoko and George, and George and Ringo, had played together often, it was the first time the three ex-Beauties had played together since – well, since they last played together. As usual, an awful lot of rumours, if not downright lies, were going on, including the possibility of impresario Allen De Klein of grABCKO playing bass for the other three in an as-yet-untitled album called *I Was A Teenage Fat Cat*. Producer Richard Perry, who planned to take the tapes along to sell them to Paul McCartney, told a friend: 'I'll take the tapes to Paul McCartney.'

The extreme humility that existed between John and Paul seems to have evaporated. 'They've spoken to each other on the telephone – and in English, that's a change,' said a McCartney associate. 'If only everything were as simple and unaffected as McCartney's new single "My Love", then maybe Dean Martin and Jerry Lewis would be reunited with the Marx Bros and *Newsweak* could get a job,' said an East African official. – Yours Up To The Teeth, John Lennon and Yoko Ono.

The two years preceding Sean's birth while the immigration battle continued were packed with dramatic events for John. As a musician, he encountered many peaks and troughs. His rock 'n' roll album produced by the legendary Phil Spector, one of his all-time heroes, was fraught with personal clashes. As a man, he descended into the worst period of his life, lurching in a drunken haze around California. The reason for that appalling episode was traceable to his marriage. In the autumn of 1973 he and Yoko split up.

'Yoko and I had a breakdown, one way or another,' John told me during their separation. 'We'd been together seven years, y'know, and it wasn't like a normal marriage where the man goes off to work all day, or even the accepted showbiz marriage where one of the partners gets involved in something that splits them up for months through work. We were together *just about twenty-four hours of every day*! So it was bound to happen that we'd snap.' Their private problem was exacerbated by the pressure of the immigration issue.

John and Yoko's split took everyone by surprise. They had been together as friends and artists, as well as man and wife, in one of the most publicly demonstrated love matches of the century. But John was a notoriously difficult, volatile, moody man to live with; during a creative lull, such as he experienced around this time, his insecurities manifested themselves in immature behaviour. He smoked too much, becoming edgy, and spent days on end in his bedroom in solitude. His hands went clammy with nervousness and worry at meeting even his closest friends. And, given the chance, he drank too much. Yoko knew only too well of the danger signs when booze was readily available, and kept a tight grip on its visibility in the Dakota.

She decided that a temporary split was essential. 'There was never any need for a divorce,' she says coolly. 'I knew we would be back together again, eventually.' But John needed time to straighten himself out and, perhaps, they should learn for a while to live without each other. If drinking and having a wild time was something he was missing, she reasoned, it was best that he got it out of his system and played out his fantasies while retaining contact with her by phone.

John was not happy about the decision. 'She kicked me out, pure and simple,' he said later. 'I was behaving stupidly and I'd lost whatever it was about me that she found good in the first place. It was grow-up time and I'm glad she made me do it.'

Yoko says: 'John and I were artists together and husband and wife together. We were competitive, also, to a point: he would write something and I'd say something like, "Well, that's nice, I've got something now *I've* just written," and we would try to stretch each other as writers. It wasn't so surprising, really that we should separate for a while. It turned out to be the best thing that could happen.'

By then, they had moved into an apartment in the Dakota building at 1 West 72nd Street in Manhattan, from where they also ran their company, Lenono. Working as their secretary at the Dakota was. a twenty-two-year old girl born in New York of Chinese parents. May Pang was trusted. She was loyal, efficient, and hardworking for two very demanding people and she loved John's music. When John and Yoko agreed on the split, Yoko suggested John should head for California; to go outside America was impossible at the time because of the Green Card problem, and anyway, Yoko said, he should experience Los Angeles.

Elliot Mintz, John's closest male friend in America since 1971, says it was Yoko who said May should accompany John. 'Obviously,' says Mintz, 'for John Lennon to go alone to Los Angeles, where he'd never been before except with the Beatles, was out of the question. Here was a man who had not driven a car in America, could not walk into a supermarket and purchase food, who couldn't take his laundry to the corner, who didn't make phone calls, didn't know how to compute a tip on a bill, didn't know where to locate restaurants, and who knew hardly anyone in Los Angeles except me. He would have been totally helpless. It was practical to send his secretary, May Pang, with him to look after him. I suppose Yoko knew it was likely there would be intimacy

between the two of them. She took a mature view, knowing John:
"Better with May than galloping around with the golden
groupies."

'And Yoko believed May could handle it. May did not smoke,
drink or take drugs, she was not part of any weird Los Angeles
orgy scene.' But it was never a love match, says Mintz, who saw
them together often. 'To think that John ran off with May to leave
Yoko Ono would require a remarkable suspension in logic. John
could not sustain May's company for more than a matter of hours
without incredible fatigue setting in. It was not a love affair. It was
a relationship born out of the convenience of the moment. I do not
wish to publicly embarrass the lady. She did a fairly effective job of
doing just that in her own book. It is one thing to merchandise the
memories but her contention that she was the other woman in
John's life is nonsense. May contrived a quasi-fictional scenario in
an attempt to give form to a relationship that was not there. From
the moment John met Yoko to the last hour of his life, she was the
only woman who shared his love. Those are not Yoko's words but
my observations.'

Elliot Mintz's closeness to John developed, curiously, from his
first association with Yoko. In 1972 Mintz was working as a disc
jockey and star television interviewer, well on the road to becoming a Dick Cavett-style commentator; in Los Angeles he reported
for *Eye-Witness News* and had a growing reputation as a penetrat-
ing interviewer of statesmen, politicians and celebrities. When
John and Yoko's controversial album, *Some Time In New York
City* was released in June of that year, Mintz conducted a
one-hour interview/profile for the radio station KLOS with Yoko,
tracing the background to her meeting with John. He asked her
unusual questions: whether the people in her dreams spoke
English or Japanese, what quotes from her book *Grapefruit* meant
to her and how she wanted to be remembered when she died. Her
answer was, 'Just say that John and I loved, lived, and died.' Next
day she called to ask for a correction to be taped to that sentence:
it was re-recorded to say: 'John and I lived, loved, and died.' Mintz
had never really understood her music or avant-garde stance but
he sensed a 'wonderful quality' in the lady over the telephone. Still,
it was one of 2,000 radio interviews he had conducted over a
decade, and he thought it would probably go no further. 'It was
really quite a beautiful interview,' said Yoko, 'and we loved the
tone of it.'

A few days later about 300 letters had arrived at Mintz's office
enthusiastically enquiring about the Yoko interview. Hesitantly

Mintz phoned Yoko to tell her about the letters. To his surprise she was fascinated to hear about every one. And that conversation began a unique telephone friendship between Yoko and Mintz that went on nightly for many months. Yoko believes it is sometimes possible to tell more of a person on the phone than in person, when appearances can sometimes distract or inhibit both parties. With Mintz in California and Yoko in New York, they spoke every night on 'everything – religion, films, politics, love, death, books, romance. And every time I spoke to Yoko her perceptions on anything we talked about, even something innocuous, brought a perspective on the subject that had never occurred to me,' says Mintz. 'I was beginning to understand why John, who had seen it all, done it all, knew it all, been around the block four million times, had to stop when he met Yoko. All her thoughts were original.'

Finally, after months of these nightly conversations, John could stand the curiosity no longer. Who was this disc jockey his wife was always talking to? Typically he decided to get in on the act and did a radio interview with Mintz.

Within months of striking up the telephone friendship, John and Yoko decided to take a car journey across America in their old station wagon, with a driver. John often remarked on how little he had seen of the country: 'We only went to America to buy records unavailable back home and give concerts in the old days. I needed to go in some of the coffee shops at four in the morning and get a chocolate milk shake, that kind of thing, just do it normally like the rest of the people do. Yoko and I wanted to experience the heartland of this country.'

A meeting with the mysterious Mintz was part of the programme. When they met him at the house they had rented in Santa Barbara, they presented him with the demonstration record of *Some Time In New York City*, the highly charged political album containing 'Woman Is Nigger Of The World' and a song about Attica State Prison. After spending the day with John and Yoko, Mintz returned to Los Angeles and broadcast the entire album, freezing all commercials and inviting listeners' reaction. Next day John and Yoko phoned him to ask how it went.

'I have the good news and the bad news,' replied Mintz. 'The good news is that it went great, the bad news is that I was fired.' The lyrical content of the album had offended the sponsors. John and Yoko thought it was hilarious.

'My radio career had just collapsed,' says Mintz, 'and they just sat there laughing.'

John said: 'Oh well, now you don't have a job, you might as well come with us. We're going up to San Francisco.' Mintz did just that, spending a month with them at the Miyako Hotel in San Francisco, and from that first meeting he became John and Yoko's close friend and confidant. Lennon trusted him completely.

Born on 16 February 1945, Mintz is, crucially, an Aquarian like Yoko. A man who speaks and moves with total precision, he shared with Lennon a similarly dry sense of humour and an interest in literature. During the fifteen-month period Lennon was away from Yoko Mintz saw him and also spoke to Yoko on the phone nearly every day. 'Don't ever ask me to keep a secret from the other,' he told both of them. 'You are both my friends.'

When John and May Pang stepped from the plane at Los Angeles airport in October 1973 Mintz was there to meet them in his 1956 Jaguar. John wanted to cash some traveller's cheques but they reached the bank – Lloyds on Sunset Boulevard – just after it had closed. 'I knocked on the window and the teller shook his head,' says Mintz. 'I took John and moved him in front of the window and suddenly the doors swung open, security guards came out and the vault opened and the president of the bank appeared.

' "Would you care for some coffee, Mr Lennon?"

'John said: "I just want to turn this into some money." '

The amount turned out to be $10,000, so John sat down and signed his name on the back of 100 cheques, each valued at $100.

'John,' said Elliot Mintz, 'maybe I should take that cash and put it in my cheque account for you. It's a lot to carry around.'

The bank manager said: 'Maybe we can interest you in a long-term checking account?'

John said: 'No, no. I'll keep the money in me pocket.' He'd never handled so much cash in his life and wanted the 'feel' of it. He took ten thousand dollars and stuffed it in his jacket. It was the very first time in his life, he said, he had been inside a bank.

Mintz joked: 'If things go well next week, I'll take you to the supermarket.' John laughed. 'How did it feel, being in a bank, then, John?'

Lennon answered: 'It felt exactly the same as anywhere else. All I did was autograph bits of paper.'

The famous record producer, Lou Adler, had loaned John and May Pang a house on Stone Canyon Road, Bel Air. 'He was incredibly unhappy because of his estrangement from Yoko during the entire "lost weekend",' says Mintz. 'It was the low point of his life. Three days after arriving, at 10 o'clock in the morning, he arrived outside my house shouting: "Wake up, wake up. I've been trying to get you on the phone." I was astonished to see him up so early. I asked: "How long have you been up?" He said: "I haven't been to sleep yet. Can you get Yoko on the phone for me?" He was having trouble with the phones and with the time difference between California and New York. I later asked him why he appeared so low, during that period, and he said that he felt alienated, lost, and consistently unhappy, especially when he was drunk. It was a vicious circle: the more morose John became, the more he drank and the more depressed he became. And the worst thing I can say about my old friend John Lennon,' says Mintz, 'is that he was a lousy drinker. He just couldn't handle booze.

'The Los Angeles months marked the end of an era for John. The wild streak that showed itself in the Lennon of the Liverpool back streets and, later, of Hamburg ended on the Sunset Strip in Hollywood. Later he told me that he just wanted to show the boys that he could get as low as any of them. He could drink more, stay awake longer, play more rock 'n' roll music and be just as outrageous as the rest of them. It was a restless farewell to a persona he had already outgrown. That crazy recording session with Phil Spector, whom he loved and admired; the bar hopping with Keith Moon, Harry Nilsson and Ringo; the Hollywood parties and the nights that knew no end; all of it was an exercise in letting go. If most people did any of those things it would mean nothing. When John Lennon did it, the effect became larger than the reality of the actual events.'

Lennon's behaviour in Los Angeles filled him with remorse and regret; it was infinitely worse than his days in Hamburg. There at least he had the excuse that he was a young man on the prowl. Now, in California with the woman he loved back in New York, monitoring his every move and telling him he was in no state to return to her, John plunged down and down. His wild behaviour included a drunken audience with Jerry Lee Lewis and a ridiculous exhibition of foul-mouthed drunkenness, interrupting the Smothers Brothers show at the Troubadour Club on Sunset Boulevard. Worst of all was when he went on the rampage in the house at Bel Air. With musicians who had been drinking at Phil Spector's record session John had returned to the house drunk on vodka. He became violent and went round smashing the gold records hanging on the wall (one for Carole King's multi-million selling *Tapestry* album), throwing vases against stained glass windows, wrecking furniture, tables, and chairs. For his own safety Spector and his bodyguard put Lennon – who had smashed

John in California: his life fell apart without Yoko. A note to jog his memory reads 'Jeans for Julian'

his spectacles – into bed, tying his wrists and ankles to prevent him doing any more damage. A horrified Mintz got an alarm call from May Pang and was at the house within minutes. May was concerned for John's safety. A drunken Lennon screamed at May: 'Keep that bastard Jew away from me.' Mintz left.

By next morning John had forgotten nearly everything. He told May Pang to assure Lou Adler that he would meet the cost of all the repairs to his house and contents. His first call of apology was to Mintz. 'In all the time I've known you,' he said contritely, 'the very worst thing I could think of to say to you was that you were a bastard Jew. I guess I really must love you.' Then he phoned everybody else.

John's drunkenness in California probably extended to about a dozen times in the whole fifteen months; unfortunately on too many occasions he got drunk in public. And he drank anything that had the right effect. 'Give me a Remy Martin, a B&B, a Courvoisier, an Amaretto, a Tia Maria, anything of that sort,' he'd tell the waitress or bartender. He ate chocolate and candies and junk food.

When John was sober, Mintz would try to tell him he was making a fool of himself. Lennon's rejoinders were as caustic as they had been during his Hamburg and Beatle days: 'Don't get real on me. If you don't like being around me when I'm that way, why don't you just fuck off?' Next day, full of regret, he would apologize – in his fashion: 'Why did you stay with me last night? God, if you were that way, I'd not stay with *you*!'

Tough, cynical, angry, bitter, and confused, John leaned on drink for the same reason he always had: he was insecure. He desperately wanted to return to Yoko after only a week but the sober lady, busy pursuing her career in New York as an avant-garde artist and poet, was not listening to his pleas. They talked frequently by telephone, sometimes for minutes, sometimes for hours. John explained that one of the reasons why he was getting drunk so easily was because his body's resistance to alcohol had been reduced by the drugs he had taken at the height of his days as a Beatle. 'All of his thoughts, all of his longing, had to do with his desperation to get back to Yoko, and to his frustration with her telling him he didn't sound ready,' says Mintz. 'Although he said he was ready to return it was clear he was not.' While he fretted, however, Yoko told her friends that she was certain she and John would re-unite one day. It was only a matter of time.

Confirming Lennon's inability to handle liquor, Mintz says: 'If he had one glass of wine, I'd have to cancel all plans for the next three days. And he was so argumentative! He would start an argument and keep it going just for the sake of having a row and winning it. The basis of the argument was not so important as the row itself. But he was never evil or terrible – just drunk. I saw him that way twice in Las Vegas, once in Japan, twice in New York, and perhaps a dozen times in Los Angeles.'

But John crossed certain personal frontiers in California. Elliot Mintz took him to see one of his favourite artists, Jerry Lee Lewis, at the Roxy in Los Angeles. 'I had only three childhood idols,' he told Mintz. 'Elvis, Carl Perkins, and Jerry Lee, and I haven't seen any live. Let's go!' John was totally immersed in the driving rock 'n' roll that had first inspired him, classics like 'Whole Lotta Shakin' ' and 'Great Balls of Fire'. Jerry Lee did his wildest show, playing the piano with his toes. Lennon led the applause at the end of each song. After the show Elliot took John backstage and introduced him to Lewis. John just sank to the floor, and kissed Jerry Lee's shoes. 'That's all right, son,' drawled Jerry Lee. 'You just get up now.'

The encounter had a strange parallel with the occasion on which he had met Elvis. There was, he decided, no future in talking to artists. 'I'm a record man,' he told me. 'I don't like live work or going to concerts. They usually let you down.'

Ten years earlier, living at Weybridge with Cynthia, John had a sign hanging in his kitchen. It said simply: 'The drunk and the glutton shall come to poverty.' It would be easy to view the California débâcle as a worthless alcoholic escapade but in many ways it was essential because John had never had a chance to grow up. It had all been done in public as a musician. This gave him the opportunity. One of his biggest dreams was to experience Las Vegas. 'What's it like, what's it like, Elliot?' he kept asking Mintz. 'Take me there. Fix me a drink and we'll go.' One drizzly day Mintz agreed to take him. 'But John, take it easy. If we're going to Las Vegas, let's at least get there sober.'

Driving down La Cienega, not far from Mintz's home, John's eye was caught by a flashing sign: 'The Losers' Topless Club'. 'Feels right,' he said to Mintz. 'Let's pull in.' Mintz was incredulous: it was two o'clock in the afternoon. Once in the bar, with the topless barmaid filling up his glass as quickly as he drank and Motown records accompanying the two topless dancers, John became more and more uneasy. He quickly realized the futility and sleaziness of it all. Even in California he was able to diagnose bad taste through his alcoholic hazes. After a few minutes John had seen enough. 'As we left The Losers,' recalls Mintz, 'John started singing softly in my ear: "We make them paint their face and dance – Woman is Nigger of the world." He could be the observer and the observed simultaneously.'

In Las Vegas John acted out all his fantasies. At Caesar's Palace John 'was enchanted by the casino atmosphere for a while, but it was the longest weekend of my life,' says Elliot Mintz. 'The house kept us supplied with drinks and we sat in the chairs by the roulette wheel for hours. He devised the John Lennon Las Vegas system; taking a ten-dollar chip and placing it on every number on the table.' John became convinced he had a system that would guarantee him a 35–1 win with each turn of the wheel. The plan was less than successful. The gambling over, we went for a walk around the casino until the spotlight fell on him and four hundred people besieged him. Cocktail hostesses began fawning over him, saying things like: "Hey, I grew up listening to the Beatles." And John was off. The plastic, crazy, neon city of Las Vegas was even more empty to him than Los Angeles. And even L.A. he had christened as "the place you stop off to buy a hamburger".'

John consoled his sorrows over drinking sessions with friends Harry Nilsson, Keith Moon, Klaus Voormann, Ringo Starr, Jim Keltner, and Mal Evans, 'Big Mal', the faithful friend from Liverpool days who had been the Beatles' road manager. Evans, whose giant frame belied his soft, warm personality, was a former telephone engineer who drifted into the Beatles camp by doing part-time work as a bouncer at the Cavern. As road manager alongside Neil Aspinall on all the Beatles' world tours, he had a particularly strong relationship – gruff but intuitive – with the moody Lennon during Beatlemania. When the Beatles split, Mal felt lost. He moved to Los Angeles, fell victim to drink and drugs, and allegedly pulled a gun on a girl in his Hollywood flat on 5 January 1976. The police were called but Mal barricaded himself in. They smashed the door down to be confronted by Mal holding a gun; they shot him dead. The news of yet another fatality in the Beatles family saddened John but he coped with it as he had with all other tragedies: by not dwelling on it for long.

George Melly, whose meetings with John seemed to punctuate key events in Lennon's life – the Beatles, meeting Yoko, and estrangement from her – was in a bungalow at Hollywood's Chateau Marmont Hotel when an aggressive John arrived at dawn with Harry Nilsson and Derek Taylor. 'I wouldn't guarantee what substances were involved in creating his condition,' says Melly, 'but certainly drink was a contributory one. They were all high on an all-night raid. Suddenly one of us mentioned Jackie Pye, the Liverpool wrestler. He was famous in Liverpool as the baddie of the wrestling circuit. Although John was much younger than me, Jackie Pye, it turned out, had spanned our youth. We had both seen him. His favourite trick was blowing his nose between his thumb and forefinger and flicking the snot at the referee. He was known as Dirty Jackie Pye. Once we hit this area of shared knowledge we were in hysterics.' Amid the palm trees of Hollywood, two lapsed Liverpudlians recalled an eccentric slice of their youth.

Four months later a similarly wild John arrived in New York and headed for Derek Taylor's suite at the Algonquin Hotel. With Harry Nilsson again, John was drunk and began trying to smash the chandeliers in Derek's suite. The next thing that happened was a 2 a.m. phone call in the hotel to George Melly's female publicity agent. 'He demanded sex with her,' says Melly. 'She replied: "I'm asleep. Go away." I couldn't help reflecting, when I heard about it next morning, on the number of girls around the world who would have received that phone call from John Lennon with a certain enthusiasm.'

As John described his songs as 'personalized diaries', it was not surprising that the music he made during the separation period comprised messages to Yoko and elements of self-pity. *Walls And Bridges*, an album made during the California period, included such songs as 'Nobody Loves You (When You're Down And Out)'. I asked him what he meant by the enigmatic album title. He answered: 'Walls you walk into and bridges you cross over. Deep stuff!'

The biggest psychological bridge John had to cross during his absence from Yoko was a meeting with Julian, who was then ten and living with Cynthia. They had spoken on the phone, on Cynthia's insistence, regularly since John had gone to America. But for nearly three years they had not met. Cynthia believed that as John was isolated in California, he should see Julian. This caused John anguish and torment right up until Julian's visit. He believed that he had been a neglectful father and he could not summon up the inner strength to pick up the pieces.

When Cynthia and Julian flew into Los Angeles Airport just after Christmas 1974, John was nervous. He had no idea of how his reunion with his son would go and whether the boy would warm to him. And he dreaded seeing Cynthia again. Once a link had been broken, especially such a strong one, John felt that it should be severed for ever. Mentally he was a million miles away from life with Cynthia in Liverpool and Weybridge. There was the extra complication of her meeting May Pang.

At the airport and in the limousine which took Cynthia and Julian to their hotel, John was jittery. He was cool with Cynthia; a 'hello' and a peck on the cheek was all he could manage. But Julian's excited chatter about the flight on a jumbo jet and arrival in America broke the ice on the car ride. John realized how thrilled he felt to see Julian and kissed him affectionately.

Next day, the plan was for John to take Julian, alone, to Disneyland. Says Cynthia: 'John wanted to whip into the hotel, take Julian away and not communicate with me which was fine by me. Unfortunately, Julian flew into a tantrum in his bedroom, screaming on the floor, hysterical.' Julian dug his heels in, insisting he wanted his mother *and* father on the outing.

'Look, John,' said Cynthia, 'I'm sorry but he won't go anywhere with you without me. You can hear him in the other room.' Reluctantly John gave in.

A tense day for John, Cynthia, and May and Mal Evans followed. 'I felt miserable trailing round Disneyland with them, but Julian had a great time and that's what mattered.' Still John would not face Cynthia, who stayed several stages behind the party for most of the time. 'John could not look me in the eyes,' says Cynthia. 'He seemed in a total panic that we might start talking and he avoided looking near me as much as he could for the whole day.' They were forced together for a lunch of bacon and flapjacks and syrup, with John talking in a stilted fashion about the virtues of American junk food, but the atmosphere was awful.

As well as being 'deeply upset' by John's aloofness, the ever-practical Cynthia was worried about Julian. 'I wanted a proper conversation with John about Julian's education, his future and what he thought should be done for our son. I pushed once or twice but John looked the other way. After two or three rebuffs I gave up. I just hoped that the relationship between John and Julian would gain strength.'

And it did. The boy went off with a handful of balloons and many hugs and kisses from his Dad. Their friendship developed warmly in later years, as Julian confirms. One of the reasons for this was Julian's own musical talent, which showed itself even at this age.

By the late seventies Julian as a teenager was establishing a friendship with John. 'It was more of one man to another than the

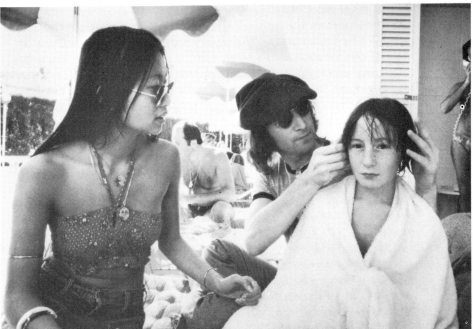

Top: John filling in time in California

Above: May Pang looks on as John attends to the styling of twelve-year-old Julian's hair during their visit to Disneyland, Los Angeles in December 1975

usual father and son relationship,' says Julian, 'because he had been away from me a lot, and he said he realized that. I was just getting through to him and growing up myself and growing out of the silly giggling I did as a young teenager that really annoyed him, when Dad was killed.' He sorely regrets being robbed of the time to develop the bond that was growing between them.

As Julian moved inexorably towards a life in music, he developed a particularly strong rapport with Sean. 'I feel a terrific blood closeness with Sean,' says Julian. 'We're going to get on well.' His relationship with his stepmother, on the other hand, will always require diplomacy. Yoko and Cynthia have kept a wary distance from each other since the divorce. 'I'll feel better with both my mother and Yoko when I'm older and more established on my own ground as a musician,' said Julian in 1984. 'I like to keep an open line with everyone and not hurt anybody's feelings.' Both personally and professionally as a singer-songwriter, being the son of John Lennon will never be easy.

By 1983, at the age of twenty, Julian had dropped his teenage plans to launch a group with the name of the Lennon Drops, and arrived in London, alone, to set up a flat and tackle, head-on, the job of becoming a singer–songwriter–bandleader. Tony Stratton Smith, boss of Charisma Records, was highly impressed with Julian's songwriting and sent him for six weeks to an obscure château in France where Julian's confidence, as well as his musicianship, improved enormously. He has now been signed to Charisma and has secured the support of the outstanding American producer Phil Ramone, who has worked with major artists of the calibre of Paul Simon, Billy Joel, Frank Sinatra, and Bob Dylan.

Julian is totally aware of the pitfalls and expects to be accused of cashing in on his father's name. Clearly he is in a 'no win' situation. However, 'I just have to do it,' he told me. 'Partly, I feel that with my father dead someone should keep the tradition alive. He was a major, successful singer and writer and it's up to me to try to carry on to keep the name Lennon going in the field of music.

'I feel music in my blood. It would be asking for trouble to do it my father's way and style.' Vocal similarities with John are obvious: 'I can tell the sound is similar when I hear myself, but I don't do it consciously. I did love the way Dad sang, and there's nothing wrong with taking a bit of inspiration from him, surely? Others do, so I don't see why I shouldn't. His work has influenced me, but I'm very self-conscious about the criticism that is bound to come. It's both an advantage and a disadvantage being the son of John Lennon. I'm determined to live it down and live it up! I feel confident I can handle it and grow as a songwriter and singer. Dad told me the Beatles thing was something he enjoyed breaking away from and in a sense I'm trying to break away from him while remaining Julian Lennon all my life. He would understand. Dad's best work came when the Beatles finished. . . . He told me the Beatles were fun while they lasted but he would never do it again.'

Cynthia's last, bitter experience of John occurred on a flight from New York to Los Angeles. Again, John was with May Pang, and Julian, who had been with him in New York during the making of the *Walls And Bridges* album; Julian had even played the drums on one track called 'Ya Ya'. While Cynthia had stayed at the Pierre Hotel in New York, Julian had stayed with John and May. After a few days a cheery John had phoned his former wife and asked her to go with them to Los Angeles. Cynthia thought that perhaps the breakthrough had come and they could have a decent relationship. She looked forward to the five-hour flight.

But when they boarded the plane, John's mental barricade went up again. He was with May and Julian in the first-class section, completely ignoring Cynthia, who was sitting behind them, for the entire journey. 'It was total and utter rejection,' she remembers. 'I couldn't get through. I'd fought hard to get John and Julian together, in ways John would never know about. But whenever we looked at each other, it was like utter panic by John. He couldn't cope with me. He must have felt threatened by me, that I was after him and wanted him and me to get back together. But I wasn't. All I wanted was mental communication for the sake of the one thing in life John and I still had in common: a son. I shall never understand why two people who had a child could not talk normally without threats or worries or fear.' Finally Cynthia broke down on the plane and wept. It was the last time she saw him.

Such was John's state during his separation from Yoko that it is amazing that he reached out to his son, establishing the basis for their future mental rapport, as well as making some superb music with lyrics sharply evocative of his mental condition. To cope with his former wife, in addition, and all memories she evoked, was impossible for him that year. At the time the estrangement from Yoko was enough of a problem.

In New York in mid-1974 I spent two days and nights with John while he was making *Walls And Bridges*. He talked openly about his depression, how he was missing Yoko, but that he expected they would re-unite. He was living with May Pang in a modest, one-roomed apartment at 434 East 52nd Street, overlooking the East River. He loved cities with rivers, he said; New York's affinity with Liverpool made him nostalgic. In the Record Plant studios John was at his mercurial best, changing lyrics and putting the gloss on some of his new songs. One evening over a Chinese meal, he talked at length to me, both about his life as a New Yorker and how he was gradually coming to terms with realizing what went on in the Beatles years.

That year George Harrison played a solo tour of America and John was rumoured to be planning to play at his New York concert. In the end he didn't because he had a row with George over what John called 'The Famous Beatles Agreement', the final dissolution of the group that required all four signatures. John was the last to sign. 'I was supposed to sign this on the day of the concert but I wouldn't. My astrologer told me it was the wrong day for business. [John finally signed the same day he visited Disneyland with Julian.] George was furious at the time because I hadn't signed it when I was supposed to and I was informed that I needn't bother to go to George's show. I was relieved because there wasn't any time for rehearsal and I didn't want it to be a case of John jumping up and playing a few chords. I went to see George at Nassau and it was a good, tight show. George's voice was shot but the atmosphere was good and George's performance was great. I saw George after the Madison Square Garden show and we were friends again.' Harrison had resolutely refused to sing major Beatles hits on the tour – 'a basic mistake,' said John, 'easy to spot when you're not making one. But people definitely wanted to hear the old stuff.' The songs George did perform included John's 'In My Life', though with slightly altered lyrics; 'Something'; 'While My Guitar Gently Weeps'; and 'For You Blue'.

In the past two years, he said, he had changed his attitude towards the Beatles. 'The period when I rejected the Beatles years in my mind was when I was just out of the Janov therapy treatment,' he explained. 'I'd been mentally stripped bare and I wanted to shoot my mouth off to clear it all away. Now it's different.

'When I slagged off the Beatles thing, it was like divorce pangs and, me being me, it was blast this, fuck the past. Remember all those articles we did together in the old *Melody Maker* – "Lennon Blasts Hollies" all over the back page? And the *Daily Mirror* piece:

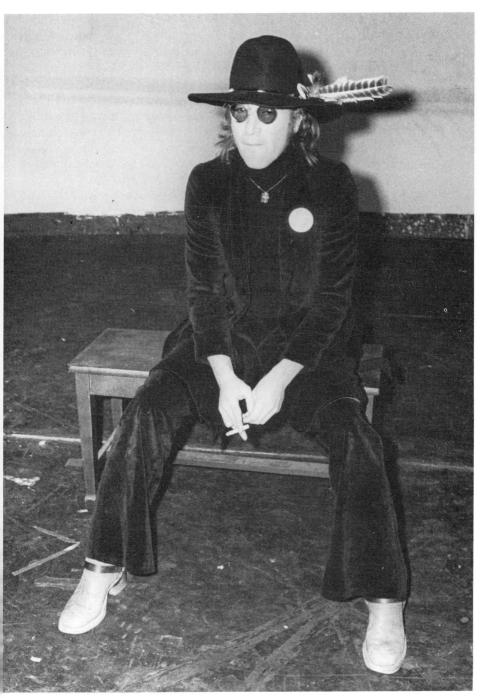

John at the opening of the *Sgt Pepper's Lonely Hearts Club Band* musical in New York in November 1974

"Lennon beats up local D.J. at Paul's 21st birthday party!" I've always had a bit of a mouth and when a thing begins that way, you have to live up to it. Then Paul and me had that fight in the pages of the *MM*. It was a period I had to go through. I sort of enjoy the fight at the time, that's the funny thing.

'Now we've all got it out and it's cool. I can see the Beatles from a new point of view. Can't remember much of what happened but I've started taking an interest in what went on while I was in that fish tank. It must have been incredible.'

Part of John's therapy in growing out of the Beatles was to recognize their importance to his life. On a long car journey across America he took a pile of Beatles cassettes to re-acquaint himself with the work which nobody would forget. And when, in 1974, America's devoted Beatles fans made it possible to stage a Beatlefest, John wanted to be counted in as a fan of his old group. Beatles films, guitars from John and Paul, Ringo's old drumsticks and other memorabilia were gathered by John when he met Mark Lapidos, who was then launching the Beatlefest at New York's Commodore Hotel, and who still runs the conventions several times a year all around America. 'John nearly even came to the first one to pick the winner of the charity raffle and see who won his old guitar,' says Lapidos. 'But he chickened out at the last minute.'

Four years later a Beatlefest assistant, Roger Berkley, bumped into John in the street and told him that the 1978 convention was coming soon. Had John any message? 'Yeah, just tell them the music was the thing,' replied John. It had taken a long time, but John Lennon had come to terms with being an ex-Beatle. He even enjoyed it.

'I'm into collecting memorabilia as well,' he told me in our interviews. 'Elton John came in with these gifts for me, stills from the *Yellow Submarine* film. Great! He gave me these four dolls of John, Paul, George, and Ringo. I thought: Christ, what's *this*? A Beatle collecting Beatle dolls? But why not? It's history, man, history. I went through a phase of hating all those years and having to smile when I didn't want to, but now I'm out of it, it's great to look back on it, man. Great! Why haven't I ever considered the good times instead of moaning about what we had to go through?'

He had even gone some way towards mending his relationship with McCartney. 'He was here in New York recently. We spent two or three nights together talking about the old days. It was cool, seeing what each other remembered from Hamburg and

Liverpool. So y'see, all that happened when I blew my mouth off was that it was like an abscess bursting, except that mine, as usual, burst in public.

'Look, when the Beatles did a tour, we hated it and loved it. There were great nights and lousy ones. . . It wasn't all pie and cookies being a Beatle but in 1970 people just wanted big-mouth Lennon to shout about the lows. So I made a quick trip [his therapy with Janov] to uncover the hidden stones of my mind and a lot of the bats flew and some of them are going to have to stay. I've got a perspective now, that's a fact.' He must have exorcized all the ghosts because he even went to the Broadway production of the successful theatrical production *Sgt Pepper*; watching it would have been like looking into the mirror of his own mind as well as his body.

John loved badges. On the nights I saw him his badge was half an apple between bread slices. 'Work that one out,' he said. 'It doesn't mean I own half of Apple. Elton gave me the badge. It means I'm schizophrenic!'

John was alive, crackling with good humour and his old rapier-like observation. Leaving the recording studio, he walked with me for five minutes before hailing a cab. I mentioned that it was a strange contrast with the police-protected limousine rides he had been used to. Ah, he said, that was precisely what he loved about New York. 'I get 'em all the time. Not in California – they're looking for stars there and it's unsafe. But here in New York, I found all the paranoia was inside my own head. It's so safe here. I feel free, walking the streets. Nobody hassles you. I reckon most of the cab drivers in New York know me, I've taken so many, and I *love* seeing the city from the inside of a cab.'

At the end of the journey, John, always an enormously generous tipper, gave the cabbie $10 for a trip that cost less than half that amount.

'Excuse me, sir,' said the cab driver, 'but aren't you John Lennon?'

'Nah,' said John. 'I wish I was. I wish I had his money.'

Inside his apartment John regaled me and photographer Bob Gruen with the bizarre story that he had seen flying saucers from his window. He was serious. 'Look,' he said, 'it's true. I was standing, naked, by this window leading on to that roof when an oval-shaped object started flying from left to right. It had a red light on the top. After about twenty minutes it disappeared over the East River and behind the United Nations Building. I wonder if it might have been carrying out some research there.

'They all think I'm potty, but it's true. I shouted after it, "Wait for me, wait for me!" But I'm not kidding, May and I saw it. I didn't believe it either.' He had phoned the police, who said there had been other reports of the sighting of a flying saucer. 'But I didn't tell them who it was on the phone. I didn't want newspaper headlines saying: "Beatle Sees Flying Saucer". I've got enough trouble with the immigration people already.'

'And you'd not been smoking or drinking?' I said.

'No, God's honest truth. I only do that at weekends or when I see Harry Nilsson.'

We watched television for hours. John watched himself on a news bulletin coming out of court earlier that day where he had been to listen to yet another round in his immigration battle. Reporters, surprised to see John formally dressed in dark suit and tie, asked him if he was confident of winning his case.

'Yes, I'm confident,' said John.

'Why?' asked a reporter.

'Because I'm big-headed, as usual,' said John. 'I like it here. I want to stay. Amnesty! Amnesty!'

'It's absolutely alive, that's why I have got to live in New York and got sick of Los Angeles,' John told me. 'There's a buzz here. I like the way you can get or do anything you like at any time of the day or night. . . . If I couldn't live here, I'd live in Paris. I love the French. They're so bloody rude.

'Look here, New York gives you television all night. It's better than the B.B.C. Light Orchestra.'

John had been consumed by the Watergate scandal. 'Any country,' he said, 'that produces the Watergate affair has got to be number one with me. I sat watching every bit of it on T.V. and couldn't believe it. They kept asking the witnesses questions and the guy replied; "That is inoperative." Everything they were asked that was meant to make 'em tell the truth, they said: "That is inoperative." I'm gonna try it when they start asking me hard questions. "Inoperative. All questions abut the Beatles inoperative." '

Part of John's fascination for Watergate can be traced to his love of causes: he loved wearing badges that championed people or attitudes and during 1975 wore one saying simply 'Elvis'. Other badges, or 'buttons' as he grew to call them when his language became peppered with Americanisms, included 'Indict Rockefeller for murder', 'Listen to this button' and 'Not Insane', a phrase coined by the parody group Firesign Theatre.

AN OPENED LETTUCE TO SODD RUNTLESTUNTLE. (from dr. winston o'boogie)

        Couldn't resist adding a few "islands of truth" of my
own, in answer to Turd Runtgreen's howl of hate (pain.)

Dear Todd,

        I like you, and some of your work, (including "I Saw The
Light", which is not unlike "There's A Place" (Beatles), melody
wise.)

   1) I have never claimed to be a revolutionary. But I
       am allowed to sing about anything I want! Right?

   2) I never hit a waitress in the Troubador. I did act
       like an ass, I was too drunk. So shoot me!

   3) I guess we're all looking for attention Rodd, do
       you really think I don't know how to get it, without
       "revolution?" I could dye my hair green and pink for
       a start!

   4) I don't represent anyone but my SELF. It sounds like
       I represented something to you, or you wouldn't be so
       violent towards me. (Your dad perhaps?)

   5) Yes Dodd, violence comes in mysterious ways it's wonders
       to perform, including verbal. But you'd know that kind
       of mind game, wouldn't you? Of course you would.

   6) So the Nazz use to do "like heavy rock" then
       SUDDENLY a "light pretty ballad". How **original**!

   7) Which gets me to the Beatles, "who had no other style
       than being the Beatles"!! That covers a lot of style
       man, including your own, TO DATE.....

        Yes Godd, the one thing those Beatles did was to affect
PEOPLES' MINDS. Maybe you need another fix?

        Somebody played me your rock and roll pussy song, but I
never noticed anything. I think that the real reason you're mad
at me is cause I didn't know who you were at the Rainbow (L.A.)
Remember that time you came in with Wolfman Jack? When I found
out later, I was cursing, cause I wanted to tell you how good you were.
(I'd heard you on the radio.)

                    Anyway,
                         However much you hurt me darling;
                    I'll always love you,

                    J. L.   *John Lennon*

                         30th Sept. 1974

John's reply to an interview conducted by *Melody Maker* with American
singer-writer Todd Rundgren in which he criticized John and the Beatles

Throughout 1974 John made a determined, conscious effort to pull himself back from the precipice of emotional and intellectual disaster which threatened him during his Californian exile. He drank less. He made music. He immersed himself in serious subjects like Watergate during his own immigration battle. He even demonstrated to Britain that the appalling international publicity he had received in Los Angeles did not reflect a numbing of his sense or his memory. When singer–songwriter Todd Rundgren criticized his activities in the *Melody Maker*, John tore into him with the same ruthlessness he had used against Paul McCartney. In a style that combined his old satire with vitriol, John wrote Todd (whom he called Sodd Runtlestuntle) the 'Opened Lettuce' which is reproduced on page 183.

One of the highlights of the year and a turning point in his life came when he went to Caribou recording studios in Colorado to record with Elton John. The two men were warm friends. Elton, a total fan of 1960s music, loved the mixture of hard man and soft romantic in John which all who knew him recognized under that sometimes manic exterior. Lennon, for his part, thought Elton's music and his industry was magnificent. He loved the nature of the man, his stage act, and his songs. Elton had worked in Dick James' music publishing office in London when the Beatles had sent in their demonstration tapes, so the link with John went back a long way. (Lennon was always attracted to extroverts; he sought only one autograph in his life, and that was Mae West's, secured for him by Elliot Mintz. 'Now, what's this fella's last name?' Mae West asked as she signed.)

John's song 'Whatever Gets You Thru The Night', on which Elton played keyboards, was his first chart-topper in America as a soloist. When they made the record Elton told John that it was a number one; John laughed at him. 'No, I'm out of favour here. It would be nice but it's not a number one.' Elton made John promise that if it did reach the top he would appear in concert with him. John was so certain it would not that he readily agreed. And so the stage was set for John to appear at Elton's Madison Square Garden concert on Thanksgiving Day, 28 November 1974.

Before he was committed to the New York show John went to see Elton's concert in Boston and he remembered thinking, Thank God it's not me, as he watched Elton dressing to go on. 'I got stage fright just looking at him!' said John. 'By the time I got on to the stage at Madison Square Garden with all the screaming and shouting [20,000 people gave Lennon a conquering hero's welcome], I thought what is *this*! I hadn't heard it since the Beatles. The place was really rocking.'

Elton wanted John to sing 'Imagine' but Lennon flatly refused. 'I didn't want to come on like Dean Martin, doing my classic hits. I wanted to have some fun and play some rock 'n' roll. And I didn't want to do more than three because it was Elton's show.' As well as the number one hit, John sang 'I Saw Her Standing There' and 'Lucy In The Sky With Diamonds'.

The significance of the show lay in much more than John's appearance. Elton had remained very friendly with Yoko during John's separation. Backstage before they went on, John received a gardenia with the message: 'Good luck, love, Yoko'. 'Hey,' John said to Elton. 'Look what Yoko sent me. I'm glad she's not here tonight. I'd never be able to go on.'

But Yoko was in the audience, shedding tears of joy at John's triumphant performance. Elton, in on the secret, had told her he wouldn't 'let on' to John, or neither Lennon nor he would have been able to perform. Backstage, John was floored when she walked into the dressing-room. Although they had spoken literally thousands of times on the phone, they had not seen each other for a year.

'You were great, John,' she said simply. She looked poised and attractive; John was palpably emotional at seeing her. It was one of the best moments of his life.

Before the show John had talked about their separation to me: 'Yoko and I, well we had this little falling out. We're two artists and we found it hard living together. We'll see what happens. I still speak to her on the phone most days. She phoned me from London the other day and said: "Hey, it's nice here. Remember the autumn with all the leaves?" And I said: "What are you trying to say, Yoko? I know it's nice, but are you trying to unsettle me in New York? It's nice *here* – remember the noise?"

January 1975 proved the watershed month. John had been for several talks with Yoko to maintain contact. Finally he phoned and told her he was fit and ready, in every way, to return. And he did, after a re-union cup of afternoon tea at the Plaza Hotel. Symbolically, that same month the Beatles as a business enterprise were finally dissolved in the High Court in London.

'I'm as happy as Larry to be back with her,' said John. 'It was a tough year for me. It's all right wondering whether the grass is greener on the other side but once you get there all you find is

more grass. I don't know whether I'll ever learn that lesson about life. We had a mutual separation and a mutual getting back together. Look, she ain't no chick that you say: "OK, I'll see you Friday," or, "I'm coming back Monday." You're dealing with a fully aware human being. There's no treating her like your chick, you know . . .

'It fell in place again. It was like I never left. I realized this was where I belonged. I think we both knew we'd get back together again sooner or later, even if it was five years, and that's why we never bothered with divorce. I'm just glad she let me back in again. I was allowed back! It was like going out for a drink but it took me a year to get it.'

In talking about his love for Yoko John was able to look at their period of separation with a new perspective. 'I'm the one who's supposed to know everything, but she's my teacher. She's taught me everything I know. The lessons are hard and I can't take it sometimes and *that's* why I freaked out. When we were separate, it was *me* making an asshole of myself in the clubs and in the newspapers. It wasn't her. She missed me as a human being and she loved me but *her* life was ordered. *I* went back to *her* life. It wasn't the other way round.' Drily, he added: 'Yoko and I are proud to say that our separation was a failure.'

The period of estrangement and the terms of the reunion were an exceptional example of one woman's love of her man. Yoko's surveillance of John's activities, particularly with May Pang in Los Angeles when she monitored their every move from the Dakota – much to their chagrin and astonishment – reached epic proportions. Yoko's telephone calls to John were often less than five minutes apart; as soon as he put the phone down she would ring again, or *he* would ring back with something that was on his mind in connection with business, or to pass the time of day by recounting his activities. She knew every twist and turn of his drunken extravaganzas. And it said much for John's desire to rehabilitate himself that not once, given the freedom and 3,000-mile distance from New York to Los Angeles, did he move anywhere without Yoko knowing his phone number.

The fifteen-month 'lost weekend' ended after many pleas by John to be allowed back. 'I'm ready to come home,' he said, so often.

'No you're not, not yet,' she replied.

Yoko kept him totally informed about the business machinery which she was keeping well oiled, increasing their prosperity. Finally, when she eventually told him by telephone to come home,

her conditions were, like her own personality, simple but serious
and demanding: he would have to act with more maturity; not
drink; travel alone frequently to keep their relationship fresh and
assert his individuality; and not relapse into the self-pitying
attitude that had caused their rift. Briefly, she demanded that he
returned to the positive thinking and firm discipline that marked
the John Lennon she once knew. John reacted well to the
unpalatable truth that he had been impossible to live with.

This reunion and John's house-husband period made Yoko
seem to many people a manipulating, psychic, power-wielding
egotist who would stop at nothing to get her way. This judgement
hid the truth from people who didn't want to face it: Yoko's
appeal, to John and the people close to her, was that she was such
a strong-minded, artistic individualist. She combined all this with
a fearsome practicality. Above all, she would not tolerate weakness in people. Many people who were aware of their own frailties
winced at Yoko's intuitive recognition of their failure to do
anything about them. John did not; he wanted his woman
forceful, intelligent, powerful, domineering, and one step ahead of
the game.

He loved Yoko and knew he needed her to reassert himself both
creatively and as a man. 'He was a simple, but complex man,'
reflects Yoko. 'I mean, when we got back together after that
separation, John said he had gone out for a walk for the morning
paper and a cup of coffee and hadn't bothered to return. In a way,
it *was* like that. At that time, we couldn't live together and we
couldn't live apart properly either. But we did know it was just a
matter of time straightening things out.'

Not for nothing did John call Yoko 'Mother' – to her face, and
to their friends, and in little notes he left on the kitchen table. As
well as being his lover, she was a distinctly maternal figure to him
and, as Yoko herself says, a substitute for his Aunt Mimi who
raised him.

7
SECLUSION

*'Sean may not have come from my belly
but I'm gonna make his bones'*

By his early thirties John Ono Lennon had travelled mental and
physical journeys that most people cannot hope for in a lifetime.
Not all of his breadth of vision had stemmed from his millionaire
status; if the money had given him freedom, it had also imprisoned
him. Material possessions, anyway, had never been his first
priority on becoming successful. As he had demonstrated when he
embraced Yoko Ono in 1966, the star trip of being a Beatle was
not enough to satisfy him. He always needed intellectual stimula-
tion and New York provided it.

Back at the Dakota, he was a totally transformed man. He
talked about the major change of direction in his life. 'The idea of
being a rock 'n' roll musician and artist sort of suited my talents
and mentality and the freedom was great,' said John. 'But then I
felt boxed in. I found out I wasn't free, and it wasn't because of a
contract. The contract was a physical manifestation of being in
prison. I might as well have gone to a nine-to-five job, as carry on
the way I was carrying on. And there's two ways to go. You either
go to Las Vegas and sing your great hits, *if you're lucky*, or you go
to hell, you know, actually literally *dying*.'

John was always a restless man, in constant need of new
challenges. It took him a long time to throw off his rock 'n' roll
restrictions but America was the melting pot in which he finally
outgrew pop stardom and impressed himself on the world as a
great man. The peace campaign had taken a long time to sink into
the world's consciousness as something real and genuine. People
had been slow to realize that even a young Beatle could have
important qualities of leadership, however much he rejected the

role. It took even longer for them to accept that the tough, loud-mouthed Lennon was, underneath, exactly the opposite. His ability to project that difference and articulate a warm humanitarianism, both in his music and by example, made him a model for generations of libertarians.

One of the popular myths about John Lennon has been that he was tough, hard-hearted, vicious, and unsentimental. One of the great myths about Yoko Ono is that she is a manipulative witch, power-hungry, and cold. The reverse is true in both cases. Lennon was incurably romantic all his life and that quality manifested itself with great intensity after his reunion with Yoko. Yoko too has always been emotional, tearful, and compassionate.

What gave her a reputation for toughness and what John loved was her industriousness, tenacity, and her enjoyment of business. Her concentration on detail and her memory are legendary. Her energy level floors everyone around her; she is not an orthodox sleeper by night but during the day takes five or six fifteen-minute 'catnaps'. Most mornings she is behind her office desk before nine.

'She's an original,' John told me. 'And she can come on as strong as any man. She's usually ahead of all of us. And at the same time, she's a woman. And when you meet someone like that, you drop everything. It's goodbye to the gang you used to drink with. Or, in my case, the guys in the band. You don't go and play football any more. Once I found *the* woman, the boys became of no interest whatsoever, other than that they were like old schoolfriends: "Hi, how are you, nice to see you. How's your wife?" That old gang of mine was over the moment I met Yoko – that was the end of the boys. It just so happened the boys were well known and weren't just the local guys at the bar. Coming face to face with anyone like her was something I never expected to do.' He was besotted with this woman who often gave him a hard time, rebuked him for his deficiencies and advised him to stop drinking and become a fanatical health enthusiast. Yoko, a non-drinker, eventually banned alcohol in the Dakota.

A few weeks after their reunion, John had good reason to heed her words. Yoko was pregnant. By spring 1975, a happy John was sending postcards to half a dozen of their closest friends: 'Here's a hard one for you to take: not only are John and Yoko back together. They're pregnant.'

Like so many major events surrounding the couple, the pregnancy was not an accident. And there had been problems leading up to it. In 1972, a year before their separation, they had visited San Francisco. There, through a journalist friend, they were introduced to a ninety-five-year-old Chinese herbalist and acupuncturist, Dr Hong. John was worried about his health. For about twelve years, since the Hamburg days and throughout Beatlemania and his early relationship with Yoko, he had abused his body. Pep pills in Hamburg had led to marijuana and L.S.D. in the Beatles years; with Yoko he had tried heroin but, being in favour of living, they had quickly rejected it.

He continued to smoke marijuana occasionally in his early days in New York. By 1972, however, John was found to have a low sperm count. It was thought it might be a result of the punishment he had meted out to his body. Dr Hong, he was advised, might be able to help. The doctor's advice was given to both: John had to renounce all drugs except cigarettes and go easy on alcohol. For Yoko, the doctor prescribed a 'magic potion' which would increase the chance of her fertility. Her age, thirty-nine then, was not a problem, said the doctor. They would eventually have a child, he said, if they lived cleanly and ate healthily. As it turned out John's 'lost weekend' got in the way of the doctor's advice but by the time he returned to Yoko he was in good shape. The Lennon I saw frequently during the last six months of 1974 was sober, lean, fit, and clearly determined to stay that way.

So when Yoko announced her pregnancy John was thrilled but not completely surprised. The child was not merely a hope on the horizon. It had been desperately wanted and planned for – something of which they were both proud. It was, says Yoko, as if their getting back together was blessed.

John made one of the most crucial decisions of his life on learning of Yoko's pregnancy. For twelve years he had been involved in music-making and being a public figure, and a break would be timely. He decided to retire from the business voluntarily. He would concentrate on being a father-to-be and then a Dad. Like a mother hen, he began fussing over Yoko in a way that amazed their friends. They perhaps did not realize that seven years earlier he had camped at Yoko's bedside during a miscarriage. True to his character John became totally immersed in every aspect of Yoko's pregnancy, reading baby books, going to health classes with her, cushioning her from stress, even to the point of being bossy. 'Stay right where you are. Don't move. If there's any rushing around to do, I'm gonna go.' He treated Yoko as if she were ill rather than pregnant. He was worried about her age – forty-two: she was very healthy but she was slight and had already suffered three miscarriages while with John. He was not taking any chances.

Many parents, according to John, conceived their children as 'Saturday night specials.' In America, the phrase he chose was unfortunate: it means handguns that have not sold well during the week and are offered as bargains on Saturdays. What John meant was that most parents conceived their babies 'after a couple of glasses of Scotch, when restraint was cast to the wind'. He was fascinated by the fact that about a hundred million people in America, half the population, were under the age of forty, and were born as a result of the 1945 post-war baby boom. John and Yoko were particularly proud that their child was sought after with love.

One of Yoko's favourite indulgences was chocolate cake. John insisted she stayed in bed every morning while he ordered it from the Silver Palette store for her, together with any other food or drink she fancied. One day Elliot Mintz arrived from Los Angeles. 'Let's go and buy Mother some clothes,' said John. John and Yoko felt strongly that the politics of pregnancy in America were bizarre: the country worshipped perfect bodies, youth and skinniness, and pregnancy seemed to be hidden. 'I think Yoko looks exquisite, beautiful,' John said as Yoko grew larger. He walked along Madison Avenue with Elliot until they saw a shop with beautiful silk and satin lingerie, and expensive dressing-gowns. Inside, he was characteristically generous, buying everything he thought Yoko might like. When it came to pay, John took out his gold American Express card, embossed with the name John Ono Lennon. Then the name of the store on the bill hit him straight between the eyes – it was called Lady Madonna. John burst out laughing.

The irony was that 'Lady Madonna' had been written by Paul. 'Another bloody McCartney song!' said John, laughing. In hotel lifts and restaurants everywhere he had been plagued for ten years by another McCartney gem, 'Yesterday'. In the Palm Court of New York's Plaza Hotel, where John liked to take afternoon tea, the violins would strike up 'Yesterday' in his honour, oblivious of the fact that he would have preferred 'Imagine'. Now 'Lady Madonna' was playing the same trick.

The usual crowd of about 300 gapers pressed against the windows of Lady Madonna. John Lennon shopping for maternity wear was special. As John sprinted away for a taxi, a chauffeur chased him and said: 'Hey, Elton's in a limousine over there. He just came in from London and wants to give you a ride.' John ran across and the two men embraced and went to Elton's hotel, the Pierre, where John told Elton of his 'retirement' plans.

Back at the Dakota Yoko looked appreciatively through the clothes which John had chosen. A woman who favoured simple and stark designs and colours, she was not particularly ena- moured, particularly by the 'I love babies so much I'm having one' T-shirt which so amused John. She was touched though by his romantic shopping spree.

John and Yoko studied natural childbirth: 'It's not just Yoko giving birth to a child,' said John. 'It's both of us.' They attended classes for months and had very few visitors or doctors at the Dakota. The natural childbirth method, whereby the woman gives birth in a dark room and the father is present to see the baby placed immediately after birth against the mother's breast, excited both of them. 'Imagine, Elliot,' he said to Mintz, 'not having the baby touched by rubber gloves on its arrival in the world, but by skin straight away!'

John expected the child to be a boy and he and Yoko went through books of names to check their meanings. When John went shopping for toys, he was incredulous at the amount of junk on sale in various shops. At Macy's department store, he looked at beds and finally decided there would be no cribs, which he described as 'wooden cages for kids'. Their child would sleep between him and Yoko for as long as possible; and he did.

At the peak of Yoko's pregnancy she looked in superb health thanks to John's nursing. He, too, was sharp, aware and enjoying life. Just as Yoko went into hospital, John's long immigration battle was nearing its end. On 8 October 1975 a triumphant Leon Wildes phoned John to explain that he thought his Green Card application would be successful. 'Do me a favour, Leon,' John replied. 'I don't quite get this. I'm not following you. Look, Yoko's at the hospital, she's going to be induced in a couple of hours . . . stay right by your phone and I'll call you as soon as I'm there – you can explain it to Yoko.'

Yoko fully understood. Lying in bed in the New York Hospital private room in which Jacqueline Kennedy Onassis gave birth to Caroline Kennedy, she said on the phone: 'Come over with Ruth [Mrs Wildes] and let's all read the report together.' The four spent the night by Yoko's side. The Wildes left the hospital at midnight. Two hours later, at 2 a.m., on John's thirty-fifth birthday, Yoko gave birth to a baby boy. It was a hazardous delivery. John was at the hospital throughout the period of the birth but when things became tense he was not allowed in. The baby was born by Caesarean section and Yoko, who had to be given a blood transfusion, nearly died.

John was well aware of the danger Yoko was in and the Lennon temper flared when Yoko was just coming round from sedation. John was jittery and wanted to get inside to see her immediately. A doctor walked up to John at a critical moment, saying: 'I love Beatle music. I just want to shake your hand.'

'Fuck off. Save my wife's life,' rasped an angry John. He was fuming with rage.

Nurses, too, had asked for his autograph. He was furious that the doctors and nurses were talking to him instead of attending to Yoko and the baby. It was an anger from which he would never recover. 'They were totally indifferent to Yoko's pain and to Sean – they wanted my *autograph* at a time like that!' Sean proved a healthy, happy baby, but both John and Yoko were sad that he had not been born by the active method, 'flesh touching flesh'.

Back home, John's first phone call was to his Aunt Mimi in her seaside bungalow in Poole, Dorset. 'It's a boy, it's a boy, Mimi,' he said excitedly. 'And we've named him Sean.'

'Oh, John, you've *branded* him,' she said.

'It's Irish for John, Mimi,' John went on, 'but don't worry, Mimi, he'll be raised internationally and he'll be a citizen of the *world*.' At 6 a.m. a jubilant John phoned Leon Wildes. 'It's John. I'm a father!' There was no controlling him, says Wildes. 'He was ecstatic, bouncing around his room as he spoke.' A Polaroid snapshot of the baby was sent, triumphantly, to Dr Hong, who had been such a psychological boost to John and Yoko.

In the months following the birth John allowed very few visitors to the Dakota. He was afraid they might spread germs. Nobody except John or Yoko was allowed to touch Sean. It was the single most important thing in his life. Elliot Mintz, visiting the family a month after the birth was asked to take the first picture of mother, father, and baby. Mintz's first view of Sean, sleeping with Yoko, was shadowed by John 'shushing' him to be quiet and not risk waking up the child. Telegrams of congratulation had poured in from all over the world, many remarking on the fact that Sean was born on John's birthday. 'It figures,' some joked, 'that the two of you would make this another one of your events!' But John took even that seriously: 'The baby decides the time and place and which family to have. Yoko did not give birth to Sean; Sean came through Yoko as a miracle and a gift to us. . . .'

'Well', said Yoko shortly after the birth, with characteristic incisiveness, 'I've carried the baby for nine months and brought him into the world. Now it's your turn to look after him.' John was in full agreement. It was a good time for a total change in emphasis in his life. Yoko went into the office downstairs full-time to manage the family business, while he raised Sean in their seventh-floor apartment. John being John, it turned into a consuming passion of incredible intensity. Both he and Yoko fulfilled their new roles with distinction. Four months after Sean's birth John's recording contract with E.M.I./Capitol expired and he decided not to renew it, the first time in fifteen years that he had not been tied to a recording deal.

During the next five years John became, as he described himself, a house-husband. His attention to Sean was total. The baby was fed, washed, bathed, dressed and taught to read by him. He hated changing his nappies but he did it all the same. No babysitters were needed. When Sean was about six months old John saw a pimple on him. Agitated, he went right round twenty office and domestic staff forbidding them to give Sean sugar of any kind in his diet: 'Sean may not have come out of my belly but I'm gonna make his bones.'

During the years of seclusion, Elliot Mintz visited John and Yoko dozens of times. 'We shared the special moments,' he recalls; 'Thanksgivings, Christmas Eves, Christmas Days, New Year's Eves, Sean's birthdays. They were the most glorious of times.

'I have never seen two people so much in love. They lived their lives with such conscious awareness. John would frequently walk over to Yoko, who might be sitting on the edge of the bed with Sean. He would hold her small hand in his and look deeply into her eyes and smile then whisper "Hello" very softly, as if he was making direct contact with her very essence. They would embrace and I would disappear. I remember reading that Brian Epstein once said he was happiest when the four Beatles and he were in a room together without anyone else, before a concert. For me, during those five years, John and Yoko and little Sean together as a family in the Dakota embodied everything that was special between lovers.'

Sean's full name is Sean Taro Ono Lennon. Says Yoko: 'John insisted that he should have one Japanese name. Taro is like Sean or John in Japanese, that kind of name. John loved it.

'In Japanese law a child belongs to the father's family. As a result of that mothers who have babies by accident sometimes have a terrible time . . . if they don't know who the father is and the mother cannot claim the child as hers. John and I wanted Sean to be as international as possible.' As well as having British and

A Japanese-style family, pictured in the Dakota apartment when
Sean was just one month old. This was the beginning of John's time
as a househusband and doting father

Japanese names and being born in New York, Sean Taro Ono Lennon has dual American and British nationality and his birth was registered in both New York and London.

There are already signs that Sean will emerge as formidable, strong-minded, and witty as his father. At the age of eight, he told me he was 'a real computer whizz'. At school, where the ever-present bodyguard accompanies him, standing within sight of him all day and every day, Sean says he is 'better at languages than adding up, but most of all I'm a real expert at using my free time'. He had a typical eight-year-old's contempt for the girls in his class, who outnumbered the boys: 'They're just not so nice as us so we beat them at dodge ball.' Although he agreed he was rather young to be considering his future, Sean said: 'I have been thinking about what to do but I haven't yet answered myself. I might be a singer or a crazy scientist or a geologist or an archaeologist.' As for his father's music: 'Sometimes it's good, sometimes not so good.' John would grudgingly have agreed with that one.

Elton John, whose concert was so instrumental in re-uniting John and Yoko, is Sean's godfather.

John scarcely needed the news of his father's death in April 1976 to persuade him to pour even more zeal into raising Sean. His own lack of parental stability as a child had nagged away at him over the years and he was determined that Sean would have a father he knew and grew up alongside. Although he could not claim to be a struggling 'mother figure', with the everyday physical pressures of millions of parents (he had a domestic staff to cushion him), John supervised everything that went into the boy's early years: food, drink, toys, books, sleep. After a year he helped Sean to toddle and walk. Television was banned. 'He's not gonna see people shooting each other,' said John. He even wheeled him in a pram around Central Park.

John was so immersed in baby-rearing that when Paul McCartney arrived, unscheduled, with a guitar at the Dakota one day and had the doorman announce him, John did not believe it could be him. Hoax phone calls were a regular problem. Paul had to be put on the phone by the doorman in the Dakota reception area to convince John that it was really him. When he went upstairs John gave him a frosty reception. 'Do you mind calling before you come round next time? This is not Liverpool, y'know. In New York, you don't just drop in on people like this without warning.' He went on to explain that he was tired from a hard day's work with Sean. Paul left in a huff. John's opinion of Paul's work at this time was very low. He described him to friends as 'like Engelbert Humperdinck'. Although he accepted that Paul was a competent songwriter, John was contemptuous of the fact that his old partner apparently wanted merely to continue as before; he referred to Mick Jagger and Paul jointly – and contemptuously – as the 'Rolling Wings'. There was more to life, implied John, than rock 'n' rolling into your forties. 'I've diarrhoead on rock 'n' roll,' he said.

As he walked around New York's Central Park during his 'house-husband' years, one of the friendly faces John occasionally encountered was that of Sid Bernstein. The man who had promoted the Beatles' American tours from their first shows in 1964 had tried several times to re-unite them for massive charity concerts. Each time there had been no official response; John said he 'didn't go for all that Al Jolson, down-on-one-knee' pleading that became Bernstein's style in expensive appeals to the Beatles in the *New York Times*. But when John saw Bernstein walking around the park or on the Upper East Side, they embraced and did not mention the Beatles. 'It was always casual talk about my family and Sean, who was sometimes with him,' says Bernstein. 'I knew not to mention the Beatles. He only ever mentioned the past to me once, describing Shea Stadium as the top of the mountain.' John's forgetfulness made an impression on Bernstein: 'I saw him several times with Yoko and he introduced me to her every time as if we'd never met. Finally Yoko had to say to him: "John, I *know* Sid now." '

Their paths crossed twice. In 1974, John phoned Bernstein and asked him for the name of a really fine Italian restaurant in New York. After he had a good dinner at Palucci's, behaving perfectly with Harry Nilsson throughout the night, John sent a huge spray of flowers to Bernstein with a note of thanks for a good recommendation. And in 1975, John phoned to ask for tickets for a concert Bernstein was promoting at Carnegie Hall. The performer was Jimmy Cliff, a star of reggae, a music style which particularly captured John's affection in the cosmopolitan atmosphere of New York. Sid Bernstein had no tickets left, but his daughters gave up theirs when they heard John Lennon wanted to go.

Bernstein later presented the New York production of a play called *Lennon*, first shown at Liverpool's Everyman Theatre in 1981. It was artistically mediocre, concentrating heavily on John's 'tough guy' image and failing to capture his multi-faceted personality and sensitivity. Nevertheless, the play was notable for establishing the huge range in ages of John's appeal: children and teenagers who were not born when John formed the Beatles attended alongside their parents whose memories of Lennon were powerful. When shots rang out at the end of the play to simulate the murder, the audience sobbed. In New York, the play failed and came off at the Entermedia Theatre, off Broadway, after only nine weeks.

While John was busy nursing Sean, Yoko revelled in her role as businesswoman. By the evening, after a long programme of meetings in her office, she would say: 'It's been a hard day. I'm tired.'

John's house-husband wit was quick: 'Well, what do you think *I've* been doing? Bringing up a baby is work, as well! Don't give me that "hard day at the office, dear" bit.'

He pointed out that he had even begun reading cookery books to improve *his* performance.

Yoko set about demonstrating her business acumen with typical determination. 'It was a two-year plan,' she says, 'which quickly ran to five years when John told me how much money he wanted and I realized I couldn't achieve *that* amount within two years.'

Hitherto Yoko had been totally unmaterialistic. 'I survived throughout my earlier years,' she says, 'by not accumulating money, partly because my mother enjoyed luxury and was always showing me diamonds. Part of me rebelled against that and despised it. I felt I never wanted to lead a life like that, thinking so much about gold and diamonds and beautiful clothes.

'So until 1975 I was the opposite of a money person. But when John and I decided that I would be a businesswoman, I told myself that in order to attract money and do the new job well I'd have to reconstruct my psyche. My old attitude of not wanting to get into money just wasn't going to do.

'I meditated on it. I visualized all the materially good things in the world – diamonds, silk, velvets, art – and tried to see those things in my mind with love, which I never did before. I just opened my mind to all those things instead of rejecting them. And John immediately bought me this diamond, heart-shaped necklace, almost as a signal that I was changing. The usual me would have said, out of snobbery: "Oh, what do I want that for?" But instead I looked at its beauty and thanked him. I tried to see the beauty in the good properties we have. And we said: "If we are going to have it, we have to *act* as if we have it already, not as if we are just starting with money."

'So I went and bought great clothes most weeks and John would really enjoy seeing what I'd bought. It wasn't a question of getting these things in order to *own* them, more like reversing all my attitudes towards possessions. I really trained my mind to enjoy the things that were positive about money.'

With no head for statistics and without making any mathematical calculations Yoko began presiding over the Lenono business with a clear mind and intuitive powers that devastated all those who dealt with her. John and Yoko's first decision was that their cash would be invested in things that were ecologically inoffensive: 'We wanted nothing to do with energy or oil or big chemical corporations or any of the other things we could have invested in,' says Yoko. 'We wanted things that were peaceful to control and caused us, and the world, no problem.'

Yoko's first business venture was the gradual acquisition of five apartments in their beloved Dakota building on West 72nd Street. The setting for the film *Rosemary's Baby*, the intimidating Dakota was not easy to gain access to: major stars before John and Yoko had been refused permission by the committee which decides who may be granted residence there. John and Yoko had to attend a screening meeting to establish that they would be peaceful, respectable residents, particularly when Yoko set about buying each apartment that fell vacant. They so loved its decorous atmosphere that there was never any danger they would abuse it. John sat watching the sun set across Central Park. The all-white room (including the furniture and the white piano on which John wrote 'Imagine' which now has Yoko's photographs of her family on it) was their *pièce de résistance*. The piano, John's gift to Yoko on her birthday in 1971, when they were living in Ascot, bears his inscription, 'This morning, a white piano for Yoko.' It remains in position. Asked why she needed all the apartments Yoko replied quixotically: 'It's just that John and I always wanted to live in a house.'

After the Dakota had been established as a major investment, Yoko turned to agriculture. Four farms were purchased, in the Catskill mountains, Virginia, Vermont, and upstate New York. Covering some 1,600 acres, the farms were reckoned to be worth nearly $1 million. Yoko's particular talent was her timing: her notoriety as a businesswoman went up several notches when one of her investments, a prize Holstein cow, one of 250 head of cattle they owned, fetched $265,000 – a world record – at the New York State Fair at Syracuse. The exceptional Lenono cow was expected to produce over 6,000 gallons of milk a year. 'Only Yoko Ono,' said an amused John, reading about the sale in a newspaper while holidaying alone in Bermuda, 'could sell a cow for a quarter of a million dollars!'

John and Yoko outside the prestigious,
Gothic-style Dakota apartment block

A vital advantage of owning the farms was that their produce –
eggs, milk, and vegetables, all produced without chemicals – was
shipped down to New York at least once a week, ensuring that
John, Yoko, and Sean had a healthy diet, which was as free of
additives as possible.

Yoko's astute purchase of properties and the hiring of staff to
run them became another time-consuming but profitable opera-
tion. For $450,000 the Lennons acquired a stunning weekend
retreat, a house at Cold Spring Harbor, Long Island, overlooking
the Atlantic. Yoko, particularly, loved this home, which was close
to Manhattan but also in the fresh air of the countryside –
important for Sean. They also bought a 63-foot ocean-going yacht
called *Isis* and a sloop which John named *Strawberry Fields*.

Then there was West Palm Beach, Florida, where $700,000
bought the Lennons a beachfront mansion, El Salano, built in
1919 and once owned by the Vanderbilt family. With seven
bedrooms, five servants' rooms, indoor and outdoor pools and its
own fifty yards of sand by the ocean, the house proved the most
expensive of all their properties: most of the year it stood empty,
except for a small staff; John and Yoko managed only one
month's visit a year. Art, a big collection of carpets, and Eastern
artefacts were other assets.

Naturally their critics had an easy target. Here was the man who
had sung 'Imagine no possessions' accumulating more, at the
behest of his shrewd wife, than he would ever need. But a changed
John had decided, as always, that if he was going to retire and be a
non-musician for a few years and father Sean, then with the
Beatles, Apple, and Allen Klein out of his system, he would have
no better manager than Yoko. And, following the dictum of his
life, 'Don't do things by halves', Yoko quickly enhanced their
fortune. By the late seventies, John's estate was conservatively
valued at $150 million with millions more coming in every year in
royalties from record sales and songwriting.

Yoko talked to me about how she reconciled her business and
her art. 'I think that most artists have this complex: they think
they should suffer and struggle and always be miserable or else
they can't be creative. John and I had that for a while. We were
very aware of that side of being artists. But we tried to reverse the
trap that artists fall into – because we didn't want to be miserable
when we obviously had money and possessions. After all, being
miserable is a pretty high price to pay for being an artist!' As to her
business methods: 'Money, and making it, is fundamentally a state
of mind. I often used to wonder why some people were rich and

naturally talented at multiplying their money and others not. It sometimes comes down to attitude. A great many very intelligent people have no money and as a Greenwich Village artist wanting only recognition, I used to be one of them. But then I also had an inverted snobbery towards money. I thought it was silly to go looking for it. I've changed.' In business deals, however, men were chauvinistically distrustful of her judgement – 'or, rather, they became upset by the fact that my judgement was right and it came from a woman. There *have* been some struggles with men in business because I am a woman.' Conversely, she had also benefited: 'Sometimes the men underestimate a woman so much that they reveal their tactics too soon. Then they find out how resilient I am.'

For John, walking away from music for a few years was much harder than carrying on: 'I know because I've done both. It was very hard because shouldn't I be going, like "to the office" or "producing something"? I don't exist if my name isn't in the charts or I'm not seen at the right club. It's like the guys aged sixty-five who've said: "Your life's over. Time for God." It's self-imposed, yes, but still the feeling was there, this whole big space that seems to be unfillable. And of course, it's naturally got to be filled because that's the law of the universe. . . . And it was filled by a fulfilling experience, to put it in a little cute phrase.'

John and Yoko did not venture out much in 1976. John's commitment to rearing Sean, supervising his every moment, was total. He explained: 'People asked me: "What are you doing now?"

'And I'd say: "Looking after the baby and baking the bread."
And they'd say: "Ha ha. No, no, what else do you do?"
And I'd say: "Are you *kidding*? It's a full-time job, as every housewife knows." There were no secret projects in the basement.'

Making music was low on his agenda but a passion for discovery was high. John's determination that Sean should be healthy was stimulated by his own splendid health. As part of a self-imposed diet he and Yoko had a forty-day fast when they drank only fruit and vegetable juice. When they came off the diet they were convinced of the importance of health foods and vitamins.

Baking bread was a passion that lasted for a few months and while he enthused about it, everybody had to know. 'Elliot,' he told Mintz by phone one afternoon, 'an extraordinary thing has happened. I've just baked my first loaf of bread. I saw it rise in the oven, I did it from start to finish.' John took a Polaroid photo of the loaf and sent it by air courier to his bemused pal 3,000 miles away. John was overjoyed and proud of his achievement. 'I feel I've conquered something,' he said to Yoko and he didn't mean merely by baking bread. The thrill wore off somewhat when the entire staff of the Dakota enjoyed his bread so much that 'drivers, and office boys, and accountants, and everyone came for one and I'd make loaves on Friday that'd be gone by Saturday afternoon.' He decided: 'Screw this for a lark. It was becoming routine. And I don't get a gold record or a knighthood . . . nothing!'

John's cooking was enthusiastic but limited. He would chop up a huge amount of vegetables, put them, occasionally with fish, into a big crockpot, which simmered for days on the cooker. Permanently beside it, loving the warmth, were the three cats, Michu, Sasha and Charo. The longer the crockpot simmered, he reasoned – quite fallaciously – the better the food would taste. That, with perfectly cooked rice, and sometimes boiled eggs – rather watery and rarely cooked properly – was his culinary height, together with the bread.

He insisted that people followed the eating method of a macrobiotic guru which he had adopted: the practice of constant chewing. Drinking anything with meals was disallowed in the Dakota, as was alcohol. Every bite had to be chewed twenty times because John had been told that if he ate and washed it down with any liquid, he would be taking away the work of the digestive enzymes, particularly ptyalin, the enzyme in saliva that begins the digestion of food. Anybody eating a Lennon crockpot combination was ordered to chew until the ptyalin naturally dissolved it. Elliot Mintz recalls a visit by John and Yoko to Manhattan's East-West macrobiotic restaurant in which about 100 people sat facing each other, chewing, with no conversation. Mintz began: 'Well, it's great to see you two, how's it been going?' John rebuked him, placing fingers across his mouth to indicate that there should be no talking.

When Sean was two John decided to try to learn Japanese. For two hours a day, three days a week, he went to a language school in Manhattan. The technique was similar to that employed in many language classes: the complete immersion method with no English spoken. John also bought a series of cassettes. Much to Yoko's chagrin he would attempt to practise on her. But his combination of Liverpudlian and American made it hard for him: after two months of battling to absorb the intonation he could manage only about forty words. He gave up after a brave try, much to Yoko's relief.

The more successful his wife became 'downstairs', the more he trusted her vision. Yoko's business moves were supported by advice from a retinue of astrologers, numerologists, and tarot card readers. Every member of the Lenono staff, and most people who came into close proximity to them, was 'checked out' through their astrological sign in infinite detail. Thus Yoko arrived at the conclusion that there were good days for business and also days when she should sign nothing and just listen, days on which neither of them should travel, and days on which it would be bad to be in contact with someone who had the wrong 'sign rising'. Yoko had always been heavily into 'vibrations', good and bad. Her application of her hunches into a science began to shape their movements and those of their closest friends: 'If Yoko said it would be advisable for John or for me to fly 6,000 miles in an easterly direction and stay at that point for exactly four and a half days,' says Elliot Mintz, 'John would say: "Go with it. Trust her. She's always right." '

In June 1977 John, Yoko, and Sean went to Japan for an extended visit of several months. They had been there for nearly eight weeks when a phone call from Elliot Mintz in Los Angeles broke the news: Elvis Presley was dead. There was a pause on the line before John said of his teenage idol: 'Elvis died in the army.' Another pause. 'How? What happened?' The information was sketchy; Mintz had just heard the news on the radio. The impact on John was minimal, his reaction almost callous. He reserved his emotion for the living. Between pauses, John said to Mintz: 'Well, the difference between the Beatles and Elvis was that with Elvis the king died and the manager lived and with the Beatles the manager died and we lived. I never wanted to be a forty-year-old who virtually died singing his golden hits in a jump-suit in Las Vegas. Oh, please send two white gardenias to Elvis's grave, saying: "Rest In Peace, Love John and Yoko." '

Next day Mintz flew out to join the Lennons for a long Japanese holiday. Mintz, clearly affected by the death of a rock legend, was chastized by John. 'Don't talk to me about Elvis. He's dead. Don't try to sell me on the dreams and myths of these people. Elvis is dead. It's all over. It's unhealthy to live *through* anybody.'

Mintz flew to Tokyo and then took a train 200 miles north to the small town of Karuizawa. The Lennon he found there was a dramatically refreshed man. In two years, he had renounced rock 'n' roll for fatherhood and house-husbandry. It was now time to concentrate on the restoration of his own mind and body. For five months John enjoyed the cleanest, wisest, physically fittest period in his life, with no alcohol, no drugs, exercises of every kind from cycling and swimming to yoga every day, and none of the foods he had leaned on so much in New York: chocolate, honey, English muffins. He cut down drastically on his beloved French cigarettes. He had a constant diet of *sushi* and rice and joked that, 'Yoko likes to feed me dead fish.'

'In Karuizawa, we all did a lot of cycling and stayed at a very old, beautiful hotel, the Mampei,' says Mintz. 'Yoko's family has a home in this town; there were no Westerners or tourists and we did not have a car. John enjoyed having Sean sit on a seat across his crossbar in front of him.'

The Japanese experience proved idyllic for John. In their constant search for strong, black coffee, which both John and Yoko loved, they would drag Mintz on five-mile mountain road expeditions, Yoko's long hair flying behind her in the wind as she led the other two, John in T-shirt and shorts, with hair almost shoulder length, keeping up with her, and Mintz trailing 'and fully expecting a cardiac arrest' behind them. The coffee café, Mintz avers, was worth it. Yoko also took them to exclusive and exotic restaurants. Often the fish for their dinner would be pulled from a stream next to the restaurant. Their search for authenticity was not always felicitous. John was a little squeamish when he was asked to drink 'the best turtle soup in Japan' from the shell of the turtle he had seen alive only a few minutes earlier.

The fifteen-course traditional Japanese dinners, during which the three of them hardly spoke, were often preceded by the mineral baths which left John's skin glowing, his hair with a brilliant sheen, and Yoko's longer hair at its best. On one occasion when the two men were taken to a bathing area and Yoko went off to a women's area, two hostesses began to undress John and Elliot. John reacted incredulously: 'What's going on? Where's Mother?' As fast as the waitresses unbuttoned his shirt buttons, he would do them up again; finally, when he entered the water, he started swimming strongly.

'It's not for swimming,' Yoko rebuked him from the other side of the partition which separated men from women. 'It's for bathing, to refresh yourself before dinner.' But John was always a powerful, enthusiastic swimmer, and enjoyed teaching Sean.

In Karuizawa, John told Elliot how wonderful it was not to be

A postcard sent to Julian from Japan

John, Yoko and their friend
Elliot Mintz during their
five-month holiday in Japan
in the summer of 1977.
Right: Outside the *sushi* bar
in Karuizawa where they
usually had lunch. *Below:*
In a restaurant in the
ancient town of Kyoto.
Opposite above: After a
long walk to the top of a
mountain John points
dramatically to the mist (the
city below was invisible).
Opposite below: In the
public gardens near their
hotel, the Mampei in
Karuizawa. 'John was at the
healthiest point in his life
during that period,' recalls
Mintz

recognized, not to have to be on guard or be attentive to strangers. A few Japanese smiled at him in recognition but he felt no pressure. At Yoko's mother's house, often wearing a suit and his old Quarry Bank school tie, he enjoyed many afternoons sitting on the porch, something similar to an old southern plantation verandah, drinking coffee, eating cakes and cycling back to the hotel later, singing songs and whistling.

In the ancient capital town of Kyoto John became immersed in the Buddhist temples. 'When we went into these and stood before the statues of Buddha, there were small areas where we wrote our prayers down,' says Mintz. 'John was genuinely into it. He clasped his hands, closed his eyes, bowed his head and prayed. . . . Yoko took us to a monastery in Kyoto where there was a religious order of very elderly women. It was irrelevant that John couldn't understand a word of the conversation. He was deeply moved. The religiosity of Japan definitely made an impression on him.'

En route home the family moved to the Okura Hotel in Tokyo, where they occupied the gigantic presidential suite. Here the throb of city life made John eager to get back to New York. 'He got out his acoustic guitar in the living-room of the suite and sang some old songs,' says Mintz. 'And he said he was getting a bit homesick.' The suite was so large that John even played football with Sean in it.

It was here that John quixotically played his last 'public' performance, which happened quite by accident. The gigantic hotel suite had lifts that arrived straight into the Lennon lounge. John was sitting quietly playing 'Jealous Guy' to himself and Elliot Mintz one evening when the lift doors opened and a Japanese couple – who had evidently arrived on the wrong floor – walked out to find a singer-guitarist whom they did not recognize. All the same they sat and listened as John continued the song. 'John was in a wonderful mood, playing gently and beautifully . . .' recalls Mintz. 'The people simply applauded and went back down the elevator.' They were the last two strangers who ever watched and listened as John performed.

When the time came to finish the Japanese holiday Yoko consulted her numerology. She decided that the 'signs' were all wrong for the two men to fly direct from Tokyo to New York. She would return straight home to the U.S. while John, Sean, and Elliot were to fly Tokyo–Hong Kong–Dubai–Frankfurt–New York. Their twenty-six-hour flight would mean changing planes at Dubai and Frankfurt. It sounded arduous but John believed implicitly in Yoko's prescience and totally trusted her ability to 'read the cards' which charted their movements.

On the long night flight from Dubai to Germany John became homesick, recalling the Beatles' early days in a conversation which Elliot Mintz will always remember as Lennon at his frankest. In the Lufthansa 747 jet Sean played with his car race track in the upper level of the plane with a nanny, while Mintz sat with Lennon with the seats on either side of them, as usual, empty. When flying he and Yoko always bought two seats on either side and in front of them to leave free. That way, John said, 'I make sure I don't sit next to somebody asking me when the Beatles will get back together again.'

Mintz had by that time known Lennon for six years but he had never seen him so sentimental, pensive, reflective, and talkative. Even his old Liverpool accent had partly returned. It was the side of John Lennon that the public had never seen. He spoke of his childhood, his sexual fantasies, how he felt when the Beatles first came to America and the feeling he had when the plane first touched down on the soil of the country that had first inspired his music. He talked of his relationship with his mother and the tears welled up as he recalled her premature death; he was in the reminiscent and confessional mood which often overcomes long-distance fliers; he repeatedly spoke of his love of Yoko, and his chattiness reassured Mintz who was a nervous flier. John was particularly proud of the fact that he had his luggage down to a fine art: a large briefcase with one change of clothing and pyjamas.

The overnight stop in Frankfurt was John's one visit to Europe in nine years. It was marked by a bizarre encounter with a hotel receptionist, aghast at unexpectedly checking in a former Beatle. Rooms were not readily available, so John introduced Mintz as Paul McCartney. Rooms were suddenly found. 'I guess,' Mintz said to an unamused John, 'the clerk liked the fact that I wrote "Yesterday".'

Next day, John, Sean, and Elliot continued their journey to New York. At Kennedy Airport John got a special thrill from the passport controller's greeting. As John handed him his British passport and remembered the four-year immigration battle he had endured, the immigration man said to him: 'Welcome home, Mr Lennon.' John turned and smiled to Elliot then caught sight of Yoko, standing alone to welcome him with an embrace. Back at the Dakota a revitalized John Lennon rediscovered with pleasure the forty hours of *Goon Show* tapes which Yoko had given him as a birthday gift.

John made other foreign trips. He went alone to Cape Town for a few days, staying at the Mount Nelson Hotel. He went to Hong Kong and Singapore and enjoyed walking incognito among the local population. His wit never deserted him. To Bob Gruen, his New York photographer friend, he sent a card from Hong Kong saying simply: 'Far East, man!' accompanied by the little doodle which told any recipient of a card that it was a genuine Lennon message. John and Yoko flew to spend one night in Cairo at the pyramids, where Yoko developed a fascination for Egyptian artefacts and bought the mummy that lies in her white room at the Dakota. John's solo journeys were a real education for a man who had been cushioned by company since his first travels out of Liverpool to Hamburg in 1960. Even dialling room service in an hotel was an adventure for him. Most of the time, he enjoyed simply sitting watching foreign television in blissful isolation in his room.

Few people recognized him on his foreign trips and in Hong Kong he enjoyed walking around the harbour among the local workers, 'just watching'. He had not enjoyed such freedom since his days in Hamburg before the lunacy of Beatlemania. The only occasions on which John was forced to admit his identity were when he handed his gold American Express card to the hotel desks. From each city he telephoned Yoko in the Dakota and Aunt Mimi in Dorset to give his hotel number, and to enthuse about the hum of a city, a skyline, a sunset, or even to crow over the fact that he was walking around shops and hotel lobbies without being hunted.

John was fortunate that he was not hounded, for in view of his name and his fame, he was astonishingly vulnerable. All public figures risk harassment by the public as soon as they step outside their front doors; for a lapsed Beatle and solo star of stature, who had a reputation as a recluse, to be travelling alone to the far-flung corners of the world, totally alone, was a brave adventure. In the case of John Lennon, it had an extra hazard: one of his most surprising flaws was an inability to detect hangers-on, phoneys, parasites or even dangerous people who sought his company, his approval, his warmth or his encouragement. There were two sides to his attitudes towards people and handling of them: the tough, abrasive, no-nonsense, street-wise Liverpudlian who believed everyone should battle their own way through life, as he had; and then there was John the sucker, the 'easy tap' for most causes that reached his ears, particularly if they were tinged with radicalism and sounded sincere. An incurable sentimentalist and

John and Yoko in New York, 1980

fundamentally kind, John leaned this way, preferring to give any dubious characters the benefit of the doubt. It made him a poor judge of people who walked up to him. He did *not* possess a sound sixth sense of those who were around him to exploit him, because he tended to take people on face value. This became dangerous as he chose to confront his stardom and fly around the world alone, or walk the streets of New York and give his autograph to anybody who appeared, to him, to be innocuous. It was a trait that enabled him to break free of the strictures of stardom. It might also have cost him his life.

Nearly twelve years after their first meeting John and Yoko had achieved a serenity in their partnership that anyone might envy. 'We would argue, of course,' says Yoko. 'We were two very temperamental, very emotional, people. Friends and lovers, musicians and artists, man and woman, husband and wife.' Even when they fought, John had a unique method of breaking the deadlock. He would write a song or poem and either play the song to Yoko or strategically place the written poem where she would see it privately. 'That was part of our communication,' she says. 'We were both shy, we didn't go out often, certainly not to parties or anything like that. So we were literally together for fourteen years with very few breaks. John and I stood for peace and love but standing for peace doesn't make either of us holier than thou. John and I together were human beings, and by no means were both of us totally peaceful. Anger, hurt, vulnerability, were all a part of John. When we met, we were like two *driven* people and it was like a fantastic meeting of two crazy souls. John was more hurt than me by the public reaction to my early work. I was the "laugh". People said: "Oh, we can't listen to *her*." And John would be choked by that. But it's like John would say, everything takes its time and in a favourite phrase of his, *it will all work out in the end*.

'What people *did* take a long time realizing was that John might not have been a great, technically proficient guitarist, but listen now to "Why" on the *Plastic Ono Band* album and his playing is fantastic, far-out. Our fusion, with my singing and his playing, was something he realized was special much later. He said he could not have played like that with anybody, it was more than a duet of artists, but a coming together of the two of us.'

Yoko likens their partnership with that of Robert Browning and Elizabeth Barrett-Browning. John thought of them more like Scott and Zelda Fitzgerald. Whichever analogy one uses, their marriage and mutual love was a quite triumphant and justly celebrated

'Farmer J. wrestling with an agricultural problem' – a postcard sent to Julian from New York. The picture had originally been included with John's *Imagine* L P, as Lennon's jibe at McCartney's *Ram* album cover

public romance. It survived many hurdles: the ridicule of the public; the taunts of John's old 'friends', in and out of the Beatles' circle, and those of millions of Beatle fans in the early days; and a lengthy separation. As Yoko comments, 'We found that the love thing was bigger than both of us.'

During the first two years of his seclusion John was so immersed in being a father and taking an interest in Yoko's business transactions that the outside world virtually passed him by. He hardly ever went out shopping after that trip for Yoko's maternity wear. He rarely answered the flashing light of the telephone. He left the staff to order the food and on the occasions when he did phone a shop, he became irritated by shop assistants' refusal to believe that he really was John Lennon.

By the time of his Japanese visit, however, John had changed. Galvanized by Yoko's exceptional success in buying property, farms, and *objets d'art* John began an excursion into acquisition. Like all his other enthusiasms, he went all the way while it lasted; this particular passion had its roots in planning Sean's life.

John decided to shower Sean with toys, games and books, practising a 'reverse materialism' on him. Lennon's theory was that he, and millions like him, were raised in the belief that he would grow up and be able to afford the first car, the first house, the first good suit, and the first guitar . . . and it was always 'tomorrow'. He wanted to try to wipe out that aspiration early in Sean's life: 'I don't want him hooked on being a consumer throughout his teenage years.' So Sean was given anything he fancied. A walk around the famous New York toy store, F.A.O. Schwarz, would cost John thousands of dollars. He spent vast sums on robot games at a store called Forbidden Planet in Greenwich Village; John also dabbled in computer games and bought Sean the most progressive ones. 'I'm giving him all the crap while he's young so that by the time he's ten, this kind of stuff won't mean anything to him. He'll have had his fix.'

It was a theory that only a rich man could apply. But it worked. By the time he was eight, Sean Lennon's proudest possession was a valueless collection of rocks. He has developed a great interest in the formation of stones, stalactites, minerals, and anything geological. His great hobby, besides computers, is hunting by the seashore for rare seashells. No expensive toys or brilliant pieces of engineering impress him: beautiful electric train sets and gadgets by the crateload lay, forgotten, in a warehouse when I visited him in 1983.

When it came to spending and collecting for himself, however,

John had immatured with age. In Japan a typical spending spree in Tokyo's 'electronic village' would find John walking down the aisles pointing out and ordering literally dozens of sophisticated amplifiers, turntables and speakers, which were shipped back to the Dakota and set up in each room. 'You know how Mother feels about wires,' he said to Elliot Mintz, who had accompanied him on the expedition, 'well, with this little lot, there'll be no need for any wires to trail around the house.'

Airline mail order catalogues fascinated him. He loved to be surprised by items he ordered on a plane, simply by filling in his American Express number; these arrived at the Dakota weeks or months afterwards, long after he had forgotten about them. A 'stereo pillow', a pillow with built-in speakers, amused him; there was a portable desk with foam-rubber backing; breakfast trays on which he would take Yoko her favourite extra strong, black coffee; and he developed a fetish for collecting attaché-cases. He had dozens in leather and other materials in all shapes and sizes, and carefully fixed the combination lock of each to include the figure nine which marked important events in his life. He was similarly attracted to manicure sets and collected dozens. If he walked into a store and found a pair of jeans that fitted him properly, he would ask for ten pairs in different colours to be sent to his home.

If that was the 'little child inside the man', there was plenty of seriousness in John to balance it out. An avid reader all his life, he spent the years of seclusion establishing a superb library of leatherbound, antiquarian books. He studied the history of the early slaves who were sent from Africa to his native Liverpool and were used, he said, to build the huge houses in the port alongside which he had grown up. He loved philosophy books, and sent Elliot Mintz *The Lazy Man's Guide to Enlightenment*.

When John and Yoko went out it was as if to re-live their early, simpler lives as student and artist. Away from the grandeur of the Dakota, light years away from rock 'n' roll, totally removed from Eastern influence, their choice was usually a small yet elegant coffee shop run by an Italian husband and wife. It was decidedly European in its atmosphere and sold only pastries and superb coffee and chocolate. For John and Yoko, for four years from the day it opened in 1976, Café La Fortuna at 69 West 71st Street, one block from their home, was a refuge.

Vincent Urwand, the owner, developed a bond with them. Only once did he have to chase away a gaggle of fans who gathered with cameras to disturb their peace. About four afternoons a week John

John and Yoko were great coffee enthusiasts. Here they are in La Fortuna,
a café round the corner from the Dakota

would wander in, with or without Yoko, and sit down for his *cappuccino* and Gitanes and a read of any newspaper that had been lying around his home. In summer they sat in the garden at the back of the café.

When Sean was a toddler, John would bring him in with a rope around him. 'You got him like a dog, strapped up round his chest!' said Vincent.

'I've gotta have him tied up or else he runs wild. I can't keep up with him when he runs off,' explained John. Special ice-cream, without sugar and containing honey, was made for Sean at John's request.

John often struck up conversations with other people in La Fortuna. One, a German religious fanatic, tried unsuccessfully to stir John up about his ambivalent attitude to organized religion. For the most part, though, it was a haven, a grass roots contact with an unpretentious café. Vincent Urwand comments, 'John told me how they used to go round second-hand shops in this neighbourhood and buy old-fashioned hats and dresses. One day John phoned me and said that he and Yoko would provide me with the picture of themselves I'd asked for, for the wall. And when it came it was John wearing a derby hat with a paper moustache, Sean with the American flag draped around him, and Yoko in a big hat and an old-fashioned dress that you'd never see her in. They loved surprising people.'

Despite banning sugar for Sean, John's craving for chocolate remained undimmed: Vincent often sold him bars of imported dark, bittersweet Italian-made Luisa chocolate: with American Hershey bars they were his favourite. Years earlier John's sweet tooth had got the better of him in a phone conversation from New York to me in London: he asked me to bring him some of his childhood favourites, chocolate-covered Bath Oliver biscuits. He often asked British visitors to bring him foods which were unobtainable in New York. When he phoned his son Julian in North Wales in 1977, he also spoke to his former art college friend Helen Anderson. When she asked him if there was anything he was missing in England, he replied: 'Yes, I could do with a string of black puddings.' Helen realized that the man she remembered from nearly twenty years ago had fundamentally changed very little . . . particularly when he went on to ask her if she still had a Liverpool Art College scarf she could send him.

'When are you coming back here?' asked Helen.

'Oh, one of these days before long,' said John.

At the café, the Urwands had little interest in modern popular music. Coincidentally John was opening out in his music tastes at the time and Vincent successfully introduced him to his own favourites, jazz and the popular music of the veteran performers. 'I gave John some 78 r.p.m. records and he asked me to make up a tape for him. Next time he came in, he said how much he'd enjoyed it.' The music consisted of songs by Al Jolson, Benny Goodman, Mae West, Duke Ellington, and the jazz of Fats Waller and Louis Armstrong. 'I had a long discussion with John on opera and classical music but as it turned out he developed a real liking for stuff which I played and he really thought they were special: Bing Crosby, the jazz violinist Stephane Grappelli, and Gracie Fields singing "Now Is The Hour". John told me he loved her singing.' The visits, each week for four years when he was in New York, made John 'one of the family' inside that little café. Yoko even took her mother there, when she visited from Japan, to demonstrate a little how she and John lived.

John ignored rock music completely during the mid-seventies. It was as if the consolidation of his love for Yoko and the birth of Sean had brought out the true romantic in him. Although he hated overt, gushing, lovey-dovey sentimentality, John was a 'pushover' when it came to romantic music. John and Yoko's favourite song and movie at this time was Barbra Streisand's 'The Way We Were'. It was some distance from 'A Hard Day's Night' and Chuck Berry.

Yoko's gift to John for his thirty-eighth birthday was a very special antique; a 'bubble-top' Wurlitzer jukebox of the style popular in American soda fountain shops in the 1950s. It took only 78 r.p.m. records and its arrival coincided with John's increasing interest in nostalgic music. The first batch of records ordered for the Wurlitzer were mostly 1950s hits by Bobby Darin like 'Dream Lover', Frankie Laine, Johnnie Ray's 'Little White Cloud That Cried', and as many Bing Crosby records as he could get. Here was real irony: Bing Crosby's 'Please', which John had heard just as the Beatles were getting started eighteen years earlier in Liverpool, had inspired John to write their first big hit, 'Please Please Me'. Another favourite was 'As Time Goes By', by Dooley Wilson.

The Wurlitzer jukebox was the centrepoint of a creation by John on New Year's Eve 1979. He decided, with Elliot Mintz, to establish a private club called the Club Dakota, one small room which would be his equivalent of an Englishman's private club. With the Yamaha electric piano bought for his birthday by Elton John, he would give private recitals to a favoured few.

The Club Dakota's only members were John Lennon and Elliot Mintz. When Yoko attended, just once on that New Year's Eve, John was dressed in tails and his old Quarry Bank brown-and-yellow school tie. The appeal of the 'club' for John was its exclusivity. He even broke the hallowed 'no alcohol' rule there, agreed between himself and Yoko, allowing himself a bottle of old cognac.

Breakfasts in the Edwardian room of the Plaza Hotel were another regular pleasure. John had a special affinity with the hotel. The Beatles had stayed there when they first visited America in 1964. In the mornings the Lennons would have a late breakfast of black coffee (John ate eggs Benedict, Yoko split pea soup), before moving across to the tea-room where the violinist greeted them playing 'The Way We Were' and 'As Time Goes By' while they held hands. On Sean's seventh birthday the same violinist visited the Dakota to play 'Happy Birthday' for him. When they were out together, John and Yoko frequently held hands. 'When their kind of 1940s music struck up,' says Elliot Mintz, 'they behaved like high school sweethearts. They were *finished*, gazing at each other. . . .'

Memories of Liverpool permeated much of John's thinking from that day in 1976 when he secured his Green Card. Most nights he would telephone Aunt Mimi. Often he would reassure her that he had triumphed magnificently over the monster that was the Beatles. Several times he tried to persuade his aunt to go and live with him and take one of their Dakota apartments: 'No fear, John. You'll never catch me over there. I never have liked Americans. And *you* shouldn't be there, either. It's no good for you. Come back and live in England.' John told her he preferred New York but he now knew better than to argue with her.

Around the world Beatles fans had regarded John as a recluse since he had got his Green Card. His world travels to Japan, Hong Kong, Singapore, and South Africa had gone unnoticed. He and Yoko travelled incognito as the Revd Fred and Ada Ghurkin. Outside the Dakota the one person who knew precisely where he was on all his trips was Aunt Mimi. When he was in New York, he would phone her at 9.30 p.m. precisely British time, 4.30 p.m. New York time. 'I knew it was him; every night it rang almost on the dot,' she says. 'And it was, "Mimi, I'm in Bermuda, Cairo, Tokyo. . ." or wherever. Always gave me his phone number and said I could reverse the charges and call him back but I never wanted to do that. . . .'

For Sean's fourth birthday and John's thirty-ninth, on 9

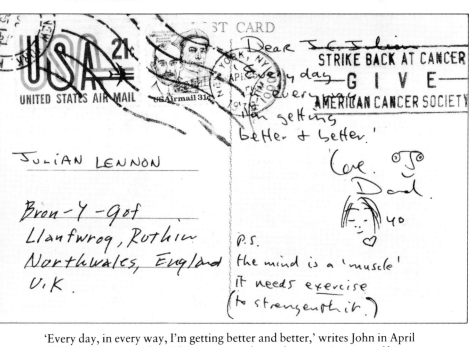

'Every day, in every way, I'm getting better and better,' writes John in April 1979 on this postcard to Julian; it was a phrase that came into one of his final songs, 'Beautiful Boy', on his penultimate album, *Double Fantasy*

October 1979, the Lennons threw a party at the Tavern on the Green, an elegant, glittering restaurant in Central Park. John was dressed soberly but wore his Quarry Bank tie to which he had grown attached. A Beatles fan sent a picture of John to a surprised Aunt Mimi, who challenged him about it. 'Who are your spies?' John said. 'Look, I've carried it around with me everywhere these past few years. I just like it.' It confirmed Mimi's lifelong suspicions about her nephew's sentimentality: 'He was a great big baby. He was no tough nut, never. I think he sometimes wanted people to think he was, but deep down, he was as soft as butter.'

Proof of this theory, which Mimi held all her life sometimes against the odds, came at the start of 1980. In one of his daily phone conversations, John said: 'Right, Mimi, now I want you to put your affairs in order.'

'What affairs?'

'Now look, Mimi, everything belonging to you, I want it.'

'What do you mean, John? If it's that important to you, you can have anything you like now. But what have you on your mind?'

The next part of John's request shattered her. The degree of his memory of all her possessions, particularly the items he had grown up with back at 251 Menlove Avenue, was almost overpowering. 'Mimi, you remember that painting that Uncle George did when he was at Liverpool Institute in Form 4A? It was a watercolour of a kind of Chinese vase. I'd like that.' It was the picture at the far end of the hall that had faced John as he had walked in from school or college every day. Mimi found it in her loft.

'John wanted every single photograph of me that I could lay my hands on,' says Mimi. And he gave her a vivid description of the china that had been on a plate rack high on the wall of the entrance hall and dining-room at Mendips. 'It's gold, Mimi, and it's got blue in it and a sort of rusty red. Coalport, Spode and Crown Derby. And don't forget to send me the teapot.' Mimi always had a weakness for collecting china; it formed a central part of the decoration of the house in which John grew up. 'He asked for the really heavy cut-glass claret jugs, an enlargement of a photograph of my mother when she was a beautiful twenty-one-year-old. John wanted all my silver, all the cutlery I was not using that he'd seen at Mendips, any old cup and saucer, salt and pepperpots, anything. He said: "There's no need to do anything with it. Just leave it for collection." And John had a removal firm ship it all to him in crates.' John was developing an increasing fascination for his roots; he told friends he intended to write a *Forsyte Saga*-type story based on his family.

His final request was for Mimi to send him something that had been passed down in her late husband's family of Smiths for generations: an antique grandfather clock, inscribed 'George Toogood, Woolton Tavern'. Uncle George, whose full name was George Toogood Smith, had taught John the time on it. The Toogoods were John's ancestors, a fact he had discovered, says Mimi, in his teenage years when he walked his Woolton girlfriends around the graveyard of St Peter's Church. Mimi had the handsome wooden clock serviced and John arranged for it to be shipped over to New York. It ticks away loudly still in the Dakota kitchen, framed symbolically by pictures carefully chosen and positioned by John: one black-and-white picture of John and Yoko above it, and a Polaroid snapshot of John and Yoko on a boat, looking at each other, next to it.

John's emotional side came over loudly and clearly during 1980. 'Remember,' he would say to Mimi, 'those holidays you sent me on in Scotland with Mater [his Aunt Elizabeth]? And the postcard I sent you: "Dear Mimi and Uncle George, I caught my first trout today. . . ." Have you still got those cards, Mimi?' And the aunt who had lectured him so sternly about getting on with his studies would find it hard to keep the tears back.

Although Mimi had never seen Sean, whom she regarded as her grandson, she must have known everything there was to know about him. John regaled her most nights with a blow-by-blow account of what Sean was doing and how he was.

'John,' she said, 'don't make the same mistake that I did and wrap your life around a little boy. That's what *I* did, and what did I get?'

'Was I that bad? A worry to you?' And they would both laugh about the years when his conscientious aunt told him he was wasting his time playing the guitar at the Cavern Club instead of getting a proper career.

Throughout 1980 John sent out clear signs to his aunt that he loved and respected her for her strictness and her care of him. 'You were right,' he told her. 'But I knew I could paint and draw . . . and *write*. I'm forty this year. I'm going to make one more record, Mimi, then I'm going to do some writing.'

8

THE MUSIC: 1972–1980

'No longer riding on the merry-go-round,
I just had to let it go'

'Nobody told me there'd be days like *these*!' chanted John, alone and simply, in a record Yoko released four years after his death. 'Everybody's smoking and no one's getting high . . . everybody's talking and no one's saying a word . . . there's U.F.O.'s over New York and I ain't too surprised. . . . Strange days indeed!'

In 1984, four years after John's murder, it was a simple, stark reminder of the powerful, allegorical word-play with which he had mesmerized millions for twenty years. There had been diversions, of course: back to the roots rock 'n' roll; the tender, loving ballads on *Double Fantasy*. But here, now, in a song that was at once danceable to and which lyrically outclassed any contemporary rock 'n' roll, the words of 'Nobody Told Me' were as relevant to the eighties as the psychedelic anthems he created earlier were for the sixties. John Lennon's posthumously released album was a far more articulate, concerned, symbolic, and creative piece of work than that produced by any living artist in popular music. Together with the searing, chilling song he wrote for Yoko, 'Grow Old With Me', the album *Milk And Honey* demonstrated to all his friends – and those who had branded *Double Fantasy* as maudlin – that Lennon was a master who had not lost his muse.

Double Fantasy and *Milk And Honey* have provided the most moving love songs from John Lennon, because they feature lyrics written and sung around the time of his happiness as a husband and father in America. They were albums that accurately reflected his mood in 1980. But the man who had arrived in New York some nine years earlier, mentally high on his fixation for Yoko and the vibrancy of the country, with his eyes wide open seeking new

John looks every inch the teenage rock 'n' roller beside the giant guitar model in New York's Record Plant where some of the mixing for the *Double Fantasy* album was done

mental horizons, provided some astonishingly provocative music and writing that demonstrated how he loved championing causes.

All the vitality Lennon felt he was getting from his new home poured into the *Some Time In New York City* album, which was released in 1972. Jerry Rubin, the political activist with whom John had become friendly, had put him in touch with a hard-rocking New York band, Elephants Memory (three of whose songs were included on the soundtrack of the film *Midnight Cowboy*). Rejuvenated politically and musically, Lennon spontaneously plunged into the recording, finishing the album in nineteen days. It was a hasty decision and one which he later came to regret. *Some Time In New York City* does have moments of energy, particularly the driving 'New York City' which conveys Lennon's enthusiasm for his new home. You can even overlook such trite lines as 'His name is David Peel/And we found that he was real', such is the vitality of the song. Yoko's songs on the record have a charm of their own. 'Sisters, O Sisters' and 'We're All Water' are lyrically invigorating. The haunting quality of her singing and the pile-driving Elephants Memory meant that the songs stood up on their own.

'Sunday Bloody Sunday' and 'The Luck Of The Irish' were drawn from Lennon's first-hand knowledge of the Irish community in Liverpool and they convey Lennon's rage at the British troops' occupation of Northern Ireland. 'The Luck Of The Irish' managed, however, to retain some of Lennon's charm.

Where the album falls down is in Lennon's trite and repetitious sloganeering. After being a leader for so long, Lennon was now being led. His direction was dominated by Rubin and Hoffman, who were hardly objective, and while the causes they championed were noble, 'John Sinclair', 'Attica State', 'Angela', and 'Woman Is The Nigger Of The World' for example, are almost offensively single-minded. The victimization of 'subversive elements' by the Nixon administration (which considered Lennon as one) was reprehensible and it was important that someone of Lennon's stature should speak out against such iniquities. Dylan's 1971 single 'George Jackson' was fired by that same sense of outrage but Dylan wisely confined his sentiments to a single. Lennon had proved throughout his career that he was one of rock's most articulate spokesmen, able to clarify and delineate problems with a perception and wry humour that few of his contemporaries could match. To hear him endlessly repeat other people's slogans was dispiriting.

Lennon resented the criticism that the album attracted – that he was writing simple lyrics – even though he had always claimed to dislike his songs 'being digested and analysed like the Mona Lisa'. 'I Want To Hold Your Hand' was simple, he said; if he constantly sought praise he could write more surrealistic material like 'I Am The Walrus'. What motivated him on his arrival in New York was the ease of writing political songs and rushing them out on a record, just as he had always wanted. 'Most other people express themselves by playing football at weekends or shouting. But here am I in New York and I hear about thirteen people shot dead in Ireland and I react immediately. And being what I am I react in four-to-the-bar with a guitar break in the middle,' he told Roy Carr in the *New Musical Express*. 'I don't say, "My God, what's happening, we should do something." I go: "It was Sunday Bloody Sunday/And they shot the people down. . ." It's not like the Bible. It's all over now. It's gone. It's finished.' Music, as a form of communication, was his main concern.

In its defence the album did possess immediacy, as Lennon remembered: 'When we made that album, we weren't setting out to make the Brandenburg Concerto or the masterpiece everybody always tries to write, paint, draw, or film. . . . The point now is that I want to say whatever it is I've got to say, as simple as the music I like. And that's rock 'n' roll, and to match the lyrics to the music. So now it's . . . AWOPBOPALOOBOP Get Outta Ireland. I suppose it looks more preachy than it really is.'

Some Time In New York City was a realization of Lennon's ideal record at that time: it should have the immediacy of a newspaper and reflect current affairs (the album packaging was based on the *New York Times*). But *Some Time In New York City* did little to enhance Lennon's reputation. Side Three was recorded at the UNICEF Lyceum Benefit in 1969. It includes a workmanlike version of 'Cold Turkey' and continues with Yoko screeching that 'Britain killed Hanratty' (the A6 murderer who was hanged). Side Four included the Zappa jam, with a competent version of the old Olympics hit 'Well (Baby Please Don't Go)' dredged up from the Cavern days.

Lennon swiftly realized he had gone too far. He had lost objectivity and his craft had suffered. He told New York writer Peter Hammill in 1975: 'It almost *ruined* [my work]. It became journalism and not poetry. And I basically feel that I'm a poet. Then I began to take it seriously on another level, saying, "Well, I am reflecting what is going on, right?" '

Lennon had laid himself wide open for criticism and the reviews that the album received were a chastening experience for him. At the beginning of 1973 he and Yoko had moved into the Dakota Building and he kept a low profile. Just before Christmas 1972 John and Yoko's 'Happy Xmas (War Is Over)' single was belatedly released in the U.K. The Christmas novelty single is a great tradition in Britain. The Lennons' single took up their 'War Is Over, If You Want It' slogan and turned it into a memorable Christmas hit. The message is simply that we should work together and shed a little love, a suitably apposite message for Christmas, and one which echoes round the world every year when it is re-released. The choir on the record is the children's Harlem Community Choir.

Not until the end of 1973 did Lennon feel confident enough to release a new album. *Mind Games* marked a return to the melodicism of *Imagine* and was a distinct departure from the polemics of his previous album. As an indication of his commitment to the project, it was the first album he had produced by himself. He gathered the best session musicians New York could offer. Names like Jim Keltner, David Spinozza, Michael Brecker, and Sneaky Pete Kleinow regularly featured on albums by Bob Dylan, Ry Cooder, the Rolling Stones, Bruce Springsteen, and the Flying Burrito Brothers. The inherent lushness and attempt to return to former glories could be found on the album's title track, which announced: 'Love is the answer, and you know that for sure.'

John was always one of the great rock 'n' roll vocalists, although he was reticent about his own vocal abilities. He had always allowed his voice to be buried on record, but on 'Tight A$', the album's second track, there is a freewheeling return to rock 'n' roll with Lennon's voice well to the fore. It is not as hard as it could have been (the backing is far too polite) but Lennon is still in great voice and the song rolls along. 'Bring On The Lucie (Freda People)' is another of those cautious rockers – 'OK boys, let's go over the hill,' he announces as the song plunges into its riff. But he doesn't go far enough and lapses back into vacuous sloganeering. The song is redeemed by some tasty dobro playing.

'Out The Blue' is a beautifully restrained love song, haunting and poignant. John's devotion to Yoko was aching: 'All my life's been a long slow knife/I was born just to get to you.' That feeling persisted on 'I Know (I Know)'. And there was the first indication of Lennon's efforts to bridge the gap between East and West with the schoolboy Japanese of 'Aisumasen (I'm Sorry)' and 'You Are Here', which overturned Kipling's maxim that 'East is East and West is West and never the twain shall meet.' Lennon maintains that the twain *shall* meet: 'From distant lands, one woman, one man. . . .'

Mind Games has several pleasant tracks – notably the title song – but it suffers from too many mid-paced rockers and lacks his usual lyrical inventiveness. The old radical Lennon had gone (as solace he offered a silent 'Nutopian International Anthem'). The love poet of *Imagine* had gone. The confessional troubador of *Plastic Ono Band* had gone. By the end of 1973 Lennon sounded listless and uninspired. After its release he went on his 'long weekend'.

Walls And Bridges, released in October 1974, was an open letter to the absent Yoko. Many of the songs were pleading, an uncharacteristic role for Lennon. The album was cockier than *Mind Games*, mainly because of Bobby Keys' raunchy sax playing and some generally fine instrumental back-up. The album was conceived and recorded while Lennon was just coming out of a bender of Dylan Thomas proportions. His old friend Harry Nilsson was closely involved. As far back as 1968 Lennon had congratulated him on his imaginative Beatle medley on his *Pandemonium Shadow Show* album and the two had collaborated on Nilsson's *Pussy Cats* L.P. in California earlier in the year.

Walls And Bridges was a beautifully packaged album, with drawings courtesy of the twelve-year-old John Winston Lennon, an imaginative cut-out sleeve, a lyric book and plenty of Dr Winston O'Boogie's (a jokey pseudonym John sometimes used) aphorisms. Elton John, an ardent Lennon fan (and at the time himself the most successful British act since the Beatles) guested on the hit single 'Whatever Gets You Thru The Night', which turned out to be the album's best track. A cocky rocker, it had suitably irreverent lyrics: 'Whatever gets you thru the night, s'alright, s'alright.'

On the slower songs like 'Old Dirt Road' and 'Nobody Loves You (When You're Down And Out)' – which he always saw Sinatra as singing – Lennon sounded maudlin. On 'Bless You' he even comes over as sluggish. '#9 Dream' was a barely marked progression from 'Aisumasen'. It had the requisite dreamy atmosphere to match the lyrics, and was as much about the number nine, which Lennon always considered lucky, as it was about his state of mind.

'Scared' could lyrically have come from his first album, Lennon laying himself open to the world at large: 'I'm scared . . . No bell, book or candle/Can get you out of this . . . I'm tired of being so alone/No place to call my own/Like a rollin' stone.' 'Going Down

On Love' was a plea to Yoko: 'Your love has gone . . . And you shoot out the light/Ain't coming home for the night.' The finished album was a definite improvement on the listless *Mind Games* but it was hardly vintage Lennon. He recalled the circumstances at the time: 'This last year has been an extraordinary one for me personally. And I'm almost amazed that I could get *anything* out. Musically, my mind was a clutter. It was apparent on *Walls And Bridges*, which was the work of a semi-sick craftsman. There was no inspiration and it gave an aura of misery.'

Significantly, two of the biggest stars of the seventies, Elton John and David Bowie, played a substantial role in getting Lennon back on the tracks: Elton because he coerced Lennon into appearing with him at his Madison Square Garden concert on Thanksgiving Night 1974 and Bowie because he asked Lennon along to help out on the sessions which made up his 1975 *Young Americans* album. In the studio Lennon backed vocals on what he said was always one of his favourite songs, Bowie's histrionic reading of 'Across The Universe'; John also co-wrote 'Fame' with Bowie and guitarist Carlos Alomar. The song gave Bowie his first American number one hit while Elton also helped Lennon there with 'Whatever Gets You Thru The Night'.

Lennon's next album to be released was *Rock 'n' Roll* in February 1975. It was a project which had fascinated him for years and the story behind the album went back to when Chuck Berry's publisher, Morris Levy, had threatened to sue John for alleged plagiarism; Levy claimed that 'Come Together' from *Abbey Road* ripped off Berry's 1956 'You Can't Catch Me'. (Both songs do include the line: 'Here comes old flat top'.) In an out of court settlement, Lennon agreed to record a number of Chuck Berry songs for a forthcoming album, which laid the seeds for *Rock 'n' Roll*.

At an artistic and emotional crossroads in 1973, Lennon felt that he needed a producer to dictate how he sang, to help recreate the feel of those rock classics, to advise, and to inspire him. Having dropped Phil Spector after *Some Time In New York City*, and having produced *Mind Games* himself, Lennon now approached Spector again and asked him to work on the new album, originally called *Oldies but Mouldies*. (This was a neat parody on the sub-title of the first Beatles' hits collection released in 1966, *Oldies But Goldies*.) Although a virtual recluse, Spector agreed and they subsequently recorded many tracks together. But a growing estrangement developed between them, and the sessions grew more and more protracted. (Studio costs alone for the four tracks

John considered to be rescuable were $90,000.) Finally Spector disappeared completely, taking the master tapes with him. There was talk of a car crash, rumour piled upon rumour, and not even John could get past the armed guards around the Spector mansion. Eventually Lennon retrieved the tapes but Spector (once again living the life of a recluse) was no longer interested in pursuing the project. In a burst of energy Lennon tore into the Record Plant in New York at the end of October 1974 and in a mere four days laid down ten new tracks to complete the album. Because of his enthusiasm for the project, and because of Levy's illegal *Roots* album suddenly being made available, *Rock 'n' Roll* was issued only four months after *Walls And Bridges*.

The cover picture alone, by Jurgen Vollmer, was worth the price of the album: John, sneering in a Hamburg doorway in 1961, fresh-faced, every inch a rocker. Blurred figures rush by hurrying to the future, while Lennon stands, as if waiting for the past to catch up with him. Lennon cherished the very *idea* of the album, and effortlessly pitched himself back in time: 'All the words to "Stand By Me" and "Be-Bop-A-Lula", I knew them all from being fifteen, they all just came back to me, just like that.'

In many ways *Rock 'n' Roll* is the definitive John Lennon album. Even when he had toyed with the avant-garde and radical politics John had remained a rocker at heart. He saw rock 'n' roll as 'the great motivator' and always paid homage to the greats who inspired him. He was genuinely modest about his own songwriting abilities and felt he had never written anything to equal 'Whole Lotta Shakin' Goin' On'. Now stripped of the peace and primals, he stands supreme as the cocky rocker who took on the world and almost beat it. *Rock 'n' Roll* is a human jukebox, with Lennon pouring his heart into his roots. It's far more than simply a rehash of twenty-year-old Chuck Berry and Little Richard songs. Each song on the album is stamped with his personality, infused with Lennon dynamism. The rockers are harder than anything Lennon had done in years, the ballads softer. While rock 'n' roll itself was looking for a direction in 1975, John Lennon was looking imaginatively back at its history.

The album spans the glory years of rock 'n' roll, from Little Richard's 1956 'Rip It Up' to Sam Cooke's 1962 'Bring It On Home To Me'. It covers John's adolescence, picking up the flickering signals of Radio Luxembourg, through art school and teenage groups, right up to the birth of the Beatles. Those songs were the soundtrack to his life, before the world went mad – the shuffle beat of Buddy Holly's 'Peggy Sue', the chilling 'Be-Bop-A-

Lula', the raucous 'Ready Teddy' and 'Bony Moronie', the rolling 'Ain't That A Shame', the poignant 'Stand By Me' – Lennon hadn't sung better since *Plastic Ono Band*. His act of homage gave him the shot in the arm he needed.

The most touching aspect of the album comes right at the end of Side Two. He finishes a tender version of Lloyd Price's 'Just Because', treating it affectionately, delivering almost a parody of fifties' recording clichés. The spoken bridge and slow fade culminate with him saying: 'This is Dr Winston O'Boogie saying goodnight from the Record Plant East. We've had a swell time. Everybody here says Hi. Goodbye.' It was as if John knew the album was a watershed. He told Andy Peebles: 'Something flashed through my mind as I said it. Am I really saying farewell to the business? I looked at the cover I'd chosen, which was a picture of me in Hamburg the first time we got there [*sic*]. I thought, this is some sort of cosmic thing. Here I am with this old picture of me in Hamburg in sixty-one and I'm saying farewell from Record Plant, and I'm ending as I started, singing this straight rock 'n' roll stuff.'

With Yoko pregnant, Lennon channelled all his energies into caring for his wife. Nothing more was heard of him on record for five long years. A fortnight after Sean was born in October 1975 *Shaved Fish* was released. It was a timely, well-assembled collection, embracing the range of his work since 1969. Opening with a snatch of 'Give Peace A Chance', and finishing with 'Happy Xmas', the album ran through the facets of his career: Lennon as junkie ('Cold Turkey'), as political activist ('Power To The People'), as idealist ('Imagine', '#9 Dream'). It was an impressive roster. Perhaps more convincingly than any of the four Beatles, Lennon proved with this L.P. that he had achieved the impossible – he had forged his own identity. He had reconciled his art with his life and proved himself able to cope with his past.

During Lennon's years of silence the English music scene became convulsed with the iconoclasm of punk. 'No more Elvis, Beatles or Stones in 1977' screamed the Clash. The young punks were bored and angry with the remote rock élite. They wanted their own heroes and were not content with second-hand idols, whose lives and music bore no relation to their own.

It marked the first generation gap in music since the broadside delivered by the Beatles and Bob Dylan all those years before. The anarchic approach of the Sex Pistols and the Clash to rock 'n' roll left many of the old guard marooned. Lennon remained one of the few rock establishment figures who was not ridiculed. Perhaps they remembered his struggles and the ridicule *he* had faced, which

John the working musician and composer: taking a guitar break and at the piano

bore comparison with their own vendetta. For his own private reasons Lennon, wisely, did not opt for punk. He had other things on his mind during the punk upheaval – being a father and a husband, and becoming a human being instead of adopting roles and causes.

During those years of silence he listened to Hank Williams, Carl Perkins, Jerry Lee Lewis, the B52s, Lene Lovich, Bruce Springsteen, Madness, John Gielgud reading Shakespeare, and 'everything Bing Crosby had ever done'. He listened but did not comment. As the punks created their own idols, he breathed a sigh of relief as he watched the mantle pass on: 'God help Bruce Springsteen when they decide he's no longer God . . . when he gets down to facing his own success and growing older and having to produce it again and again, they'll turn on him and I hope he survives it.' John watched his idols and contemporaries fall, succumbing to the sort of pressures he had wisely managed to avoid.

During those five private years the anger seeped out of John Lennon. There is a school of rock theory that says the only *great* music comes out of anger and frustration, from the energy of youth. It has its point; that *is* where much of rock's motivation has come from. It• follows that comfort and contentment see the original intentions vanish and disappear (McCartney's domesticity, Dylan's pulpit-bashing). And yet we have no right to expect our idols to suffer for the sake of their music. If they are enjoying security and happiness, then, inevitably, that is what will be reflected in their music. It is that feeling of contentment and domesticity which permeates *Double Fantasy*.

'(Just Like) Starting Over' was released on 24 October 1980, the first single from John Lennon in five years. Despite the convulsions in pop music during his silence, despite the contempt with which most icons of the sixties were held, a tremor ran through the music industry – Lennon was back! John now had something fresh to say musically. Sean was five, and he wanted to reflect the parental bliss he was experiencing. He also wanted to give his son a birthday present. And he chose the method he knew best.

The songs for the album were mostly written in a three-week burst in Bermuda. But then Lennon was never one to labour over a song. He once told David Bowie: 'Look, it's *very* simple: Say what you mean, make it rhyme and put a backbeat to it!' John and Yoko had a ball in the studio – Lennon was exultant at being back. 'We cut twenty-two tracks in two weeks!'

Double Fantasy was released at the end of November 1980 on the newly inaugurated Geffen label. With its release some ardent Lennon fans felt twinges of disappointment. They thought it simply showed John and Yoko washing their clean linen in public. Gone was the old *Angst*-ridden Lennon, the poet who carried the world's troubles on his shoulders. With the tracks evenly split between them, the Lennons now offered domestic bliss as the solution. It should have been obvious to everyone what public face the inscrutable Lennon would present. His wife and child were now his whole world. What else could he (or did he want to) write about? *Double Fantasy* was the most honest Lennon album since *Plastic Ono Band* in that it perfectly reflected his state of mind. The demons were vanquished. The past was firmly put in its place. With Yoko and Sean, and after forty years of trial and torment, John Lennon had found peace.

In all truth, and ridding ourselves of the poignancy which irrevocably surrounds *Double Fantasy*, it is not a great album. In retrospect it is, of course, John Lennon's final vinyl statement in which the tracks were produced, mixed, and sequenced exactly as he intended. A song like 'Beautiful Boy (Darling Boy)' takes on a terrible beauty in the aftermath of Lennon's murder, as he sings to his son: 'Close your eyes and have no fear/The monster's gone and your Daddy's here.' The morning he promised Sean at the end of the song never came.

'Starting Over' was the album opener, ushered in by the ringing of Yoko's personal 'wishing bell' – it was a deliberate ploy: 'I put it on *Double Fantasy* to show the likeness and difference from "Mother" to "Starting Over",' said John. Before, tolling bells had emphasized doom. Now there was a chirpy cheerful bell, indicating a willingness to start again. What was appealing was the diehard rock 'n' roll voice he chose (à la Elvis): 'It was the fifties-ish sound because I had never really written a song that sounded like that period, although that was my period, the music I identified with. So I just thought, why the hell not? In the Beatle days, that would have been taken as a joke. One avoided clichés. But of course now those clichés are not clichés any more.'

'Woman' was a beautifully sustained Lennon ballad, written in fifteen minutes; it is already a classic. It recalls the fragility of 'Imagine' and touchingly recognizes that Yoko understands 'the little child inside the man'. 'Dear Yoko' finds Lennon again in fine fifties voice, pleading his love. It is a rockier version of 'Oh Yoko!' from 1971 and perfectly summarizes the intensity of their relationship: 'Without you I'm a one-track mind, dear Yoko/After all is really said and done/The two of us are really one. . . .' (Yoko's seven songs on the album were her most accessible to date and proved she had an even more contemporary edge than her husband.)

'Watching The Wheels' is Lennon's answer to all those who speculated on his state of mind during his five-year silence: 'People have been saying I'm lazy, dreaming my life away, all my life,' John commented. 'Pop stars were getting indignant in the Press that I wasn't making records. I couldn't believe it, they were acting like mothers-in-law. . . .' To counter that speculation Lennon wrote of what he actually was doing: 'watching shadows on the wall . . . No longer riding on the merry-go-round/I just had to let it go.' Finally, after years of pressure, Lennon could slide off the helter skelter and leave the fairground.

It could come as no surprise to him, though, that people were fascinated by his silence. Rock 'n' roll is a notoriously short-lived profession. The only comparable absences were when Elvis entered the army in 1958 and Dylan's enforced seclusion following his motorcycle crash of 1966. Rumours spread. The remote rock star becomes a mythical figure. People couldn't believe that John Lennon, probably the most talented rocker of his generation, could be *happy* simply making bread! He realized people still looked to him for answers but by 1980 the only answer he could offer was: 'Just sitting here watching the wheels go round/I really love to watch them roll. . . .' He told *Rolling Stone* in 1980: 'They're my own wheels, mainly. But you know, watching myself is like watching everybody else. The hardest thing is facing yourself. It's easier to shout "Revolution" and "Power To The People" than it is to look at yourself and try to find out what's real inside you and what isn't, when you're pulling the wool over your own eyes.' Lennon was well aware of the disappointment that his new-found peace would cause his fans but had no wish to compromise his own feelings to satisfy them: 'I cannot be a punk in Hamburg and Liverpool any more. I'm older now, I see the world through different eyes. . . . As Elvis Costello said – "What's so funny 'bout peace, love and understanding?" '

In the terrible aftermath of John's death in December 1980, 'Starting Over', 'Imagine', and 'Woman' all reached number one on the British charts. The three songs he performed with Elton John in 1974 appeared on a single and *The John Lennon Collection* was the number one album for Christmas 1982. Lennon's name was subsequently evoked by many of his disciples:

John makes a point to Yoko at the recording console, autumn 1980

on Elton John's 'Empty Garden', on Queen's 'Life Is Real', and on Paul Simon's 'The Late Great Johnny Ace'.

Paul McCartney movingly remembered Lennon on a song called 'Here Today', on his 1982 album *Tug of War*. McCartney admitted the gulf which had grown between the two men but, accompanied by a discreet string quartet, he unashamedly sang: 'I am holding back the tears no more/I love you.' In conversation with the late Alexis Korner he spoke of that song: 'It was being heralded as a kind of tribute album. Which I hadn't thought of, you know – "I will now make this a tribute album" . . . John would have been the first one to laugh at that kind of stuff. . . . He'd probably laugh and say that we're worlds apart anyway . . . but we weren't. I know if we had you back here right now you'd say, "Oh, load of bollocks." But it's not true, you know, that would be just bluff. We actually did know each other, we actually were very close. . . . There was always the competitive thing with John and I, which I know was very good for me and I think he appreciated it as it was very good for him too.'

When the shock of Lennon's murder eventually subsided, the *Milk and Honey* album was released in January 1984. Recorded at the *Double Fantasy* sessions in August 1980, the album follows the format of its predecessor, the tracks evenly divided between John and Yoko. The single, 'Nobody Told Me', was among John's best since 'Imagine', a jerky compelling rocker with Lennon again favouring that fifties vocal style which raced into the British charts. It stands as a tribute to his innate musical ability that 'Nobody Told Me' sounds as ebullient and infectious as anything Lennon had ever done.

Milk and Honey has a harder feel to it than *Double Fantasy* because of the obvious rawness of the Lennon tracks. As Yoko told Andy Peebles, the temptation for any outside producer would have been to over-produce the whole album (as Norman Petty did with Buddy Holly's posthumous recordings). So the resultant album retains its charm and spontaneity, notably on the lovely 'Grow Old With Me', with Lennon on piano, accompanied by a rhythm box. There is a grittiness on the album's rockier tracks, showing that, right to the end, Lennon was a rocker. Rock was both his heritage and his legacy.

There are moments of mawkishness as in '(Forgive Me) My Little Flower Princess', but on the whole it is the moments of touching greatness we remember. 'I Don't Wanna Face It' carries on the theme developed in 'Watching The Wheels' with Lennon advocating that people find another hero, he has had enough: 'Say

John and Yoko perched on their favourite bench in Central Park. They used to spend hours walking and talking there

you're looking for a place to go/Where nobody knows your name/You're looking for oblivion, with one eye on the Hall of Fame/I don't wanna face it . . . Well I can dish it out/But I just can't take it.' 'I'm Stepping Out' opens the album with Lennon taking on the character of Lonnie Donegan of 'Rock Island Line', vintage, before stepping into traditional blues territory, with John revelling in his role as house-husband.

The perfect marriage occurs at the end of Side One, as Lennon's 'Three, four. . .' ushers in 'Nobody Told Me', with his ruminating on Nazis in the bathroom and little yellow idols, punctuated by wistful cries of, 'Strange days indeed Momma'. Next to it, Yoko's poignant, brief ' "O" Sanity', probably her most incisive recorded song, ends with the terse: 'Let it go, cut it out!'

'Borrowed Time' has Lennon facing the uncertainties of middle age in a world no longer conveniently divided into black and white: 'The more I see, the less I know for sure,' he sings, although maintaining that 'It's good to be older.' For John, 'Grow Old With Me' had become a pleasant vision of his and Yoko's future. He wanted to include it on *Double Fantasy* but couldn't decide on the song's arrangement. As the album's deadline drew closer, it was held over for the follow-up and appears here in this charming, uncluttered version.

The album is peppered with Lennon's on-mike asides, his count-ins, and snatches of studio conversation, which add to the casual eavesdropping atmosphere for the listener. *Milk and Honey* is full of charm and tragedy. The tragedy lies in the fact that as a musician and poet John Lennon was back finding his musical feet. On the sleeve of his 1975 *Rock 'n' Roll* album, Dr Winston O'Boogie simply wrote: 'You should have been there.' Thanks to the music of John Lennon, we were and always will be.

9

THE COMEBACK

'Life begins at forty'

The word spread like a forest fire at the beginning of August 1980: John Lennon, the hermit, the Howard Hughes of rock, the man who had freaked out to become a house-husband and led a mysterious, reclusive life for five years, was back. At a New York recording studio he was recording a new album. With Yoko Ono. Amid U.S. election fever (Carter was to lose to Reagan in November), and as 100 Americans were held hostage in Iran, the news from the Lennon camp was like a beacon of light.

John's decision to return to recording had been made in Bermuda a month earlier. Bermuda proved yet another watershed for John. He had gone there because he felt that up until then he had done so few things alone in his life. He decided to go by sea with a five-man crew on his yacht *Isis*. The crossing from Newport, Rhode Island, is notoriously rough at certain times of the year and the yacht was tossed around in heavy seas. With the crew falling sick one by one, it fell to John to take the controls, which he did successfully. 'There was crockery falling all over the place and it was really rough with the waves coming up over the boat,' John recalled later. 'I thought I was supposed to be the passenger but I had a go.' He told Aunt Mimi of it by phone when he reached Bermuda; he had felt like an old sea captain, the sort that sailed into Liverpool. John said he had sung himself songs as he steered the yacht to keep up his morale: mostly Beatles oldies, 'Strawberry Fields Forever', 'Getting Better', 'Please Please Me'. Mentally he was slowly turning full circle.

In Bermuda, in a rented house, the idea was for John to relax totally and go swimming and sailing. But he could hardly stay off

245

the phone each day, trying to reach Yoko. Incredibly he sometimes found his busy wife in business meetings, unable to be interrupted. It was then that he wrote the evocative song 'I'm Losing You', which he played to her over the telephone.

> Here in some stranger's room
> Late in the afternoon
> Can't even get you on the telephone
> There ain't no doubt about it . . . I'm losing you.

At the Forty Thieves discothèque and also on the radio John heard the music he was listening to being described as 'new wave'. It struck him that there was nothing new about it. Yoko had been writing and performing much more imaginative material, in the same genre, ten years earlier. At the time she was rejected as a freak. Perhaps, he mused, the world was ready for her now. It inspired him to write songs furiously. One of his first was 'Woman', that paean not only to Yoko but to women everywhere, which laid bare his deepest affections for them. Over the next week or two, on his daily phone conversations with Yoko, he sang and played her his latest compositions and she reciprocated with her new work. The stage was set. On his return to Manhattan he and Yoko had around twenty songs between them, some finished, some unfinished.

'(Just Like) Starting Over' epitomized precisely what John felt about his return to recording. His earliest influences in rock 'n' roll – Elvis Presley and Roy Orbison – were recalled on the sound and atmosphere of the song. The album's concept, a combination of songs by both husband and wife, was poetically captured by the title, *Double Fantasy*. John had been enraptured by a flower of this name while out walking in the summer in botanical gardens in Bermuda. It suited the tone of the album perfectly.

Back in New York, John was in superb mental and physical shape for the recording sessions. Seen outside the Hit Factory Studios on West 54th Street, Manhattan, he looked sprightly and smiling. For the first time in eighteen years he was free of a contract: he had written the songs and was making the record purely for himself. No record deal was in the offing – the plan was to find a label when they had completed the work. The working pattern and atmosphere at the recording studios was both civilized and organized: there was no alcohol but Yoko arranged for the musicians to have a plate of *sushi* and fruit in front of them when they arrived. Potted plants and flowers were ordered; there was a

Yoko and John in New York, 6 December 1980

rest-room with comfortable chairs for everyone to relax; the musicians chosen to accompany John and Yoko were kindred spirits whom they admired as players: Andy Newmark (drums), Hugh McCracken (bass guitar), Earl Slick (guitar), Tony Levin (bass guitar). The competition among New York musicians to be on John Lennon's comeback album was enormous.

Yoko knew John was hungry for a successful return to work. He was particularly anxious for success in Britain. Phone calls to Aunt Mimi, imported tapes of British television shows like *Fawlty Towers* and *Monty Python*, and anything that gave him a sighting of the green British countryside, had made John almost misty-eyed when he thought of his native land. 'But England's not gonna go away,' he told anyone near him who asked when he was planning to return. 'It's still going to be there when I want to go and have a look at it. . . .'

He was in majestic form in the recording studios. His voice had achieved a resonance that was still the quintessential John Lennon but with a worldliness brilliantly mirrored in the lyrics of his songs.

Elliot Mintz had attended a number of *Double Fantasy* recording sessions. They were unlike any recording session for a John and Yoko album, he remembers. 'Yoko made it very clear to everyone that there was to be no alcohol or drugs of any kind during the making of that album. When it was time to break for dinner she had exquisite servings of fresh *sushi* delivered to the studio for the musicians and crew. A large colour photograph of Sean was taped over the television screen that faced the mixing console. There were dishes of raisins and sesame seeds placed around the control room. An assistant set up a small room with an interior look that resembled one of the rooms in the Dakota. Some pieces of furniture and art were placed in there so they would both feel comfortable and at home during the breaks.'

In November 1980 Elliot again flew in from Los Angeles to hear the final tape of *Double Fantasy*. John and Yoko had received the first complete master cassette on the night he arrived. 'John escorted me into the old bedroom and asked me to sit at the foot of the bed, while John and Yoko lay down with their heads propped up on the pillows – the stereo speakers were on the mantelpiece behind them. It was about ten at night and John dimmed the lights as he pushed the play button on the cassette. He played it loudly.'

As Mintz listened to the music he was reminded of another time. 'We had met for the first time almost ten years before. I thought about that first experience in California when we listened to the acetate of *Some Time In New York City*. John once told me he remembered points in his life by recalling the songs he was writing at the time. That night I was consciously reviewing the decade of adventure I had shared with John and Yoko; the birthdays, Christmases, trips around the world, months in Japan, John's Lost Weekend in California, the first time I saw Sean.'

The cassette ended and the three of them chatted excitedly into the night. When Elliot finally left John walked him to the front door of the apartment. He was wearing pyjamas under an antique Japanese robe. Elliot thought he had never looked better or seemed more optimistic. 'His enthusiasm was contagious – it was the best time of his life.'

'If you wake up before noon,' John said to his best male pal, 'we can meet for breakfast in the old hotel'. As he turned the brass doorknob Mintz recalls hearing the sound of bells.

'They used to have a string of chimes draped around the doorknob. Whenever anyone came or went, the bells would make a delicate sound as they rubbed against the door. We used to joke about it being a subtle, Zen-like alarm system.'

As the lift door closed, Mintz heard the bells chime again as John closed the door. They spoke by phone in the weeks ahead, but Elliot Mintz never saw John again.

With enough songs to make an album and plans for two more beyond that, John became apprehensive about signing a contract with the right record company. Free of both E.M.I./ Capitol and Apple, John was anxious not to sign with a major corporation. The album was sought by many companies but too many wanted to hear the music before talking about a deal. John regarded that as an insult to his integrity after eighteen years of making records. The album eventually went to David Geffen, whose empathy with major artists for more than a decade was matched by his acceptance of the record 'on trust', with not a note played to him before the deal was done. Geffen had been instrumental in discovering Joni Mitchell, Jackson Browne, and the Eagles. His Asylum label had also boasted Tom Waits and Linda Ronstadt. Before signing the Lennons his biggest coup had been to persuade Bob Dylan away from C.B.S. for two albums in the mid-seventies. *Double Fantasy* helped establish his label, which would later also attract Elton John, Asia and Peter Gabriel.

For the fans, the five-year wait had been a long one during pop music's darkest and least creative decade since its birth in 1955. John's return was a timely marker of rock's silver anniversary. He wanted to start a new decade and one which pointed up not down.

John autographing copies of *Double Fantasy* in his office at the Dakota

As far as he was concerned the sixties were hip and the seventies appalling. Only the birth of Sean had redeemed the previous decade for him. Family relationships, love, and personal communication were now the foundation of his music and he applied all the passion and articulacy to his mature love songs that he had to his Beatles hits. John had too much sense to wade back with all the sounds of yesteryear and he avoided the trap of becoming an embarrassing forty-year-old rocker. For her part, Yoko responded to John telling her that her music of a decade before was now fashionable with the remark: 'I'm not going to do all that *old* stuff.' Fittingly sub-titled 'A Heart Play' *Double Fantasy* traced the path for family relationships which John had found so enriching and now wanted others to share.

It was a natural evolution for a man who had come full circle. When John had returned from seclusion and Bermuda he was heavily in favour of survival. He had seen too many of his rock 'n' roll contemporaries die prematurely, martyrs to their own myths: Elvis Presley, Jimi Hendrix, Brian Jones, Buddy Holly, Eddie Cochran, and also James Dean and Marilyn Monroe. John did not believe in any 'live fast die young' philosophy. He did not want to be a hero. He wanted to carry on making his marriage better, making music, raising his son. And in the year 1981 he would sail to Britain as part of a short concert tour, also taking in New York, Los Angeles, San Francisco, and Hamburg. 'Yes, we'll have real fun on this tour,' John said. To mark the new album Yoko gave John a gold watch inscribed on the back: 'To John. Just Like Starting Over. Love Yoko.'

At the age of thirty-nine, when he re-entered the recording studios, Lennon was at a mental peak. No other major rock star had achieved such intellectual and physical maturity yet maintained an aura of rugged warmth. As John put it succinctly but with his customary edge, when he spoke of people who wanted to carry on in rock bands into their forties: 'So the Stones have been going for a hundred and twelve years. Yippee!' That, he implied, was no achievement. *His* success could be measured by the fact that he had grown up, not grown old, in the same field. Many middle-aged pop stars from the sixties invited the question: 'What are you going to do when you grow up?' John was determined it would never be addressed to him. He confounded the cynics by returning with his own, highly personal stance, that somehow reached out to old and new music fans. In defeating all the odds John had also beaten the system that chewed artists up before spitting them out as tired and worn.

John crystallized his outlook and his life as a family man on his new song 'Cleanup Time':

Moonlight on the water
Sunlight on my face
You and me together
We are in our place
The gods are in the heavens
The angels treat us well
The oracle has spoken
We cast the perfect spell. . .

The queen is in the counting home
Counting out the money
The king is in the kitchen
Making bread and honey
No friends and yet no enemies
Absolutely free
No rats aboard the magic ship
Of (perfect) harmony

However far we travel
Wherever we may roam
The centre of the circle
Will always be our home.

'I'm not interested in being a sex symbol,' John said. He reiterated his pride and the unity with his wife and family: 'It was an enlightening experience for me, as the house-husband . . . because it was a complete reversal of my upbringing . . . I did it to experience what it was like being the women who've done it for me. And it's the way of the future. I'm glad to be in on the forefront of that.'

He felt that for a period he had lost the initial freedom of the artist by 'becoming enslaved to the image of the artist'. Many artists killed themselves because of that, John said. Yoko had been his mental liberation, salvation, inspiration.

'Life begins at forty, so they promised. I believe it, too. I feel fine. I'm . . . excited. It's like twenty-one, and saying: "Wow, what's gonna happen?" '

10
THE END

*'What does it mean that when you're such
a pacifist you get shot?'*

On the afternoon of Saturday 6 December 1980 John went alone to Café La Fortuna for his customary *cappuccino* and read of the newspapers. Vincent Urwand playfully teased him about his comeback album.

'Look, you've had all those years of wildness and success in the Beatles. You don't need the money. What are you doing all this for? You're enjoying being a husband and father!'

John laughed. 'I swore I'd look after that boy until he was five, and he's five and I feel like getting back to my music,' he replied. 'The urge is there. It's been a long time since I wrote a song, but they're coming thick and fast now.' John sent Vincent a demonstration copy of *Double Fantasy*, autographed by him and Yoko.

That same evening John phoned Aunt Mimi. Enthusing about his record he told her about its success, how pleased he was with it, and how he was thinking about a world tour. Mimi, used to his capriciousness and visions of Utopia, was unconvinced by his *bonhomie*. 'John,' she said, in the peremptory voice he knew and secretly loved, 'John, you're an idealist looking for a lost horizon. You would make a saint cry!' For thirty-five years she had listened to him articulating his dreams. They both enjoyed banter.

'Oh, Mimi don't be like that. . . . You see, I'll *see you soon* and we'll bring Sean. Goodnight, God bless, Mimi.'

Two nights later John was dead.

John was acutely aware of the fact that the number nine had dominated his life.

'I love New York because I can walk around feeling so free,' said John. In
T-shirt and jeans, he and Yoko stroll the sidewalks in September 1980

He was born on 9 October 1940. Sean was born on 9 October 1975. Brian Epstein first saw John and the Beatles at Liverpool's Cavern on 9 November 1961 and he secured their record contract with E.M.I. in London on 9 May 1962. The début record, 'Love Me Do', was on Parlophone R4949.

John met Yoko Ono on 9 November 1966. John and Yoko's apartment was located on West 72nd Street, New York City (seven plus two making nine) and their main Dakota apartment number was also, at first 72. The bus he had travelled on as a student each morning from his home to Liverpool Art College had been the 72.

John's songs included 'Revolution 9', '#9 Dream', and 'One After 909', which he had written at his mother's home at 9 Newcastle Road, Wavertree, Liverpool. When he moved his Aunt Mimi from Liverpool to Sandbanks in Dorset her new address was 126 Panorama Road, the combination of figures striking John as his lucky number.

He even joked to me that one of his most important songs had nine key words: 'All we are saying is Give Peace A Chance'.

When John went gambling in Las Vegas, the number he repeatedly chose on the roulette wheel was nine . . . and he usually lost with it.

In Paris in 1964 during the Beatles' tour he received a death threat letter which made him nervous: 'I am going to shoot you at nine tonight.' John sold Tittenhurst Park to Ringo on 9 September 1973. He believed the sign of a marriage 'written in the stars' was that the names of John Ono Lennon and Yoko Ono Lennon together featured the letter 'o' nine times.

When John was killed, at 10.50 p.m. in New York on 8 December 1980, the five-hour time difference meant that it was 9 December in Britain. His body was taken to Roosevelt Hospital. It was situated on Ninth Avenue, Manhattan.

At the Dakota John and Yoko were among the most popular residents. The exclusive apartment block's vetting committee, which had allowed them to buy up five apartments comprising thirty-four rooms in nine years, had been vindicated. The surest test of their acceptance came from the doormen and desk staff. While some celebrated Dakota residents treated the staff dismissively and bossily, John and Yoko always treated them as equals, with, in the words of several, perfect manners. John was so popular and such a generous tipper that the staff almost fought to deliver his packages to the seventh floor. Throughout his life John trusted everyone. A fatal flaw in him was a lack of perception in judging which people were 'on the level' with him. He was honest and expected the same of everyone.

Jay Hastings was a twenty-seven-year-old front desk clerk in the oak-panelled entrance hall of the Dakota. He checked every arrival and every package and phoned through to any apartment for permission to release the door lock and allow a visitor access. With the constant stream of artists, businessmen, and delivery people arriving at the Dakota's forbidding Gothic entrance, 'You get to be a pretty shrewd judge of character,' he says.

Growing a beard in midsummer 1980, John quizzed Jay Hastings about how he kept his facial hair looking so trim. Hastings told him he must buy a pair of plastic, snap-on guides for his razor. 'You mean as if I'm cutting grass?' said John. 'That's amazing. They make *that* kind of thing for people with beards?' But within a few weeks Lennon was in the lobby with neither beard nor spectacles, carrying a guitar case and *en route* for Bermuda. Jay asked him where the beard had gone. 'Oh, there was a picture of me with it in the paper and people recognized me everywhere after that,' replied John. 'I just wanna roam *free*! Nobody will expect me to look like this.'

On so many nights Jay Hastings had awaited John's cheery whistle as his five foot eleven frame strode distinctively the thirty-second walk from West 72nd Street up the steps into the hallway. '*Bonsoir*, Jay!' John would often say.

At the beginning of December 1980 John was particularly 'up', Hastings recalls. 'He had the album out, *Double Fantasy*. He was going back and forth two miles to the studio most days, leaving late afternoon and returning between ten-thirty and eleven-thirty, with Yoko. I'd listen out for the slam of their black limousine door. I could always tell his walk. And I waited for that whistle.'

The night of 8 December was particularly balmy. After spending five hours in the studio John and Yoko returned, their car pulling up at 10.49 p.m. José, the doorman, left his sentry box to open their car door. John walked ahead of Yoko into the archway. A man's voice called out: 'Mr Lennon?' As John turned round his murderer shot five bullets from a .38 revolver into his back. Contrary to popular belief, John was not shot in his chest. The bullets caught his arm and, mostly, his back as he turned his head to face his murderer.

Horrifying, chaotic scenes followed. Yoko, hysterical, screamed for an ambulance. John staggered up the six steps to Jay Hastings' office, eventually falling on his left side on to the floor, moaning, 'I'm shot, I'm shot.' Hastings ripped his own jacket off and covered John with it; then he immediately pressed an alarm button connected directly to the police precinct. Within two minutes a police car had arrived. They decided there was no time to wait for an ambulance. Jay Hastings helped the police carry John to their car which sped to Roosevelt Hospital. There doctors tried instant heart massage but to no avail. John died from a massive loss of blood.

At the Dakota the cassette recorder and tape which John was carrying when he fell were slowly picked up. Yoko later took possession of his spectacles. The music in his hand, destined for their next album, was Yoko's 'Walking On Thin Ice'. Back home from the hospital Yoko composed herself enough to issue a simple statement to a shattered world: 'John loved and prayed for the human race. Please do the same for him.'

As the news of his murder broke, the world's airwaves were filled with his music. Tragically, incredibly, the moment of his death was also the time he came alive in the minds of millions. He was guaranteed immortality on a scale that neither he, nor the world's ageing Beatles fans, would ever comprehend. Not since the murder of President John F. Kennedy in 1963 had the world been so enraged, stunned, and simply hurt by an assassination. Lennon's murder transcended that of even a major statesman because John was so much closer to his public. For one awful moment, a world that didn't care was brought together, and in its grief remembered *how* to care. As shock turned to anger, as statesmen paid their tributes to his talent and human qualities, as the Dakota flag hung at half mast in his honour, the bitter irony sank in: the rebel who had finally found tranquillity in his life and who had preached peace and love, offered hope, inspired millions with his imagination, self-deprecating wit, compassion, and new example of family commitment, had died by the gun.

John was cremated at Hartsdale Crematorium, New York State. Millions mourned him, often with celebrations of his music which eclipsed the desire for revenge. Tributes poured in from around the world as people went on pilgrimages: to Menlove Avenue; to Liverpool College of Art; to Mathew Street, once the home of the Cavern; to New York's Central Park, where Yoko's request for a world-wide ten-minute silence was marked by 400,000 people assembling opposite John's home, heads bowed; and to Hamburg, where Astrid Kirchherr still remembers the terrible depression. 'The city seemed to close for days,' she says. Millions mourned the loss of their adolescence, for John had supplied the soundtrack to it. At a time when we could expect no more from rock 'n' roll, its voice as a form of youthful rebellion long gone and the battle for teenage assertiveness won, John had survived with a rare dignity. He had made the transition so few manage, from young rocker to artist and in forty years he had always refused to be bought. When he outgrew the Beatles he stayed true to himself. The world mourned the loss of his arrogance, his humour, his warmth, his frailties, and, above all, his humanity.

Within two hours of the shooting Elliot Mintz was on American Airlines Flight 10 from Los Angeles to New York. His mother had phoned from there to say she had heard a radio bulletin that John had been shot. Mintz's car radio was not working; as he drove to Los Angeles airport he hoped and believed that Lennon had survived. 'Just after take-off, I was sitting alone when the cockpit door opened. A stewardess appeared with tears streaming down her face. A lady asked her what was the matter. "John Lennon is dead," I overheard her say.' For the five-hour flight, Elliot remained in his seat in the darkened cabin in a state of shock. He went direct to the Dakota to be with Yoko.

'It was about six in the morning when I arrived. The police had not disturbed the spot where it happened. The image of the broken glass and the chalk marks and John's blood on the cement will haunt me for ever.

'I stood by the door to the old bedroom. For a long time I just listened to Yoko crying before I knocked.'

'It's me,' Mintz whispered. 'I'll be right here if you need me.' He stayed for the next two months, answering phones, sorting mail, meeting reporters, co-ordinating security, following up calls from psychics and psychotics and generally supporting Yoko and Sean. Later he was asked to inventory all John's precious possessions, noting the many photographs which Aunt Mimi had posted to her surrogate son months before.

'No one ever gets over a tragedy of this magnitude,' says Mintz. 'You just learn to readjust, to cope, to deal with a different reality. Yoko and Sean have been an inspiration to me. They are now the keepers of the wishing well. Her optimism and sense of dignity prevail. John and Yoko represent a prototype for couples of the future. Their love and honesty and conviction are now part of everyone whom they touched. He was very special.'

On the streets of
Manhattan, a few days
before the murder.
John is wearing his Quarry
Bank High School tie

On 10 December 1980 Yoko, who had the appalling job of breaking the news to five-year-old Sean, issued the following statement from the Dakota:

> I told Sean what happened. I showed him the picture of his father on the cover of the paper and explained the situation. I took Sean to the spot where John lay after he was shot. Sean wanted to know why the person shot John if he liked John. I explained that he was probably a confused person. Sean said we should find out if he was confused or if he really had meant to kill John. I said that was up to the court. He asked what court – a tennis court or a basketball court? That's how Sean used to talk with his father. They were buddies. John would have been proud of Sean if he had heard this. Sean cried later. He also said, 'Now Daddy is part of God. I guess when you die you become much more bigger because you're part of everything.'
>
> I don't have much more to add to Sean's statement. The silent vigil will take place December 14th at 2 p.m. for ten minutes.
>
> Our thoughts will be with you.
>
> Love, Yoko and Sean

None of the public responses were as simple and eloquent as those of the hundreds of fans who stood vigil for days outside the Dakota, with banners bearing quickly scrawled slogans like: 'Strawberry Fields Forever, John', 'We'll never forget him', and, movingly, 'Christmas In Heaven'.

Upstairs in her bedroom as the fans stayed there playing transistors with a non-stop, twenty-four-hour soundtrack of John's music, Yoko could scarcely stand the pressure. 'It began,' she recalls, 'on the night of the murder. As it wore on, throughout the week, it nearly drove me crazy. All day and all night, the music . . . after what had just happened, it was unbearable.' She valued the fans' touching letters, which still arrive every day.

Such spontaneous, heartfelt emotion came through a love of a man, his music and what he represented. For, although John shunned the role of leader, he was, despite his reluctance, the inspiration for a generation's ideals. He never wanted to be a god, certainly not a dead martyr. 'Make your own dreams and do things for yourself. I can't wake you up. You wake *you* up,' he said. All he had done, he implied, was leave a few signposts; but he positively rejected any theory that he was saying 'Follow me, this is how it is.' Gandhi and Martin Luther King were great examples, he pointed out, of non-violent people who had died violently. He never understood that, he said. Unnervingly, one of the last sentences he said to a friend, was: 'What does it mean that when you're such a pacifist you get shot?'

In the weeks that followed, as the world's media were flooded with discussions of John's life and music, Yoko went into seclusion in the Dakota. She decided to cut off all her hair as a mark of respect for her husband. She closed off the bedroom they used to sleep in. Out of all the hundreds of gifts John had showered on her in the red velvet boxes he knew she loved, she took only two items to keep by her side – ironically they were *her* final gifts to *him*: the inscribed gold watch she had given him a month before he died, and a tiny American flag pin made up of red rubies, white diamonds, and blue sapphires. Yoko is rarely seen without the diamond necklace which John bought at Tiffany's and which she wears in the picture on the sleeve of *Double Fantasy*.

Inside the apartment Yoko instructed staff that every picture and painting on all the walls was to be left, for ever, precisely as John had wanted. There were, interestingly, no Beatles pictures or gold records hanging there. Significantly, the only one of John as a musician was the original picture of the twenty-year-old Lennon standing in a Hamburg doorway, every inch a rock 'n' roller.

'I think,' said Yoko when I met her a few months after the murder, 'that in many ways he was a simple Liverpool man right to the end. He was a chameleon, a bit of a chauvinist, but so human. In our fourteen years together he never stopped trying to improve himself *from within*. We were best friends but also competitive artists. To me, he is still alive. Death alone doesn't extinguish a flame and a spirit like John.'

John and Yoko probably saw more of each other in fourteen years than most married couples see of each other in a lifetime. It was hardly surprising that, in the wake of his assassination, Yoko became severely depressed alone in her bedroom. Staring out of the window, she ate only mushrooms and chocolate cake for nearly three months and smoked her Nat Sherman brown cigarettes until she felt that there was a clear choice facing her: she could either return to work, managing the family business as before or she could go back to making a record. She finally decided on both: John would have liked that.

Her first decision astonished those who did not know her. She wanted to stay at the Dakota. John was part of the place. She felt him over her shoulder. And when she finally emerged, walking every day past the very spot where John was shot, she felt the inner strength of his invisible presence.

'I have strong emotions of sorrow, and hate, and resentment, but where do you put them?' she said to me. Gaunt, nervous of her first newspaper interview since the murder, she chainsmoked throughout and had carefully checked all the signs, astrologically, beforehand to ensure that we should talk. (The interviews, which took place at the Dakota, appeared in London's *Daily Mirror* on 12 and 13 August and subsequently in dozens of international publications.)

Scorned and vilified no more, Yoko Ono as a widow ironically gained a respect she would have preferred not to have earned. The world which had once jeered suddenly applauded her dignity. 'Do you know how that feels? For ten years I was the devil,' she said to me. 'Now suddenly I'm an angel. Did the world have to lose John for people to change their opinion of me? It's unreal. If it brought John back, I'd rather remain hated.'

To regain her sanity and to make some statements, Yoko went back to the recording studio. When she went into the Hit Factory to record *Season Of Glass* with many of the musicians who had worked on *Double Fantasy*, she conquered a voice choking with emotion and sang her compositions charged with grief and anger. 'Making the record was definitely a therapy, the only way I could survive,' she says. 'I felt John with me all the time in the studio.' Her songs 'Goodbye Sadness' with the sound of four gunshots and the ambulance siren on 'No, No, No', are stunningly evocative of the murder. And at one point she shouted on the record, 'You *bastards*. We had *everything*!' Yoko ran into a major controversy on her choice of photograph for the sleeve which showed John's blood-covered spectacles, which she had retrieved on the night of the murder. 'Tasteless,' said her critics.

Yoko disagreed: 'John would have approved and I will explain why. I wanted the whole world to be reminded of what happened. People are offended by the glasses and the blood? The glasses are a tiny part of what happened. If people can't stomach the glasses, I'm sorry. There was a dead body. There was blood. His whole body was bloody. There was a load of blood all over the floor. That's the reality. I want people to face up to what happened. He did not commit suicide. He was *killed*. People are offended by the glasses and the blood? John had to stomach a lot more.'

John's assassin, Mark David Chapman, was twenty-five. He came originally from Decatur, Georgia, but had been living in Honolulu with his wife Gloria. He had worked as a hospital security guard

For years, Sean had been asking his parents to take him to Liverpool. In January 1984, Yoko took him on a tour of the city to all his father's old haunts . . . the Art College, the Cavern Mecca where they pinned a Cavern badge on Sean, and finally to John's childhood home in Woolton. This picture, taken outside the house, shows Yoko and Sean flanked by their ever-present bodyguards

and a printer but had left, alone, for New York several days before 8 December 1980. He stayed at the Olcott Hotel on West 72nd Street, just 200 yards from the scene of the murder. That day, clutching a copy of John and Yoko's *Double Fantasy* album, he loitered outside the Dakota building and succeeded in getting John's autograph. Nobody had any reason to regard the fans who often stood outside the Dakota as a threat.

In a fifteen-minute hearing on 9 December in a packed Manhattan Criminal Court, the district attorney said: 'This man came to New York with a specific purpose. He has done it. Chapman deliberately premeditated the execution of John Lennon in a cool, calm, rational and intelligent manner.' Chapman's lawyer said the murderer had told him he had always been a great fan of Lennon: 'He told me he had admired him very much ever since he was ten years old. My impression was of a very confused character.'

Chapman was subsequently sentenced to between twenty years and life imprisonment, first going to Rikers Jail and later to the top-security Attica State Prison, New York, as convict number 81A3860. There, he became arguably the most closely guarded man in the world, because of the distinct possibility of reprisals from other prisoners irate about having Lennon's murderer near them. Letters of hatred and requests from the world's media for interviews to discover his reasons for murdering John Lennon continued to arrive every day; not one, however, could equal the spine-chilling letter Chapman wrote to Yoko in 1982, seeking her approval in writing his story and giving the proceeds of any such book to charity. The letter, the content, and its signature which Yoko could scarcely absorb, still less reply to, brought back floods of tears. 'I was numbed by it,' she says. Chapman said he had written to her previously to apologize for what he had done. If Yoko objected to his book idea he would not do it, he added. This letter went unanswered but Yoko kept it 'for historical reasons, for future generations'.

A quarter of a million letters of sympathy arrived by the sackload at the Dakota within two months of John's murder. The *Double Fantasy* album sold 7 million copies around the world within seven months. John's friend, the singer–songwriter Harry Nilsson, involved himself in a campaign to ban handguns in America.

Yoko, warily opening John's drawers and books in the months after his death, found notes from him to her which she had never seen. 'Mother, don't forget the clocks are one hour fast ...

Julian Lennon clasps the shoulders of Sean Lennon at the dedication ceremony for 'Strawberry Fields', a garden in New York's Central Park, in March 1984; on the far left is long-time John Lennon supporter Mayor Ed Koch

Daddy.' Others, more affectionate, brought her to tears. 'Don't forget the kettle's on.' 'Mother, I'll be back in an hour.' She cries often, and speaks of John in the present tense: 'His spirit is in the world for ever,' she declares.

It was three years before she could bear to listen to the songs he planned for their follow-up album to *Double Fantasy*. Finally, weeping openly when she re-discovered his aching love song to her, 'Grow Old With Me', she had a cassette recording of it encased in sweet-smelling, rare Bermudan cedarwood, a favourite aroma of John's. The music box, engraved 'Milk And Honey, Love Yoko and Sean, Xmas '83, N.U.C.', was sent to her friends one month before the final album, *Milk and Honey*, was released.

Back in England Aunt Mimi, suffering from a respiratory illness, sold Sandbanks in Dorset and went to live with her sister Anne near Liverpool. Heartbroken, she turned off the radio whenever John's voice came on. 'I shall never recover,' she says.

Liverpool was appallingly dilatory and mean in recognizing its four most famous sons. Not until 1982 was there any tangible civic recognition of the Beatles, when four roads were named after them (including John Lennon Drive). And when, in 1984, a statue was unveiled, and Beatle City and Cavern Walks established, it was through private enterprise and not civic pride.

In 1982, the twentieth anniversary year of the Beatles' first record release, the Performing Right Society in Britain launched its John Lennon Memorial Scholarship. This annual award supports postgraduate work incorporating recording techniques in the University of Surrey's department of music. John was a member of the Performing Right Society, an association of composers, authors, and music publishers, throughout his songwriting career. The scholarship was launched by two men instrumental in John's earliest work: George Martin and Dick James.

On a visit to Liverpool in 1984 with Sean, Yoko gave £10,000 for educational aid to students at Liverpool Polytechnic, once called the College of Art. She took Sean to the Pier Head, to all John's old haunts, to look at Menlove Avenue, and to meet an Aunt Mimi tearful with joy. 'Just like John,' said Mimi when she saw Sean.

John's will left half his wealth, calculated at the time of his death at more than $150 million and growing by more than $50,000 a day from songwriting and record royalties, to Yoko, with the other half held on trust for undisclosed beneficiaries. The will contained a provision that if any named beneficiary objected or took court action they were to receive nothing. Many of the beneficiaries would have been charities.

John and Yoko had launched the Spirit Foundation, a charitable organization which distributes money to all kinds of causes ranging from old people's homes to handicapped children. Their income was 'tithed' – 10 per cent of it was automatically deducted and covenanted to the foundation. In what turned out to be an appalling irony, a year before he was shot dead John had donated $1,000 to a campaign to help provide New York policemen with bullet-proof vests.

Yoko continues to be heavily involved, anonymously, with a great deal of charity work. In 1983, she decided to simplify her life. After selling the house in West Palm Beach and their farms she planned to give approximately £3 million to charities and orphanages around the world. These included the Salvation Army hostel in Liverpool's Strawberry Field, John's childhood inspiration.

In New York's Central Park a triangular-shaped piece of land was designated Strawberry Fields in John's honour. At the opening ceremony, performed by long-time John Lennon admirer, Mayor Ed Koch, on 21 March 1984, Yoko broke down. It was a project she had begun shortly after John died. Sixteen years earlier John and Yoko had planted acorns in the precincts of Coventry Cathedral. That acorn was now symbolically a tree, she said. As a mark of world love and sharing, which John cared about, she had written to heads of state throughout the world asking for a plant, rock or stone of their nation to be sent for Strawberry Fields in Central Park. 'This is the nicest tribute we could give to John,' says Yoko. It was, fittingly, the place they had sat down and talked after their last walk together. Julian Lennon, in New York recording his début album, attended the ceremony. On 20 March, the date of John and Yoko's wedding anniversary, Yoko presented Sean with a full collection of his parents' recorded work.

In a bittersweet evening, Sean chose 'Instant Karma!' as his first favourite. Yoko broke down again when 'Imagine' came on. They played record after record through the night, totally absorbed in the music of the man they loved.

John Lennon was not only a genius. He was also a man of profound commitment, total integrity and intensive activity: a glance at the sheer volume and pattern of his life's work confirms that. His honesty and wit, his vulnerability, his lack of pomposity, his unique spirit and romanticism endeared him to millions. The grief that followed his murder, and the celebrations of his life and work, spanned the world.

As a twentieth-century philosopher, he set an example of imagination and humanitarianism. Although he would hate to be deified, a light went out on 8 December 1980. But his music and his spirit shine on.

CHRONOLOGY
1967–1980

1966

26 Dec. John appears in Peter Cook and Dudley Moore's *Not Only . . . But Also* T.V. programme in a comedy sketch, telerecorded on 27 November. The 'granny glasses' from the *How I Won The War* film are still there and they stay with John, forming part of his new image.

1967

17 Feb. E.M.I. release a revolutionary new Beatles single – John's 'Strawberry Fields Forever' backed with Paul's 'Penny Lane'. Ironically it becomes their first record to fail to reach the coveted number one spot on some charts since 'Please Please Me', released four years earlier.

20 May The B.B.C. ban John's 'A Day In The Life' from the forthcoming Beatles L.P. because its lyrics might encourage drug-taking.

1 June *Sgt Pepper's Lonely Hearts Club Band*, the Beatles' most ambitious L.P. yet, is released.

25 June The Beatles appear before an estimated audience of 400 million people from twenty-four countries, singing 'All You Need Is Love' on the world-wide T.V. link-up show *Our World*.

24 Aug. Various Beatles with wives and relations, including John and Cynthia, attend a lecture on transcendental meditation by the Maharishi Mahesh Yogi at the Hilton Hotel, London.

25 Aug. The Beatles and their wives travel by train from Lon-

don's Euston Station to Bangor, North Wales to attend a weekend seminar on meditation by the Maharishi. John's wife Cynthia, after a frantic dash, misses the train by seconds. John's disappearance down the platform without her seems symbolic of the future of their unsteady marriage.

27 Aug. While the Beatles are away in Bangor, Brian Epstein is found dead in his flat at 24 Chapel Street, Belgravia, London S.W.1. The Beatles hurriedly return to London.

11 Sept. Shooting of the ill-fated *Magical Mystery Tour* T.V. film starts in Cornwall.

30 Sept. John and George appear with the Maharishi on *The Frost Programme* on I.T.V. with presenter David Frost.

11 Oct. John anonymously sponsors an exhibition at the Lisson Art Gallery, London N.W.8. entitled *Yoko Plus Me*. It runs until 14 November.

17 Oct. John, Paul, George, and Ringo attend a memorial service for Brian Epstein at the New London Synagogue, Abbey Road, London N.W.8.

18 Oct. The world première of *How I Won The War* in London.

20 Nov. The B.B.C. ensure that John's composition 'I Am The Walrus' receives no radio or T.V. exposure although they officially deny actually banning it.

4 Dec. A new Beatles venture, the Apple Boutique, opens in Baker Street, London N.W.1.

16 Dec. John, George, and the Maharishi attend a UNICEF gala in Paris.

26 Dec. The world première of *Magical Mystery Tour* on B.B.C. television. A critical disaster, it is the Beatles' first public failure.

1968

5 Jan. John and his father Fred meet at John's Weybridge home. John gives his blessing to his father's impending marriage to nineteen-year-old former Exeter University student, Pauline Jones. The couple announce that the wedding may have to wait until the bride is twenty-one years old as her mother refuses to give her consent. Instead they travel to Scotland, outside the English court jurisdiction, and marry there.

16 Feb. John and Cynthia, with George and his wife Pattie, fly to Rishikesh, India for an extensive course of

meditation under the Maharishi. Paul, with fiancée Jane Asher, and Ringo and his wife Maureen, follow on four days later.

12 April   John and George with their wives hurriedly leave Rishikesh two weeks earlier than expected. They feel that the Maharishi is not such a holy man after all. Paul, Jane, Ringo, and Maureen have already left.

15 May   John and Paul appear on the *Tonight* show on American television to announce the formation of Apple Corps. John also takes the opportunity to denounce the Maharishi publicly.

15 June   John and Yoko Ono plant two acorns outside Coventry Cathedral as part of the National Sculpture Exhibition. It is the couple's first 'event'.

18 June   John and Yoko attend the opening night of *In His Own Write* at London's National Theatre, a play adapted from John's two books by his friend, actor Victor Spinetti.

21 June   Apple Corps buys grandiose premises at 3 Savile Row, London W.1.

1 July   The opening of John's first art exhibition, *You Are Here*, dedicated to Yoko, at the Robert Fraser Gallery in Duke Street, London W.1. Prior to the opening John and Yoko release 365 helium-filled balloons over London.

17 July   World première of the Beatles' *Yellow Submarine* cartoon film in London.

31 July   The Apple Boutique closes after two days of stock clearing free of charge to the general public.

22 Aug.   Cynthia sues John for divorce on the grounds of adultery with Yoko Ono Cox.

18 Oct.   Police raid the flat at 34 Montagu Square, London W.1., owned by Ringo but the temporary home of John and Yoko. They discover 219 grains of cannabis resin. The couple are also charged with obstructing police in the execution of a search warrant.

19 Oct.   At Marylebone Magistrates' Court John and Yoko are remanded on bail until 28 November.

25 Oct.   John and Yoko announce they are expecting a baby in February 1969.

8 Nov.   Cynthia is granted a decree nisi in the Divorce Court because of John's adultery with Yoko. The petition is uncontested but it is announced that John has made

	'generous and proper provision' for his wife and child.
21 Nov.	Yoko has a miscarriage. John stays with her at Queen Charlotte's Maternity Hospital in Hammersmith, London W.6. in a spare bed. When that is no longer free he sleeps on the floor beside her.
28 Nov.	John pleads guilty to unauthorized possession of cannabis at Marylebone Magistrates' Court. He is fined £150 plus 20 guineas costs. Both John and Yoko are found not guilty of obstructing the police.
29 Nov.	*Unfinished Music No.1: Two Virgins*, John and Yoko's first avant-garde album together is released. Its content is completely overshadowed by the furore over the album cover, which shows the couple stark naked in full-frontal pose on the front cover with a rear view on the back cover.
10 Dec.	Kenwood, John's Weybridge home, is put up for sale.
11 Dec.	John and Yoko participate in the never-completed Rolling Stones T.V. special *Rock and Roll Circus* at Wembley T.V. studios.
18 Dec.	John and Yoko appear onstage in a large white bag at the Royal Albert Hall during *Alchemical Wedding*, the underground art movement's Christmas party.
23 Dec.	John and Yoko dress up as Father and Mother Christmas, handing out presents, at the Apple Christmas party at Savile Row.

1969

2 Jan.	Shooting of the disastrous *Let It Be* film commences at the cold Twickenham Film Studios.
3 Jan.	30,000 copies of John and Yoko's *Two Virgins* are confiscated in New Jersey on the grounds that the sleeve is pornographic.
18 Jan.	John tells Ray Coleman in an interview for *Disc and Music Echo*: 'Apple's losing money every week . . . if it carries on like this, all of us will be broke in the next six months.'
30 Jan.	The Beatles perform live on the roof of the Apple building in Savile Row. The event is captured on film for the *Let It Be* project.
2 Feb.	Yoko Ono is divorced from Anthony Cox in the Virgin Islands.
3 Feb.	An American, Allen Klein, is appointed to look after the Beatles' financial affairs at the insistence of John,

George, and Ringo. Paul opposes Klein's involvement.

2 Mar. John and Yoko appear in an avant-garde jazz concert at the Lady Mitchell Hall in Cambridge.

20 Mar. John and Yoko fly from Paris to Gibraltar where they stay for just seventy minutes. During that time they are married by registrar Cecil Wheeler in the British Consulate building. They then return to Paris. John comments: 'It was all very quick, quiet and British.'

24 Mar. John and Yoko lunch with Salvador Dali in Paris.

25–31 Mar. John and Yoko's first big 'event' – the Amsterdam bed-in for peace. For seven days the couple hold court in Room 902 of the Amsterdam Hilton and give literally hundreds of interviews and messages about peace.

31 Mar. John and Yoko fly from Amsterdam straight to Vienna for the world T.V. première of their film *Rape*, shown later that evening. The couple also hold a quick press conference at the Hotel Sacher to launch the film and appear completely encased in a white bag, their voices being the only clue to their identity.

1 April Back in London, John and Yoko appear on Thames Television's *Today* programme, inviting host Eamonn Andrews to join them in bed before the cameras.

21 April Bag Productions, John and Yoko's film and production company, is formed.

22 April In a formal ceremony before Señor Bueno de Mesquita, the Commissioner of Oaths, John changes his middle name from Winston to Ono. The ceremony is on the roof of the Apple building at 3 Savile Row, London W.1.

4 May John and Yoko buy Tittenhurst Park, a mansion in Sunningdale, Ascot, Berkshire. They move in during August.

8 May John, George, and Ringo sign a business management contract with Allen Klein. Paul refuses.

9 May *Unfinished Music No.2: Life With The Lions*, John and Yoko's second 'experimental' album, is released on the Zapple label, Apple's newly-formed avant-garde record label.

16 May John's application for a United States visa is rejected because of his drug conviction in November 1968. He planned to stage a New York bed-in.

24 May John and Yoko with Kyoko, Yoko's daughter from her

marriage to Anthony Cox, fly to the Bahamas to stage
their bed-in for peace at the Sheraton Oceanus Hotel.
They leave the island within twenty-four hours because
it is further from the United States than John had
believed and because the humid 86° temperature is not
conducive to seven days in bed.

25 May   The Lennons arrive in Toronto but are detained at the
airport for two and a half hours by the Canadian
Immigration authorities. They are eventually released
on their own recognizance. It is nearly midnight before
they are able to check into a downtown motel.

26 May   The Lennons and their entourage fly to Montreal and
announce their intention to hold a bed-in at the Queen
Elizabeth Hotel. John invites Canadian Prime Minister,
Pierre Trudeau, to join him and also to plant acorns for
peace. Says Trudeau: 'I don't know about his acorns,
but I'd like to see him if he's around. He's a good poet.'

26 May–   John and Yoko hold another seven-day bed-in in Room
2 June   1742 of the Queen Elizabeth Hotel.

30 May   The Australian Broadcasting Commission (A.B.C.) ban
the new Beatles single, 'The Ballad of John And Yoko'
on the grounds that it is blasphemous.

1 June   From their bed John and Yoko record 'Give Peace A
Chance'. They are assisted by a roomful of people
including the Smothers Brothers, Timmy Leary, the
Canadian Radha Krishna Temple, Derek Taylor,
Murray The K, and the local rabbi.

2 June   John and Yoko leave the hotel early in the afternoon
and quickly move on to Ottawa for a university conference on peace. Later that evening they fly back to
London.

1 July   After visiting John's aunt in Durness, Sutherland, Scotland, John, Yoko, Kyoko, and Julian, John's first child,
have a car accident in Golspie. No other vehicle is
involved. They are taken to the Lawson Memorial
Hospital where John receives seventeen stitches in a
facial wound, Yoko fourteen stitches and Kyoko four.
Julian suffers shock.

2 July   Cynthia travels to Scotland to see and retrieve Julian.

3 July   Still hospitalized after their car crash, John and Yoko
are unable to attend the press launch of the Plastic Ono
Band at Chelsea Town Hall, London S.W.1. In their
place stand perspex tubes with fitted microphones, tape

recorders and amplifiers.

4 July   'Give Peace A Chance', John's first solo single, credited to the Plastic Ono Band, is released.

6 July   John, Yoko and Kyoko fly back to London from the Golspie Hospital in a specially chartered helicopter. John tells the delighted Golspie local newspaper: 'If you're going to have a car crash try to arrange for it to happen in the Highlands. The hospital there was just great.'

10 Sept.   An evening of John and Yoko films at the New Cinema Club in the Institute of Contemporary Arts (I.C.A.) in London's Pall Mall. Those shown are *Self Portrait, Smile, Honeymoon, Two Virgins*, and *Rape*. An unidentified couple sit on stage throughout encased in a white sack though nobody is quite sure whether it is John and Yoko themselves. The audience reaction to the evening is filmed by an infra-red camera hidden out of view.

12 Sept.   At very short notice John and Yoko are asked to appear live at a Rock 'n' Roll Revival concert in Toronto, scheduled for the following day. John hurriedly gathers together Eric Clapton, Klaus Voormann and Alan White to join him and Yoko in forming a makeshift Plastic Ono Band.

13 Sept.   The Plastic Ono Band fly from Heathrow to Toronto, grabbing their only chance to rehearse on board the plane. Later that night they take the stage at the Varsity Stadium and perform 'Blue Suede Shoes', 'Money', 'Dizzy Miss Lizzy', 'Yer Blues', 'Give Peace A Chance', and a new Lennon composition, 'Cold Turkey', as well as two lengthy Yoko compositions, 'Don't Worry Kyoko' and 'John, John (Let's Hope For Peace)'.

25 Sept.   After months of protracted dealings in the City, John and Paul lose control of Northern Songs and thereby the full rights to all of their past – and a good deal of their future – compositions, to Lew Grade's A.T.V. Music.

Oct.   John invites his father to his house at Tittenhurst Park for what is to be their last meeting.

12 Oct.   Yoko loses a baby expected in December – her second miscarriage – at King's College Hospital, Denmark Hill, London S.E.5.

3 Nov.   An evening of John and Yoko films at Nash House,

	London S.W.1. under the collective title of *Something Else*. A second such evening is held a week later, on 10 November.
7 Nov.	Apple release John and Yoko's *Wedding Album*. The luxurious package contains not only a record but a copy of their marriage certificate, various pictures, two booklets, a poster, and a photograph of a slice of wedding cake.
13 Nov.	A group of hippies travel to Ireland to inspect a tiny uninhabited island, Dornish, off the coast of County Mayo. It is being offered to them rent free by John Lennon who bought it in 1966 at a cost of £1,500.
25 Nov.	(Announced 26 November) John returns his M.B.E. medal to Buckingham Palace 'in protest against Britain's involvement in the Nigeria–Biafra thing, against our support of America in Vietnam, and against 'Cold Turkey' slipping down the charts.' His letter is signed 'With love, John Lennon of Bag'.
27 Nov.	Buckingham Palace reports that Mr Barry Hearn, who returned his B.E.M. medal in 1965 when the Beatles were awarded the M.B.E.s, has asked for its return following John's return of his medal. Unfortunately Buckingham Palace cannot locate it.
1 Dec.	John and Yoko offer to buy a 32-foot caravan school for gypsy children to be situated on an unofficial site at Caddington, near Luton, Bedfordshire.
3 Dec.	John is asked to play the part of Christ in the Tim Rice/Andrew Lloyd Webber musical *Jesus Christ Superstar*, to be staged in St Paul's Cathedral.
4 Dec.	Rice and Lloyd Webber withdraw their offer, stating that the part would be better suited to an unknown actor.
9 Dec.	Apple announce that John and Yoko are to make a film about James Hanratty, the convicted and executed 'A6' murderer. It would reveal facts never before disclosed, they claim.
11 Dec.	John startles a crowd of 200 people outside the Kensington Odeon, there for the première of *The Magic Christian*, which starred Ringo, by slowly carrying past a banner reading 'Britain Murdered Hanratty'.
12 Dec.	*The Plastic Ono Band – Live Peace in Toronto 1969* is released by Apple.
14 Dec.	A white sack labelled 'A Silent Protest For James

Hanratty', with two anonymous wriggling occupants (John and Yoko?) is taken to Speakers' Corner, Marble Arch, London W.1., where Hanratty's father calls for a public inquiry into his son's hanging. A petition is later handed in to 10 Downing Street.

15 Dec. The Plastic Ono Supergroup – John augmented by Yoko, George Harrison, Eric Clapton, Billy Preston, Keith Moon, and many more – play at a *Peace for Christmas* concert at the Lyceum Ballroom in London in aid of UNICEF.

16 Dec. Huge posters and billboards go up in various locations in eleven cities world-wide reading: 'War Is Over! If You Want It. Happy Christmas from John and Yoko.'

23 Dec. Back in Canada for the third time in seven months John and Yoko have a fifty-one-minute private conference with Prime Minister, Pierre Trudeau in Ottawa. They later describe him as 'more beautiful than we expected' and add, 'If all politicians were like Trudeau there would be world peace.'

24 Dec. Back in England John and Yoko briefly join a sit-in and fast outside Rochester Cathedral in Kent to call for peace and spotlight world poverty.

29 Dec. John and Yoko fly to the small village of Aalborg in Denmark to holiday with Kyoko at the home of Anthony Cox and his new wife, Belinda.

30 Dec. I.T.V. transmit *Man Of The Decade* – a sixty-minute television programme split into three twenty-minute segments featuring John F. Kennedy, Mao Tse-Tung, and John Lennon. John's section includes a lengthy, newly recorded interview filmed at Tittenhurst Park.

1970

5 Jan. From Denmark John announces that all future proceeds from his songs and records will go towards promoting peace on earth.

15 Jan. An exhibition of fourteen John Lennon lithographs opens at the London Arts Gallery in New Bond Street, London W.1.

16 Jan. Detectives from Scotland Yard raid the exhibition and confiscate eight of the lithographs, which are deemed to be erotic and indecent.

19 Jan. It is reported that sales of *Bag One*, the collection of John's lithographs, have rocketed since the police raid.

Three hundred sets are for sale at £550 each.

20 Jan.   Still in Denmark John and Yoko have their hair crop-
            ped in the barn of Anthony Cox's north-Jutland retreat.

22 Jan.   All fourteen John Lennon lithographs go on show at the
            London Gallery in Detroit, U.S.A. – to no reaction.

27 Jan.   Back in England John writes, records, and mixes his
            next single, 'Instant Karma!', all in one day. Phil
            Spector produces. It is released just ten days later.

28 Jan.   The London exhibition of John's lithographs – with
            only six remaining on show – comes to its scheduled
            end at the London Arts Gallery.

 4 Feb.   John and Yoko swap their shorn hair, neatly tied up in
            plastic bags, for a pair of blood-stained Muhammad Ali
            boxing trunks in a ceremony with Michael X, the
            notorious Black Power leader, on the roof of X's 'Black
            House' in Holloway, north London. John and Yoko
            intend auctioning the trunks to raise money for peace.

11 Feb.   John pays the outstanding fines, totalling £1,344, im-
            posed on ninety-six people involved in protests against
            the South African rugby team who played a match in
            Scotland in December 1969.

12 Feb.   The Plastic Ono Band appear live in the studio on the
            B.B.C. programme *Top Of The Pops* singing 'Instant
            Karma!' (The entire show was tele-recorded on 11
            February.)

25 Feb.   A summons is served on the London Arts Gallery for
            showing John's lithographs – 'an indecent exhibition
            contrary to the Metropolitan Police Act, 1839'.

22 Mar.   In an interview with the French magazine *L'Express*
            John reveals that the Beatles smoked marijuana in the
            toilets at Buckingham Palace prior to their M.B.E.
            investiture in 1965. A Palace spokesman curtly replies:
            'Obviously when people come along to an investiture
            toilet facilities are available.'

29 Mar.   John sends a telephone message, broadcast to 8,000
            people at a Campaign for Nuclear Disarmament
            (C.N.D.) rally in Victoria Park, Bethnal Green, east
            London. During his message he reveals that Yoko is
            expecting a baby in October. Later in the year she
            miscarries again.

 1 April   Defence lawyers in the London Arts Gallery prosecu-
            tion trial compare John Lennon's works with those of
            Picasso.

10 April	Paul McCartney announces his resignation from the Beatles.
Late April	John and Yoko travel to Los Angeles to undergo four months of primal therapy under Dr Arthur Janov.
27 April	The lithographs court case is dismissed in favour of the London Arts Gallery and the exhibits are returned.
13 May	World première of the Beatles' *Let It Be* film in New York. None of the four attend.
1 Aug.	John's first wife Cynthia re-marries, to Italian hotelier Roberto Bassanini.
8 Dec.	John records a mammoth interview with *Rolling Stone* magazine.
11 Dec.	*Plastic Ono Band*, John's stark and brilliant first true 'solo' album is released.
31 Dec.	Paul begins proceedings in the London High Court to end the Beatles partnership.

1971

21 Jan.	*Rolling Stone* publish Part One of their extensive John Lennon interview. Part Two follows on 4 February.
3 Mar.	South African Broadcasting Corporation (S.A.B.C.) finally lift their ban on Beatles music implemented on 8 August 1966, although John Lennon compositions, vocals, and solo work remain blacklisted.
12 Mar.	Paul wins Beatles court case in London. A receiver, James Douglas Spooner, is appointed to look after the group's business and financial affairs, superseding Allen Klein.
23 April	In Palma, Majorca, John and Yoko are escorted by Spanish police to the magistrates' court and questioned over the alleged abduction of Yoko's daughter, Kyoko. Anthony Cox complained to the police after her disappearance from a playground.
3 May	John and Yoko pass through Heathrow Airport on their way from Trinidad back to Majorca to see the Justices there about the custody of Kyoko.
15 May	World première of two more Bag productions, *Apotheosis (Balloon)* and *Fly* at the Cannes Film Festival, attended by John and Yoko.
1 June	John, in possession of a nine-month U.S. visa issued on 31 May, jets to New York with Yoko in an attempt to locate and gain custody of Kyoko.
6 June	John and Yoko make a surprise appearance on stage

	with Frank Zappa and The Mothers of Invention at the Fillmore East in New York City.
July	John records his *Imagine* album over seven days at Tittenhurst Park and two days at the Record Plant in New York.
15 July	John and Yoko attend a promotion and book-signing session at Selfridges giant department store on Oxford Street, London, for the re-publication of Yoko's *Grapefruit*.
17 July	John and Yoko are interviewed on the B.B.C. *Parkinson* T.V. show. It turns out to be their last public appearance before leaving the U.K. for good.
19 July	John and Yoko hold a press conference at the Apple H.Q. in Savile Row to talk about *Grapefruit*. John says: 'In England I'm regarded as the guy who won the pools. She's [Yoko] regarded as the lucky Jap who married the guy who won the pools. In America we are both treated as artists.'
11–31 Aug.	A programme of five John and Yoko films are shown at *Art Spectrum*, a pot pourri exhibition of modern art held in the Great Hall at London's Alexandra Palace.
11 Aug.	More than 1,000 demonstrators, including John and Yoko, march past the Ulster Office in London. The demonstration is split between those supporting the *Oz* editors, who are being tried for publishing an obscene underground paper, and those against internment and the use of troops in Northern Ireland. John says: 'The two matters are integral and cannot be divided.'
12 Aug.	John and Yoko send £1,000 to the 'fighting fund' of the Upper Clyde [Scotland] Shipbuilding union who are refusing to stop work after being made redundant. The previous week they had sent roses.
3 Sept.	John and Yoko leave English soil for the last time and fly to New York.
9 Sept.	John on the *Dick Cavett* U.S. television show, says that the Beatles broke up 'because of Beatlemania and screaming crowds that drowned out the music, not because of Yoko Ono'.
8 Oct.	John's classic *Imagine* album is released.
9–27 Oct.	Yoko's art exhibition, with John as a guest artist, entitled *This Is Not Here*, takes place at the Everson Museum of Art in Syracuse, New York. A television special about the show is transmitted on 11 May 1972.

6 Nov.   After a day of large scale demonstrations in New York City, a benefit concert for the casualties of the Attica prison riots at the Apollo Theatre includes a surprise stage appearance by John and Yoko. (On 13 September, four days after prison camp guards had been taken hostage, 1,000 New York State troopers had invaded the prison under a pall of tear gas, killing twenty-eight prisoners and nine hostages in the process.)

11 Dec.   John and Yoko perform live at a benefit rally held in the Chrysler Arena, Ann Arbor, Michigan, for left-wing writer John Sinclair who had been jailed for ten years in 1969 for possession of two marijuana cigarettes. Fifty-five hours after the rally, on 13 December, Sinclair is freed on bail.

15 Dec.   John and Yoko attend a reception in honour of U Thant, the retiring United Nations Secretary-General.

18 Dec.   John and Yoko visit Houston, Texas to try to gain access to Kyoko.

22 Dec.   Houston, Texas. Anthony Cox is jailed for five days after refusing to allow Yoko to visit Kyoko.

1972

13 Jan.   John and Yoko appear on the U.S. television *David Frost Show*.

5 Feb.   John and Yoko, in temperatures well below freezing, are among 400 demonstrators outside the New York building of British Overseas Airways Corporation (B.O.A.C.), supporting union leaders' boycott of British exports as a protest against British policy in Northern Ireland.

14–18 Feb.   John and Yoko co-host *The Mike Douglas Show* on U.S. television in the absence of Douglas. Every night they feature interviews and music and on one show John plays live and jams with his teenage idol, Chuck Berry.

17 Feb.   John and Yoko's forty-minute colour film of the campaign for an inquiry into the Hanratty execution of 1961 is shown in the crypt of St Martin in the Fields, London.

29 Feb.   John and Yoko's U.S. visas expire. They are granted a routine fifteen-day extension in order to make a fresh application.

3 Mar.   Yoko is finally awarded custody of Kyoko but Anthony

Cox flees with the child and cannot be found.

6 Mar.   The temporary extensions of John and Yoko's visas are cancelled at the instigation of the Deputy Attorney-General and the couple's four-year battle against deportation begins.

16 Mar.   John and Yoko are served with deportation orders because of his 1968 London drugs conviction. Yoko says it will cause the couple to lose the custody of Kyoko, although both she and the child's father, Anthony Cox, are still in hiding.

22 April   John and Yoko address the crowd at the National Peace Rally in New York, protesting against the bombing of North Vietnam.

27 April   (Announced 29 April) John Lindsay, the Mayor of New York City, appeals in a letter to the Commissioner of Immigration and Naturalization in Washington, D.C., for John and Yoko's deportation order to be dropped. He says that the proceedings are 'a grave injustice' and adds that the real reason behind the order is not John's 1968 London drug conviction but because the couple 'speak out with strong and critical voices on the major issues of the day'.

11 May   John appears on *The Dick Cavett Show* and claims he is being followed by government agents and that his telephone is being tapped.

17 May   At a deportation hearing before the immigration authorities in New York, John says, 'I don't know if there is any mercy to plead for, but if so, I would like it for both us and our child.'

12 June   *Some Time In New York City*, John and Yoko's angry and heavily political album is released in America. Its anti-British content, together with copyright problems, prevents simultaneous U.K. release, which does not happen until 15 September.

2 July   John and Yoko's lawyers prepare a final brief, outlining the reasons why the couple want to stay in the U.S.A.

4 July   On American Independence Day, Lord Harlech, former British Ambassador to the U.S.A., writes to the Immigration and Naturalization Service in John's defence.

30 Aug.   The Madison Square Garden arena in New York City hosts two *One To One* concerts in aid of retarded children and adults. John and Yoko with the Elephants Memory band appear on the bill with Stevie Wonder,

Roberta Flack, and Sha Na Na. A total of $1½ million is raised including $60,000 donated by the Lennons. A T.V. special recorded at the concerts is aired on 14 December 1972.

6 Sept.   John and Yoko with Elephants Memory appear live on Jerry Lewis' Muscular Dystrophy telethon.

23 Dec.   *Imagine*, a film made to accompany the album of the same name, receives its belated world première on U.S. television.

1973

22 Jan.   Northern Songs and Maclen Music of London and New York sue John for over $1 million claiming that he, with Allen Klein's encouragement, intentionally and unlawfully violated a 1965 agreement that the companies would have exclusive rights to his compositions, whether written solo or in collaboration with someone else. Five songs are in dispute, all written with Yoko and with half-copyright claimed by Ono Music Ltd. Ironically Paul McCartney had recently gone through a similar ordeal when he tried to write with *his* wife, Linda.

23 Mar.   John is ordered to leave the U.S. within sixty days but Yoko is granted permission to remain as a permanent resident. The couple are not present at the hearing but issue a statement from the West Coast: 'Having just celebrated our fourth wedding anniversary, we are not prepared to sleep in separate beds. Peace and love, John and Yoko.'

24 Mar.   John formally appeals against the sixty-day deportation order.

31 Mar.   John, George, and Ringo's management contract with Allen Klein and his company ABCKO expires and is not renewed.

28 June   Allen Klein and ABCKO Industries sue John for a total of $508,000 over allegedly unrepaid loans.

9 Sept.   Tittenhurst Park, John and Yoko's Ascot home, is put up for sale.

18 Sept.   Ringo Starr buys Tittenhurst Park.

Oct.   John and Yoko separate after four and a half years of marriage. John flees to Los Angeles.

Oct.–Dec. John records a prospective album of rock 'n' roll standards with Phil Spector producing. The sessions eventually disintegrate into a drunken nightmare and Spector runs off with the tapes. After much wrangling John finally retrieves them in June 1974.

24 Oct.   John sues the U.S. government, demanding it admit or deny whether he and/or his lawyer, Leon Wildes, have been the subject of illegal wiretapping or surveillance by the F.B.I.

2 Nov.   John, George, and Ringo bring legal action in the High Court against Allen Klein and ABCKO (nicknamed grABCKO by John), claiming damages for alleged misrepresentation. Klein responds with a counter-action, suing for lost fees, commissions and expenses.

16 Nov.   John's *Mind Games* album is released.

11 Dec.   John sends £1,000 to the ailing British underground paper *IT* (formerly *International Times*). It eventually folds eight months later.

1974

1 Feb.   It is reported that the costs of all three appeals to stop the hanging of Michael X (real name Michael Abdul Malik) have been met by John. X was found guilty of murder in Trinidad. (After many further appeals and much deliberation Malik was eventually executed on 16 May 1975.)

Mar.–   Mayhem and drunkenness abound during the recording
May   of *Pussy Cats*, a Harry Nilsson album, produced by John at the Record Plant in Los Angeles. Similar scenes are rife at the Santa Monica home they share with Keith Moon and Ringo Starr.

13 Mar.   John is ejected from the Troubadour night club in West Hollywood after hurling insults and foul language at the Smothers Brothers during their act. Encouraged by his drinking pal Harry Nilsson, John tries to assault the Smothers' manager Ken Fritz, and Brenda Mary Perkins, a waitress-cum-'photographer' who tries to take a polaroid snapshot of John while he is being thrown out of the club.

27 Mar.   The Los Angeles District Attorney dismisses a citizen's complaint filed against John by Brenda Mary Perkins who claims to have been slapped during the fracas at the Troubadour.

17 July   John is again ordered to leave the U.S. within sixty days and again he lodges an appeal.

31 Aug.	John claims in court what people have come to realize over the previous few months: that the Nixon administration tried to have him deported not because of his 1968 London drug conviction but because they mistakenly believed that he was one of the organizers of a possible anti-war demonstration to be held at the Republican Convention in 1972.
4 Oct.	John's *Walls And Bridges* album is released.
8 Oct.	John meets music publishing and record company executive, Morris Levy, to discuss an out-of-court settlement over his copyright infringement of the Levy-owned Chuck Berry composition 'You Can't Catch Me' on 'Come Together', recorded for the Beatles' *Abbey Road* album in 1969.
1 Nov.	John requests a Federal judge the right to allow him to question immigration officials in connection with an alleged police vendetta led by former Attorney General, John N. Mitchell, which arose after John began supporting the Democrats in 1972.
16 Nov.	John's first 'solo' U.S. number one as 'Whatever Gets You Thru The Night' tops the *Billboard* singles chart. Elton John, who had played keyboards on the recording, had made John vow that if it reached number one he would have to join him on stage some time in the future.
28 Nov.	John keeps his promise and makes a surprise appearance onstage during Elton's Thanksgiving Day concert at the Madison Square Garden, New York, singing three songs.
27 Dec.	John, accompanied by his son Julian, and May Pang, spends the New Year holidays at Disneyland, Los Angeles.

1975

Jan.	John returns to New York and is re-united with Yoko at the Dakota. Yoko is soon pregnant.
9 Jan.	The partnership of The Beatles and Co. is finally dissolved in the London High Court.
Mid–Jan.	David Bowie, in New York to record his *Young Americans* album, invites John to play guitar on his version of the Lennon song 'Across The Universe'. While together they also write and record 'Fame'.
8 Feb.	American T.V. advertisements appear for the semi-legal

Lennon album *Roots*, available by mail order from Morris Levy's Adam VIII label.

21 Feb.   E.M.I./Capitol rush release John's *Rock 'n' Roll* album to counteract *Roots*. Litigation looms large again as Morris Levy sues for $42 million.

1 Mar.   John and Yoko make their first public appearance together since their reunion at the annual Grammy Awards ceremony in Los Angeles.

6 Mar.   John issues a statement that his eighteen-month separation from Yoko 'was not a success' and that he has returned to live with her in New York.

18 April   B.B.C. Television transmit their famous *Old Grey Whistle Test* interview with John.

13 June   U.S. Television airs a *Salute to Lew Grade* T.V. special in which John appears live, singing 'Imagine' and 'Slippin' and Slidin' ' backed by a 'two-faced' band – John's none too subtle dig at Grade. It was his last live appearance before an audience.

19 June   John sues former Attorney-General John N. Mitchell, and other U.S. law officers, for 'improper selective prosecution' arising from the deportation attempt.

13 July   John awarded a total of $144,700 by a New York court for lost royalties and damaged reputation over the *Roots* album.

23 Sept.   John's deportation order is temporarily halted on humanitarian grounds because of Yoko's pregnancy which has reached a critical stage.

7 Oct.   The New York State Supreme Court votes by a two-to-one decision to reverse the deportation order, instructing the Immigration Service to re-consider John's request for resident status. The chief judge adds: 'The court cannot condone selective deportation based upon secret political grounds.'

9 Oct.   At the age of forty-two and on John's thirty-fifth birthday, after three previous miscarriages, Yoko gives birth at the New York Hospital to their first child – a son – named Sean Taro Ono Lennon. 'I feel higher than the Empire State Building,' says John.

1976

5 Jan.   Mal Evans, the Beatles' former road manager, aide, gofer and confidant, is shot dead by police in Los Angeles.

6 Feb.	John's recording contract with E.M.I./Capitol expires and is not renewed. For the first time in nearly fifteen years John is not tied to a contract.
1 April	Freddy Lennon, John's father, dies in Brighton General Hospital, England, aged sixty-three.
April	During the Los Angeles recording of Ringo Starr's *Rotogravure* album John makes his last commerical studio appearance for four years, playing piano on his own composition 'Cookin' (In The Kitchen Of Love)'.
27 July	John's battle to remain in the U.S. is finally over when his application to become a permanent resident is formally approved at a special hearing in New York. He is awarded his precious Green Card, number A17–597–321, and proclaims: 'It's great to be legal again.' The judge, Ira Fieldsteel, informs John that he can apply for U.S. citizenship in 1981.
20 Sept.	New York promoter Sid Bernstein, the man behind the Beatles' American tours in the sixties, places a page advertisement in the *International Herald Tribune* asking the Beatles to perform a reunion concert for charity – possible revenue $230 million.
Oct.	John begins his 'retirement' and house-husband period, bringing up Sean at the Dakota.

1977

10 Jan.	All outstanding litigation between the Beatles/Apple Corps and Allen Klein/ABCKO is dropped after a scttlement costing Apple $5 million and ABCKO $800,000.
20 Jan.	John and Yoko attend Jimmy Carter's Presidential inauguration gala in Washington D.C.
June	The Lennon family travel to Japan for five months.

1978

4 Feb.	John and Yoko pay more than $178,000 for several plots of land in Delaware County, New York, for use as a vacation retreat and to raise Regis Holstein cows. It is also revealed that the couple are buying every apartment which becomes available at the Dakota Building.
16 June	John unsuccessfully tries to prevent the London *News of the World* newspaper publishing extracts from *A Twist of Lennon*, the book written by his first wife, Cynthia.

1979

27 May   John and Yoko place whole-page advertisements in the *New York Times*, the London *Sunday Times*, and a Tokyo newspaper, entitled: 'A Love Letter From John And Yoko. To People Who Ask Us What, When and Why.'

 9 Sept.   Sid Bernstein makes a public plea for three Beatles reunion concerts – to be held in Cairo, Jerusalem, and New York, in aid of the Vietnamese 'boat people'. Possible revenue, $500 million.

21 Sept.   Kurt Waldheim, Secretary-General of the United Nations, gets in on the act and also asks the Beatles to perform a reunion concert in aid of the 'boat people'.

15 Oct.   John and Yoko contribute $1,000 to a campaign to provide New York City policemen with bullet-proof vests.

31 Dec.   Bag Productions, John and Yoko's film and production company formed in 1969, is dissolved, along with several other late sixties ventures.

1980

28 Jan.   John and Yoko buy a beachside mansion in Palm Beach, Florida to add to their ever-growing list of property investments.

20 Mar.   John and Yoko celebrate their eleventh wedding anniversary in West Palm Beach, Florida. John gives Yoko a diamond heart and 500 fresh gardenias. Yoko gives John a vintage Rolls-Royce.

23 May   To gain independence and boost his confidence John goes alone to Cape Town, South Africa for a holiday.

July   John and a five-man crew sail to Bermuda on *Isis*, his 63-foot yacht. While there he begins to compose music again.

 2 July   A Holstein cow owned by John and Yoko is sold for a world record $265,000 to buyer Steve Potter at an auction in New York State Fairgrounds, Syracuse, New York.

 4 Aug.   John and Yoko enter the Hit Factory recording studios in Manhattan to record their first album for six years.

Sept.   Over three weeks John and Yoko record a mammoth interview for *Playboy* magazine.

22 Sept.   David Geffen, former top executive with Warner Brothers and Asylum Records, signs John and Yoko to

his newly formed independent record label, Geffen Records, and announces that their new album will be entitled *Double Fantasy*.

29 Sept.   The first publication of a 'comeback' interview – in *Newsweek*.

9 Oct.   Yoko celebrates John's fortieth birthday and Sean's fifth, by having a message of love sky-written over Manhattan.

17 Nov.   *Double Fantasy* is released.

5 Dec.   John records an interview for *Rolling Stone*.

6 Dec.   B.B.C. disc jockey Andy Peebles flies to New York to record a lengthy radio interview with John and Yoko.

8 Dec.   John gives an interview for R.K.O. Radio.

8 Dec.   (9 December in the U.K.) John Ono Lennon is shot dead.

DISCOGRAPHY
1967–1984

This list is based on British record releases. Songs either completely written or co-written by John Lennon are printed in capitals. But songs to which John contributed a few words, a line or a phrase – and there are a great many – are *not* ascribed to him.

SINGLES

February 1967	'Penny Lane'/'STRAWBERRY FIELDS FOREVER' *(The Beatles)**
July 1967	'ALL YOU NEED IS LOVE'/'BABY, YOU'RE A RICH MAN' *(The Beatles)*
November 1967	'Hello, Goodbye'/'I AM THE WALRUS' *(The Beatles)*
March 1968	'Lady Madonna'/'The Inner Light' *(The Beatles)*
August 1968	'Hey Jude'/'REVOLUTION' *(The Beatles)*
April 1969	'Get Back' *(The Beatles with Billy Preston)*/ 'DON'T LET ME DOWN' *(The Beatles)*
May 1969	'THE BALLAD OF JOHN AND YOKO'/'Old Brown Shoe' *(The Beatles)*
July 1969	'GIVE PEACE A CHANCE'/'Remember Love' *(Plastic Ono Band)*
October 1969	'COLD TURKEY'/'Don't Worry Kyoko (Mummy's Only Looking For Her Hand In The Snow)' *(Plastic Ono Band)*
October 1969	'Something'/'COME TOGETHER' *(The Beatles)**
February 1970	'INSTANT KARMA!'/'Who Has Seen The Wind?' *(Lennon/Ono with the Plastic Ono Band)*

March 1970	'Let It Be'/'YOU KNOW MY NAME (LOOK UP THE NUMBER)' *(The Beatles)*
March 1971	'POWER TO THE PEOPLE' *(John Lennon/Plastic Ono Band)*/'Open Your Box' *(Yoko Ono/Plastic Ono Band)*
November 1972	'HAPPY XMAS (WAR IS OVER)' *(John and Yoko/ The Plastic Ono Band with the Harlem Community Choir)*/'Listen, The Snow Is Falling' *(Yoko Ono and the Plastic Ono Band)*†
November 1973	'MIND GAMES'/'MEAT CITY' *(John Lennon)*
October 1974	'WHATEVER GETS YOU THRU THE NIGHT' *(John Lennon with the Plastic Ono Nuclear Band)*/ 'BEEF JERKY' *(John Lennon with the Plastic Ono Nuclear Band/Little Big Horns and Booker Table and the Maitre D's)*
January 1975	'#9 DREAM'/'WHAT YOU GOT' *(John Lennon)*
April 1975	'STAND BY ME'/'MOVE OVER MS.L' *(John Lennon)*
October 1975	'IMAGINE'/'WORKING CLASS HERO' *(John Lennon)*
October 1980	'(JUST LIKE) STARTING OVER' *(John Lennon)*/'Kiss Kiss Kiss' *(Yoko Ono)*
January 1981	'WOMAN' *(John Lennon)*/'Beautiful Boys' *(Yoko Ono)*
March 1981	'WATCHING THE WHEELS' *(John Lennon)*/'I'm Your Angel' *(Yoko Ono)*
November 1982	'LOVE'/'GIVE ME SOME TRUTH' *(John Lennon)*
January 1984	'NOBODY TOLD ME' *(John Lennon)*/' "O" Sanity' *(Yoko Ono)*
March 1984	'BORROWED TIME' *(John Lennon)*/'Your Hands' *(Yoko Ono)*
July 1984	'I'M STEPPING OUT' *(John Lennon)*/'Sleepless Night' *(Yoko Ono)*

* Denotes a double A-sided record
† Denotes released in the U.S.A. December 1971

ALBUMS

June 1967	**Sgt Pepper's Lonely Hearts Club Band**

'Sgt Pepper's Lonely Hearts Club Band'; 'WITH A LITTLE HELP FROM MY FRIENDS'; 'LUCY IN THE SKY WITH DIAMONDS'; 'Getting Better'; 'Fixing A Hole'; 'SHE'S LEAVING HOME'; 'BEING FOR THE BENEFIT OF MR KITE!'.

'Within You Without You'; 'When I'm Sixty-Four'; 'Lovely Rita'; 'GOOD MORNING GOOD MORNING'; 'Sgt Pepper's Lonely Hearts Club Band' *(Reprise)*; 'A DAY IN THE LIFE'.   *(The Beatles)*

November 1968   The Beatles

'Back in the U.S.S.R.'; 'DEAR PRUDENCE'; 'GLASS ONION'; 'Ob-La-Di, Ob-La-Da'; 'Wild Honey Pie'; 'THE CONTINUING STORY OF BUNGALOW BILL'; 'While My Guitar Gently Weeps'; 'HAPPINESS IS A WARM GUN'.

'Martha My Dear'; 'I'M SO TIRED'; 'Blackbird'; 'Piggies'; 'Rocky Raccoon'; 'Don't Pass Me By'; 'Why Don't We Do It In The Road'; 'I Will'; 'JULIA'.

'Birthday'; 'YER BLUES'; 'Mother Nature's Son'; 'EVERYBODY'S GOT SOMETHING TO HIDE EXCEPT ME AND MY MONKEY'; 'SEXY SADIE'; 'Helter Skelter'; 'Long Long Long'.

'REVOLUTION 1'; 'Honey Pie'; 'Savoy Truffle'; 'CRY BABY CRY'; 'REVOLUTION 9'; 'GOOD NIGHT'.   *(The Beatles)*

November 1968   Unfinished Music No.1: Two Virgins

'TWO VIRGINS NO.1'; 'TOGETHER'; 'TWO VIRGINS NO.2'; 'TWO VIR-GINS NO.3'; 'TWO VIRGINS NO.4'; 'TWO VIRGINS NO.5'; 'TWO VIRGINS NO.6'.

'HUSHABYE HUSHABYE'; 'TWO VIRGINS NO.7'; 'TWO VIRGINS NO.8'; 'TWO VIRGINS NO.9'; 'TWO VIRGINS NO.10'.
        (John Lennon and Yoko Ono)

January 1969   Yellow Submarine

'Yellow Submarine'; 'Only A Northern Song'; 'All Together Now'; 'HEY BULLDOG'; 'It's All Too Much'; 'ALL YOU NEED IS LOVE'.

(The remainder of the album comprises original film score by George Martin.)   *(The Beatles)*

May 1969   Unfinished Music No.2: Life With The Lions

'CAMBRIDGE 1969'.

'NO BED FOR BEATLE JOHN'; 'BABY'S HEARTBEAT'; 'TWO MINUTES SILENCE'; 'RADIO PLAY'.   *(John Lennon and Yoko Ono)*

September 1969   **Abbey Road**

'COME TOGETHER'; 'Something'; 'Maxwell's Silver Hammer'; 'Oh! Darling'; 'Octopus's Garden'; 'I WANT YOU (SHE'S SO HEAVY)'.

'Here Comes The Sun'; 'BECAUSE'; 'You Never Give Me Your Money'; 'SUN KING'; 'MEAN MR MUSTARD'; 'POLYTHENE PAM'; 'She Came In Through The Bathroom Window'; 'Golden Slumbers'; 'Carry That Weight'; 'The End'; 'Her Majesty'.   *(The Beatles)*

November 1969   **Wedding Album**

'JOHN AND YOKO'.
'AMSTERDAM'.   *(John and Yoko)*

December 1969   **Live Peace in Toronto 1969**

'Blue Suede Shoes'; 'Money (That's What I Want)'; 'Dizzy Miss Lizzy'; 'YER BLUES'; 'COLD TURKEY'; 'GIVE PEACE A CHANCE'.

'Don't Worry Kyoko (Mummy's Only Looking For Her Hand In The Snow)'; 'John John (Let's Hope For Peace)'.
                                          (The Plastic Ono Band)

May 1970   **Let It Be**

'Two Of Us'; 'DIG A PONY'; 'ACROSS THE UNIVERSE'; 'I Me Mine'; 'DIG IT'; 'Let It Be'; 'MAGGIE MAE'.

'I'VE GOT A FEELING'; 'ONE AFTER 909'; 'The Long and Winding Road'; 'For You Blue'; 'Get Back'.   *(The Beatles)*

December 1970   **John Lennon/Plastic Ono Band**

'MOTHER'; 'HOLD ON'; 'I FOUND OUT'; 'WORKING CLASS HERO'; 'ISOLATION'.

'REMEMBER'; 'LOVE'; 'WELL WELL WELL'; 'LOOK AT ME'; 'GOD'; 'MY MUMMY'S DEAD'.   *(John Lennon)*

October 1971   **Imagine**

'IMAGINE'; 'CRIPPLED INSIDE'; 'JEALOUS GUY'; 'IT'S SO HARD'; 'I DON'T WANT TO BE A SOLDIER'.

'GIVE ME SOME TRUTH'; 'OH MY LOVE'; 'HOW DO YOU SLEEP?'; 'HOW?'; 'OH YOKO!'
          (John Lennon/Plastic Ono Band [with the Flux Fiddlers])

September 1972   Some Time In New York City*

'WOMAN IS THE NIGGER OF THE WORLD'; 'Sisters, O Sisters'; 'ATTICA STATE'; 'Born In A Prison'; 'NEW YORK CITY'.

'SUNDAY BLOODY SUNDAY'; 'THE LUCK OF THE IRISH'; 'JOHN SINCLAIR'; 'ANGELA'; 'We're All Water'.
(John and Yoko/Plastic Ono Band with Elephants Memory and The Invisible Strings)

'COLD TURKEY'; 'Don't Worry Kyoko (Mummy's Only Looking For Her Hand In The Snow)'.
(John and Yoko/Plastic Ono Band with a cast of thousands)

'Well (Baby Please Don't Go)'; 'JAMRAG'; 'SCUMBAG'; 'AU'.
(John and Yoko/Plastic Ono Band with Frank Zappa and the Mothers of Invention)

November 1973   Mind Games

'MIND GAMES'; 'TIGHT A$'; 'AISUMASEN (I'M SORRY)'; 'ONE DAY (AT A TIME)'; 'BRING ON THE LUCIE (FREDA PEOPLE)'; 'NUTOPIAN INTERNATIONAL ANTHEM'.

'INTUITION'; 'OUT THE BLUE'; 'ONLY PEOPLE'; 'I KNOW (I KNOW)'; 'YOU ARE HERE'; 'MEAT CITY'.   *(John Lennon)*

October 1974   Walls And Bridges

'GOING DOWN ON LOVE'; 'WHATEVER GETS YOU THRU THE NIGHT'; 'OLD DIRT ROAD'; 'WHAT YOU GOT'; 'BLESS YOU'; 'SCARED'.

'#9 DREAM'; 'SURPRISE, SURPRISE (SWEET BIRD OF PARADOX)'; 'STEEL AND GLASS'; 'BEEF JERKY'; 'NOBODY LOVES YOU (WHEN YOU'RE DOWN AND OUT)'; 'Ya Ya'.   *(John Lennon)*

February 1975   Rock 'n' Roll

'Be-Bop-A-Lula'; 'Stand By Me'; 'Rip It Up/Ready Teddy'; 'You Can't Catch Me'; 'Ain't That A Shame'; 'Do You Want To Dance'; 'Sweet Little Sixteen'.

'Slippin' and Slidin''; 'Peggy Sue'; 'Bring It On Home To Me/Send Me Some Lovin''; 'Bony Moronie'; 'Ya Ya'; 'Just Because'.
(John Lennon)

October 1975   Shaved Fish

'GIVE PEACE A CHANCE'; 'COLD TURKEY'; 'INSTANT KARMA!'; 'POWER

TO THE PEOPLE'; 'MOTHER'; 'WOMAN IS THE NIGGER OF THE WORLD'.

'IMAGINE'; 'WHATEVER GETS YOU THRU THE NIGHT'; 'MIND GAMES'; '#9 DREAM'; 'HAPPY XMAS (WAR IS OVER)'; 'GIVE PEACE A CHANCE (live reprise)'.   *(John Lennon/Plastic Ono Band)*

November 1980   Double Fantasy

'(JUST LIKE) STARTING OVER'; 'Kiss Kiss Kiss'; 'CLEANUP TIME'; 'Give Me Something'; 'I'M LOSING YOU'; 'I'm Moving On'; 'BEAUTIFUL BOY (DARLING BOY)'.

'WATCHING THE WHEELS'; 'I'm Your Angel'; 'WOMAN'; 'Beautiful Boys'; 'DEAR YOKO'; 'Every Man Has A Woman Who Loves Him'; 'Hard Times Are Over'.   *(John Lennon and Yoko Ono)*

November 1982 The John Lennon Collection

'GIVE PEACE A CHANCE'; 'INSTANT KARMA!'; 'POWER TO THE PEOPLE'; 'WHATEVER GETS YOU THRU THE NIGHT'; '#9 DREAM'; 'MIND GAMES'; 'LOVE'; 'HAPPY XMAS (WAR IS OVER)'.

'IMAGINE'; 'JEALOUS GUY'; 'Stand By Me'; '(JUST LIKE) STARTING OVER'; 'WOMAN'; 'I'M LOSING YOU'; 'BEAUTIFUL BOY (DARLING BOY)'; 'WATCHING THE WHEELS'; 'DEAR YOKO'.   *(John Lennon)*

December 1983   Heart Play – Unfinished Dialogue

(Conversation. Tracks not banded.) *(John Lennon and Yoko Ono)*

January 1984   Milk And Honey

'I'M STEPPING OUT'; 'Sleepless Night'; 'I DON'T WANNA FACE IT'; 'Don't Be Scared'; 'NOBODY TOLD ME'; ' "O" Sanity'.

'BORROWED TIME'; 'Your Hands'; '(FORGIVE ME) MY LITTLE FLOWER PRINCESS'; 'Let Me Count The Ways'; 'GROW OLD WITH ME'; 'You're The One'.   *(John Lennon and Yoko Ono)*

MISCELLANEOUS

December 1967 **Magical Mystery Tour** (E.P.)

'Magical Mystery Tour'; 'Your Mother Should Know'/'I AM THE WALRUS'.

'The Fool On The Hill'; 'FLYING'/'Blue Jay Way'.　　　*(The Beatles)*

December 1969　　　**No One's Gonna Change Our World** (L.P.)

(Album using various artists. Contains early version of 'ACROSS THE UNIVERSE').

July 1971　　　　　**Elastic Oz Band** (single)

(B-side, 'DO THE OZ', John Lennon/Plastic Ono Band under a pseudonym)

March 1981　　**Elton John/John Lennon** (single)

'I Saw Her Standing There'/'WHATEVER GETS YOU THRU THE NIGHT'; 'LUCY IN THE SKY WITH DIAMONDS'.

(Note: 'I Saw Her Standing There' was also released previously as the B-side of Elton John's 'Philadelphia Freedom' in February 1975.)
(Elton John Band featuring John Lennon and the Muscle Shoals Horns)

* Denotes released in the U.S.A. June 1972

Songs written or co-written by John Lennon, not commercially recorded by him but instead 'given' to other artists.

'THE BALLAD OF NEW YORK CITY' – David Peel and the Lower East Side, 1972
'COOKIN' (IN THE KITCHEN OF LOVE)' – Ringo Starr, 1976
'FAME' – David Bowie, 1975
'GOD SAVE US' – Bill Elliot and the Elastic Oz Band, 1971
'I'M THE GREATEST' – Ringo Starr, 1973
'(IT'S ALL DA-DA DOWN TO) GOODNIGHT VIENNA' – Ringo Starr, 1974
'MUCHO MUNGO' – Harry Nilsson, 1974
'ROCK AND ROLL PEOPLE' – Johnny Winter, 1974

Guest Appearances

John Lennon appeared many times as a guest on other artists' recordings. A selection of titles on which John had particular influence is given below.

David Bowie: 'ACROSS THE UNIVERSE' and 'FAME', 1975
Elephants Memory: *Elephants Memory*, 1972
Elton John: 'LUCY IN THE SKY WITH DIAMONDS' and 'ONE DAY (AT A TIME)', 1974
Harry Nilsson: *Pussy Cats*, 1974
Yoko Ono: All albums pre-1981 – *Yoko Ono/Plastic Ono Band*, 1970; *Fly*, 1971; *Approximately Infinite Universe*, 1973; *Feeling The Space*, 1973. All singles, including 'Walking On Thin Ice', 1981, which John was producing on the night of his murder.
David Peel and the Lower East Side: *The Pope Smokes Dope*, 1972

JOHN LENNON'S CLASSIC SONG LYRICS 1967–1980

Strawberry Fields Forever

Let me take you down
'cos I'm going to Strawberry Fields
Nothing is real
And nothing to get hungabout
Strawberry Fields forever
Living is easy with eyes closed
Misunderstanding all you see
It's getting hard to be someone
But it all works out
It doesn't matter much to me
Let me take you down
'cos I'm going to Strawberry Fields
Nothing is real
And nothing to get hungabout
Strawberry Fields forever
No one, I think, is in my tree
I mean, it must be high or low
That is you can't, you know, tune in
But it's alright
That is, I think it's not too bad
Let me take you down
'cos I'm going to Strawberry Fields
Nothing is real
And nothing to get hungabout
Strawberry Fields forever

Always, no, sometimes, think it's me
But, you know, I know when it's a dream
I think, er, no, I mean, er, yes
But it's all wrong
That is, I think I disagree
Let me take you down
'cos I'm going to Strawberry Fields
Nothing is real
And nothing to get hungabout
Strawberry Fields forever
Strawberry Fields forever
Strawberry Fields forever.

Lucy In The Sky With Diamonds

Picture yourself in a boat on a river
With tangerine trees and marmalade skies
Somebody calls you, you answer quite slowly
A girl with kaleidoscope eyes
Cellophane flowers of yellow and green
Towering over your head
Look for the girl with the sun in her eyes
And she's gone.
Lucy in the sky with diamonds
Lucy in the sky with diamonds
Lucy in the sky with diamonds
Follow her down to a bridge by a fountain
Where rocking-horse people eat marshmallow pies
Everyone smiles as you drift past the flowers
That grow so incredibly high
Newspaper taxis appear on the shore
Waiting to take you away
Climb in the back with your head in the clouds
And you're gone.
Lucy in the sky with diamonds
Lucy in the sky with diamonds
Lucy in the sky with diamonds
Picture yourself on a train in a station
With plasticine porters with looking-glass ties
Suddenly someone is there at the turnstile
The girl with kaleidoscope eyes
Lucy in the sky with diamonds

Lucy in the sky with diamonds
Lucy in the sky with diamonds
Lucy in the sky with diamonds
Lucy in the sky with diamonds
Lucy in the sky with diamonds
Lucy in the sky with diamonds
Lucy in the sky with diamonds
Lucy in the sky with diamonds.

A Day In The Life

I read the news today, oh boy
About a lucky man who made the grade
And though the news was rather sad
Well I just had to laugh
I saw the photograph
He blew his mind out in a car
He didn't notice that the lights had changed
A crowd of people stood and stared
They'd seen his face before
Nobody was really sure if he was from the House of Lords
I saw a film today, oh boy
The English army had just won the war
A crowd of people turned away
But I just had to look
Having read the book
I'd love to turn you on.
Woke up, fell out of bed
Dragged a comb across my head
Found my way downstairs and drank a cup
And looking up I noticed I was late
Found my coat and grabbed my hat
Made the bus in seconds flat
Found my way upstairs and had a smoke
And somebody spoke and I went into a dream.
I read the news today, oh boy
Four thousand holes in Blackburn, Lancashire
And though the holes were rather small
They had to count them all
Now they know how many holes it takes to fill the Albert
 Hall
I'd love to turn you on.

Across The Universe

Words are flowing out like endless rain into a paper cup
They slither wildly as they slip away across the universe
Pools of sorrow, waves of joy
Are drifting through my opened mind
Possessing and caressing me
Jai Guru Deva OM
Nothing's gonna change my world
Nothing's gonna change my world
Nothing's gonna change my world
Nothing's gonna change my world
Images of broken light which dance before me like a million eyes
They call me on and on across the universe
Thoughts meander like a restless wind inside a letter-box
They tumble blindly as they make their way across the universe
Jai Guru Deva OM
Nothing's gonna change my world
Nothing's gonna change my world
Nothing's gonna change my world
Nothing's gonna change my world
Sounds of laughter, shades of love
Are ringing through my opened ears
Inciting and inviting me
Limitless, undying love which shines around me like a million suns
It calls me on and on across the universe
Jai Guru Deva OM
Nothing's gonna change my world
Nothing's gonna change my world
Nothing's gonna change my world
Nothing's gonna change my world
Jai Guru Deva, Jai Guru Deva, Jai Guru Deva
Jai Guru Deva, Jai Guru Deva, Jai Guru Deva.

Revolution

You say you wanna revolution
Well, you know we all wanna change the world
You tell me that it's evolution
Well, you know we all wanna change the world
But when you talk about destruction
Don't you know that you can count me out?
Don't you know it's gonna be alright, alright, alright?

You say you got a real solution
Well, you know we'd all love to see the plan
You ask me for a contribution
Well, you know we're all doing what we can
But if you want money for people with minds that hate
All I can tell you is brother, you have to wait.
Don't you know it's gonna be alright, alright, alright?
You say you'll change the constitution
Well, you know we all want to change your head
You tell me it's the institution
Well, you know you better free your mind instead
But if you go carrying pictures of Chairman Mao
You ain't gonna make it with anyone anyhow.
Don't you know it's gonna be alright, alright, alright?
Alright, alright, alright, alright
Alright, alright, alright – alright!

Glass Onion

I told you about Strawberry Fields
You know, the place where nothing is real
Well here's another place you can go
Where everything flows
Looking through the bent-backed tulips
To see how the other half live
Looking through a glass onion
I told you about the walrus and me – man
You know that we're as close as can be – man
Well here's another clue for you all:
The walrus was Paul
Standing on the Cast Iron Shore – yeah
Lady Madonna trying to make ends meet – yeah
Looking through a glass onion
Oh yeah, oh yeah, oh yeah!
Looking through a glass onion
I told you about the fool on the hill
I tell you man, he's living there still
Well here's another place you can be
Listen to me!
Fixing a hole in the ocean
Trying to make a dovetail joint – yeah
Looking through a glass onion.

Julia

Half of what I say is meaningless
But I say it just to reach you, Julia
Julia, Julia, oceanchild, calls me
So I sing a song of love, Julia
Julia, seashell eyes, windy smile, calls me
So I sing a song of love, Julia
Her hair of floating sky is shimmering, glimmering in the sun
Julia, Julia, morning moon, touch me
So I sing a song of love, Julia
When I cannot sing my heart
I can only speak my mind, Julia
Julia, sleeping sand, silent cloud, touch me
So I sing a song of love, Julia
Hmm hmm hmm calls me
So I sing a song of love for Julia
Julia, Julia.

The Ballad Of John And Yoko

Standing in the dock at Southampton
Trying to get to Holland or France
The man in the mac said you've gotta go back
You know they didn't even give us a chance
Christ! You know it ain't easy
You know how hard it can be
The way things are going
They're gonna crucify me
Finally made the plane into Paris
Honeymooning down by the Seine
Peter Brown called to say, you can make it OK
You can get married in Gibraltar, near Spain
Christ! You know it ain't easy
You know how hard it can be
The way things are going
They're gonna crucify me
Drove from Paris to the Amsterdam Hilton
Talking in our beds for a week
The news people said, say what're you doing in bed?
I said we're only trying to get us some peace
Christ! You know it ain't easy
You know how hard it can be

The way things are going
They're gonna crucify me
Saving up your money for a rainy day
Giving all your clothes to charity
Last night the wife said, oh boy, when you're dead
You don't take nothing with you but your soul
Think!
Made a lightning trip to Vienna
Eating chocolate cake in a bag
The newspapers said, she's gone to his head
They look just like two gurus in drag
Christ! You know it ain't easy
You know how hard it can be
The way things are going
They're gonna crucify me
Caught the early plane back to London
Fifty acorns tied in a sack
The men from the Press said, we wish you success
It's good to have the both of you back
Christ! You know it ain't easy
You know how hard it can be
The way things are going
They're gonna crucify me
The way things are going
They're gonna crucify me.

Give Peace A Chance

Two, one two three four
Everybody's talking about
Bagism, Shagism, Dragism, Madism, Ragism, Tagism, Thisism,
   Thatism, Ismism
All we are saying is give peace a chance
All we are saying is give peace a chance
Everybody's talking about
Ministers, sinisters, banisters and canisters
Bishops and fishops and rabbis and popeyes
Bye bye, bye bye
All we are saying is give peace a chance
All we are saying is give peace a chance
Let me tell you now
Everybody's talking about

Revolution, evolution, masturbation, flagellation, regulation,
   integration, meditation, United Nations, congratulations
All we are saying is give peace a chance
All we are saying is give peace a chance
Everybody's talking about
John and Yoko, Timmy Leary, Rosemary, Tommy Smothers,
   Bobby Dylan, Tommy Cooper, Derek Taylor, Norman Mailer,
   Alan Ginsberg, Hare Krishna, Hare Hare Krishna
All we are saying is give peace a chance
All we are saying is give peace a chance
All we are saying is give peace a chance
All we are saying is give peace a chance
All we are saying is give peace a chance
All we are saying is give peace a chance
All we are saying is give peace a chance
All we are saying is give peace a chance
All we are saying is give peace a chance
All we are saying is give peace a chance
All we are saying is give peace a chance
All we are saying is give peace a chance
All we are saying is give peace a chance.

Cold Turkey

Temperature's rising
Fever is high
Can't see no future
Can't see no sky.
My feet are so heavy
So is my head
I wish I was a baby
I wish I was dead.
Cold turkey has got me on the run.
My body is aching
Goosepimple bone
Can't see nobody
Leave me alone.
My eyes are wide open
Can't get to sleep
One thing I'm sure of
I'm in at the deep freeze.

Cold turkey has got me on the run.
Cold turkey has got me on the run.
Thirty-six hours
Growing in pain
Praying to someone
Free me again.
Oh I'll be a good boy
Please make me well
I'll promise you anything
Get me out of this hell.
Cold turkey has got me on the run.

Mother

Mother, you had me
But I never had you
I wanted you
You didn't want me
So I, I just gotta tell you
Goodbye, goodbye.
Father, you left me
But I never left you
I needed you
You didn't need me
So I, I just gotta tell you
Goodbye, goodbye.
Children, don't do
What I have done
I couldn't walk
And I tried to run
So I, I just gotta tell you
Goodbye, goodbye.
Mama don't go, daddy come home
Mama don't go, daddy come home
Mama don't go, daddy come home
Mama don't go, daddy come home
Mama don't go, daddy come home
Mama don't go, daddy come home
Mama don't go, daddy come home
Mama don't go, daddy come home
Mama don't go, daddy come home
Mama don't go, daddy come home.

God

God is a concept by which we measure our pain
I'll say it again
God is a concept by which we measure our pain – yeah
I don't believe in magic
I don't believe in I Ching
I don't believe in Bible
I don't believe in tarot
I don't believe in Hitler
I don't believe in Jesus
I don't believe in Kennedy
I don't believe in Buddha
I don't believe in mantra
I don't believe in gita
I don't believe in yoga
I don't believe in kings
I don't believe in Elvis
I don't believe in Zimmerman
I don't believe in Beatles
I just believe in me
Yoko and me
And that's reality.
The dream is over
What can I say?
The dream is over
Yesterday
I was the dreamweaver
But now I'm reborn
I was the walrus
But now I'm John
And so, dear friends
You'll just have to carry on
The dream is over.

Isolation

People say we got it made
Don't they know we're so afraid?
Isolation
We're afraid to be alone
Everybody got to have a home
Isolation

Just a boy and a little girl
Trying to change the whole wide world
Isolation
The world is just a little town
Everybody trying to put us down
Isolation
I don't expect you to understand
After you've caused so much pain
But then again, you're not to blame
You're just a human, a victim of the insane
We're afraid of everyone
Afraid of the sun
Isolation
The sun will never disappear
But the world may not have many years
Isolation.

Working Class Hero

As soon as you're born they make you feel small
By giving you no time instead of it all
Till the pain is so big you feel nothing at all
A working class hero is something to be
A working class hero is something to be
They hurt you at home and they hit you at school
They hate you if you're clever and they despise a fool
Till you're so fucking crazy you can't follow their rules
A working class hero is something to be
A working class hero is something to be
When they've tortured and scared you for twenty odd years
Then they expect you to pick a career
When you can't really function you're so full of fear
A working class hero is something to be
A working class hero is something to be
Keep you doped with religion and sex and T.V.
And you think you're so clever and classless and free
But you're still fucking peasants as far as I can see
A working class hero is something to be
A working class hero is something to be
There's room at the top they are telling you still
But first you must learn how to smile as you kill
If you want to be like the folks on the hill
A working class hero is something to be

A working class hero is something to be
If you want to be a hero well just follow me
If you want to be a hero well just follow me.

My Mummy's Dead

My mummy's dead
I can't get it through my head
Though it's been so many years
My mummy's dead.
I can't explain
So much pain
I could never show it
My mummy's dead.

Imagine

Imagine there's no heaven
It's easy if you try
No hell below us
Above us only sky
Imagine all the people
Living for today.
Imagine there's no countries
It isn't hard to do
Nothing to kill or die for
And no religion too
Imagine all the people
Living life in peace.
You may say I'm a dreamer
But I'm not the only one
I hope someday you'll join us
And the world will be as one.
Imagine no possessions
I wonder if you can
No need for greed or hunger
A brotherhood of man
Imagine all the people
Sharing all the world.
You may say I'm a dreamer
But I'm not the only one
I hope someday you'll join us
And the world will live as one.

Crippled Inside

You can shine your shoes and wear a suit
You can comb your hair and look quite cute
You can hide your face behind a smile
One thing you can't hide is when you're crippled inside
You can wear a mask and paint your face
You can call yourself the human race
You can wear a collar and a tie
One thing you can't hide is when you're crippled inside
Well now you know that your cat has nine lives, babe
Nine lives to itself
You only got one, and a dog's life ain't fun
Mama, take a look outside
You can go to church and sing a hymn
You can judge me by the colour of my skin
You can live a lie until you die
One thing you can't hide is when you're crippled inside
Well now you know that your cat has nine lives, babe
Nine lives to itself
You only got one, and a dog's life ain't fun
Mama, take a look outside
You can go to church and sing a hymn
Judge me by the colour of my skin
You can live a lie until you die
One thing you can't hide is when you're crippled inside
One thing you can't hide is when you're crippled inside
One thing you can't hide – is when you're crippled inside.

Jealous Guy

I was dreaming of the past
And my heart was beating fast
I began to lose control
I began to lose control
I didn't mean to hurt you
I'm sorry that I made you cry
I didn't want to hurt you
I'm just a jealous guy
I was feeling insecure
You might not love me any more
I was shivering inside
I was shivering inside

I didn't mean to hurt you
I'm sorry that I made you cry
I didn't want to hurt you
I'm just a jealous guy
I didn't mean to hurt you
I'm sorry that I made you cry
I didn't want to hurt you
I'm just a jealous guy
I was trying to catch your eyes
Thought that you was trying to hide
I was swallowing my pain
I was swallowing my pain
I didn't mean to hurt you
I'm sorry that I made you cry
I didn't want to hurt you
I'm just a jealous guy
Watch out, I'm just a jealous guy
Look out, babe, I'm just a jealous guy.

Give Me Some Truth

I'm sick and tired of hearing things
From uptight, short-sighted, narrow-minded hypocritics
All I want is the truth
Just gimme some truth
I've had enough of reading things
By neurotic, psychotic, pig-headed politicians
All I want is the truth
Just gimme some truth
No short-haired, yellow-bellied son of Tricky Dicky
Is gonna mother-hubbard, soft-soap me
With just a pocketful of hope
Money for dope
Money for rope.
No short-haired, yellow-bellied son of Tricky Dicky
Is gonna mother-hubbard, soft-soap me
With just a pocketful of hope
Money for dope
Money for rope.
I'm sick to death of seeing things
From tight-lipped, condescending, mummy's little chauvinists
All I want is the truth

Just gimme some truth now
I've had enough of watching scenes
Of schizophrenic, egocentric, paranoiac, prima donnas
All I want is the truth now
Just gimme some truth
No short-haired, yellow-bellied son of Tricky Dicky
Is gonna mother-hubbard, soft-soap me
With just a pocketful of soap
It's money for dope
Money for rope
Aah, I'm sick to death of hearing things
From uptight, short-sighted, narrow-minded hypocrites
All I want is the truth now
Just give me some truth now
I've had enough of reading things
By neurotic, psychotic, pig-headed politicians
All I want is the truth now
Just gimme some truth now
All I want is the truth now
Just gimme some truth now
All I want is the truth!
Just gimme some truth!
All I want is the truth!
Just gimme some truth!

How Do You Sleep?

So Sgt Pepper took you by surprise
You better see right through that mother's eyes
Those freaks was right when they said you was dead
The one mistake you made was in your head
How do you sleep?
How do you sleep at nights?
You live with straights who tell you you was king
Jump when your mama tell you anything
The only thing you done was Yesterday
And since you've gone you're just Another Day
How do you sleep?
How do you sleep at nights?
How do you sleep?
How do you sleep at nights?
A pretty face may last a year or two

But pretty soon they'll see what you can do
The sound you make is Muzak to my ears
You must have learned something in all those years
How do you sleep?
How do you sleep at nights?

Oh Yoko!

In the middle of the night
In the middle of the night I call your name
Oh Yoko!
Oh Yoko!
My love will turn you on.
In the middle of a bath
In the middle of a bath I call your name
Oh Yoko!
Oh Yoko!
My love will turn you on
Our love will turn you on.
In the middle of a shave
In the middle of a shave I call your name
Oh Yoko!
Oh Yoko!
My love will turn you on.
In the middle of a dream
In the middle of a dream I call your name
Oh Yoko!
Oh Yoko!
My love will turn you on
Our love will turn you on.
In the middle of a cloud
In the middle of a cloud I call your name
Oh Yoko!
Oh Yoko!
My love will turn you on.
Oh Yoko!
Oh Yoko!
Oh Yoko!

Woman Is The Nigger Of The World

Woman is the nigger of the world
Yes she is. . .think about it
Woman is the nigger of the world
Think about it. . .do something about it.
We make her paint her face and dance
If she won't be a slave, we say that she don't love us
If she's real, we say she's trying to be a man
While putting her down we pretend that she's above us.
Woman is the nigger of the world
Yes she is. . .
If you don't believe me, take a look at the one you're with
Woman is the slave of the slaves
Ah yeah, better scream about it.
We make her bear and raise our children
And then we leave her flat for being a fat old mother hen
We tell her home is the only place she should be
Then we complain that she's too unworldly to be our friend.
Woman is the nigger of the world
Yes she is. . .
If you don't believe me, take a look at the one you're with
Woman is the slave to the slaves
Yeah, alright.
We insult her every day on T.V.
And wonder why she has no guts or confidence
When she's young we kill her will to be free
While telling her not to be so smart we put her down for being so
    dumb
Oh well, woman is the nigger of the world
Yes she is . . .
If you don't believe me, take a look at the one you're with
Woman is the slave to the slaves
Yes she is . . .
If you believe me, you better scream about it.
We make her paint her face and dance
We make her paint her face and dance
We make her paint her face and dance
We make her paint her face and dance
We make her paint her face and dance
We make her paint her face and dance
We make her paint her face and dance.

Sunday Bloody Sunday

Well it was Sunday bloody Sunday
When they shot the people there
The crys of thirteen martyrs
Filled the free Derry air.
Is there anyone amongst you
Dare blame it on the kids?
Not a soldier boy was bleeding
When they nailed the coffin lids!
Sunday bloody Sunday
Bloody Sunday's the day!
Well, you claim to be majority
Well, you know that it's a lie
You're really a minority
On this sweet emerald isle.
When Stormont bans our marches
They've got a lot to learn
Internment is no answer
It's those mothers' turn to burn!
Sunday bloody Sunday
Bloody Sunday's the day!
Sunday bloody Sunday
Bloody Sunday's the day!
Well, you Anglo pigs and Scotties
Sent to colonize the North
You wave your bloody Union Jack
And you know what it's worth!
How dare you hold to ransom
A people proud and free?
Keep Ireland for the Irish
Put England back to sea!
Sunday bloody Sunday
Bloody Sunday's the day!
Sunday bloody Sunday
Bloody Sunday's the day!
Well, it's always bloody Sunday
In the concentration camps
Keep Falls Road free forever
From the bloody English hands!
Repatriate to Britain
All of you who call it home
Leave Ireland for the Irish
Not for London or for Rome!

Sunday bloody Sunday
Bloody Sunday's the day!
Sunday bloody Sunday
Bloody Sunday's the day!
Sunday bloody Sunday
Bloody Sunday's the day!
Sunday bloody Sunday
Bloody Sunday's the day!

Out The Blue

Out the blue you came to me
And blew away life's misery
Out the blue life's energy
Out the blue you came to me
Every day I thank the Lord and lady
For the way that you came to me
Anyway it had to be
Two minds one destiny
Out the blue you came to me
And blew away life's misery
Out the blue life's energy
Out the blue you came to me
All my life has been a long slow knife
I was born just to get to you
Anyway I survived
Long enough to make you my wife
Out the blue you came to me
And blew away life's misery
Out the blue life's energy
Out the blue you came to me
Like a U.F.O. you came to me
And blew away life's misery
Out the blue life's energy
Out the blue you came to me.

The Luck Of The Irish

If you had the luck of the Irish
You'd be sorry and wish you were dead
You should have the luck of the Irish
And wish you was English instead!
A thousand years of torture and hunger
Drove the people away from their land
A land full of beauty and wonder
Was raped by the British brigands!
Goddamn, goddamn!
If you could keep voices like flowers
There'd be more shamrock all over the world
If you could drink dreams like Irish streams
Then the world would be high as the mountain of Mourne.
In the 'Pool they told us the story
How the English divided the land
Of the pain and the death and the glory
And the poets of old Ireland.
If we could make chains with the morning dew
The world would be like Galway Bay
Let's walk over rainbows like leprechauns
The world would be one big Blarney Stone.
Why the hell are the English there anyway?
As they kill with God on their side
Blame it all on the kids and the I.R.A.
As the bastards commit genocide
Aye, aye, genocide!
If you had the luck of the Irish
You'd be sorry and wish you were dead
You should have the luck of the Irish
Yes, you'd wish you was English instead!
Yes, you'd wish you was English instead!

Attica State

What a waste of human power
What a waste of human lives
Shoot the prisoners in the towers
Forty-three poor widowed wives.
Attica State, Attica State, we're all mates with Attica State.
Media blames it on the prisoners
But the prisoners did not kill
'Rockefeller pulled the trigger'
That is what the people feel.
Attica State, Attica State, we're all mates with Attica State.
Free the prisoners, nail the judges
Free all prisoners everywhere
All they want is truth and justice
All they need is love and care.
Attica State, Attica State, we're all mates with Attica State.
They all live in suffocation
Let's not watch them die in sorrow
Now's the time for revolution
Give them all a chance to grow
Attica State, Attica State, we're all mates with Attica State.
Come together, join the movement
Take a stand for human rights
Fear and hatred clouds our judgement
Free us all from endless night.
Attica State, Attica State, we're all mates with Attica State.
Attica State, Attica State, we all live in Attica State.
Attica State, Attica State, Attica, Attica, Attica State.

Scared

I'm scared, I'm scared, I'm scared
I'm scared, so scared
I'm scared, I'm scared, I'm scared
As the years roll away
And the price that I paid
And the straws slip away
You don't have to suffer
It is what it is
No bell, book or candle

Can get you out of this, oh no!
I'm scarred, I'm scarred, I'm scarred
I'm scarred
I'm scarred, I'm scarred, I'm scarred
Every day of my life
I just manage to survive
I just wanna stay alive
You don't have to worry
In heaven or hell
Just dance to the music
You do it so well, well, well!
Hatred and jealousy, gonna be the death of me
I guess I knew it right from the start
Sing out about love and peace
Don't wanna see the red raw meat
The green-eyed goddamn straight from your heart!
I'm tired, I'm tired, I'm tired
Of being so alone
No place to call my own
Like a rolling stone.

Steel And Glass

(This here is a story about your friend and mine – who is it?
   Who is it?)
There you stand, with your L.A. tan
And your New York walk, and your New York talk
Your mother left you when you were small
But you're gonna wish you wasn't born at all
Steel and glass
Steel and glass
Steel and glass
Steel and glass
Your phone don't ring, no one answers your call
How does it feel to be off the wall?
Well, your mouthpiece squawks as you spread your lies
But you can't pull string if your hands are tied.
Well, your teeth are clean but your mind is capped
You leave your smell like an alley cat
Steel and glass
Steel and glass
Steel and glass
Steel and glass.

Nobody Loves You
(When You're Down and Out)

Nobody loves you when you're down and out
Nobody sees you when you're on cloud nine
Everybody's hustlin' for a buck and a dime
I'll scratch your back and you scratch mine
I've been across to the other side
I've shown you everything, I got nothing to hide
And still you ask me, do I love you?
What it is, what it is
All I can tell you is, it's all showbiz
All I can tell you is, it's all showbiz.
Nobody loves you when you're down and out
Nobody knows you when you're on cloud nine
Everybody's hustlin' for a buck and a dime
I'll scratch your back and you knife mine
I've been across the water now so many times
I've seen the one-eyed witchdoctor leading the blind
But still you ask me do I love you?
What you say, what you say
Everytime I put my finger on it, it slips away
Everytime I put my finger on it, it slips away.
Well I get up in the morning and I'm looking in the mirror to see
Then I'm lying in the darkness and I know I can't get to sleep.
Nobody loves you when you're old and grey
Nobody needs you when you're upside down
Everybody's hollerin' 'bout their own birthday
Everybody loves you when you're six foot in the ground.

Beautiful Boy
(Darling Boy)

Close your eyes
Have no fear
The monster's gone
He's on the run and your daddy's here
Beautiful, beautiful, beautiful
Beautiful boy
Beautiful, beautiful, beautiful
Beautiful boy
Before you go to sleep
Say a little prayer
Every day in every way
It's getting better and better
Beautiful, beautiful, beautiful
Beautiful boy
Beautiful, beautiful, beautiful
Beautiful boy
Out on the ocean, sailing away
I can hardly wait
To see you come of age
But I guess we'll both just have to be patient
It's a long way to go
A hard row to hoe
Yes, it's a long way to go
But in the meantime
Before you cross the street
Take my hand
Life is what happens to you
While you're busy making other plans
Beautiful, beautiful, beautiful
Beautiful boy
Beautiful, beautiful, beautiful
Beautiful boy
Before you go to sleep
Say a little prayer
Every day in every way
It's getting better and better
Beautiful, beautiful, beautiful
Beautiful boy
Darling, darling, darling
Darling Sean
(Goodnight Sean, see you in the morning, bright and early!)

Watching The Wheels

People say I'm crazy doing what I'm doing
Well they give me all kinds of warnings to save me from ruin
When I say that I'm OK, well they look at me kind of strange
Surely you're not happy now you no longer play the game?
People say I'm lazy, dreaming my life away
Well they give me all kinds of advice, designed to enlighten me
When I tell them that I'm doing fine watching shadows on the wall
Don't you miss the big time, boy, you're no longer on the ball?
I'm just sitting here watching the wheels go round and round
I really love to watch them roll
No longer riding on the merry-go-round
I just had to let it go
People asking questions lost in confusion
Well I tell them there's no problems, only solutions
Well they shake their heads and they look at me
As if I've lost my mind
I tell them there's no hurry, I'm just sitting here doing time
I'm just sitting here watching the wheels go round and round
I really love to watch them roll
No longer riding on the merry-go-round
I just had to let it go
I just had to let it go
I just had to let it go.

Woman

Woman, I can hardly express
My mixed emotions at my thoughtlessness
After all, I'm forever in your debt
And woman, I will try to express
My inner feelings and thankfulness
For showing me the meaning of success
Woman, I know you understand
The little child inside the man
Please remember my life is in your hands
And woman, hold me close to your heart
However distant, don't keep us apart
After all, it is written in the stars
Woman, please let me explain

I never meant to cause you sorrow or pain
So let me tell you again and again and again
I love you – yeah, yeah
Now and forever
I love you – yeah, yeah
Now and forever
I love you – yeah, yeah
Now and forever
I love you – yeah, yeah
Now and forever.

Borrowed Time

When I was younger
Live in confusion and deep despair
When I was younger
Live in illusion of freedom and power
When I was younger
Full of ideals and broken dreams (my friend)
When I was younger
Everything simple but not so clear
Living on borrowed time
Without a thought for tomorrow
Living on borrowed time
Without a thought for tomorrow
Now I am older
The more that I see
The less that I know for sure
Now I am older
The future is brighter and now is the hour
Living on borrowed time
Without a thought for tomorrow
Living on borrowed time
Without a thought for tomorrow
Good to be older
Would not exchange a single day or a year
Good to be older (you bet)
Less complications, everything clear
Living on borrowed time
Without a thought for tomorrow
Living on borrowed time
Without a thought for tomorrow.

Grow Old With Me

Grow old along with me
The best is yet to be
When our time has come
We will be as one
God bless our love
God bless our love
Grow old along with me
Two branches of one tree
Face the setting sun
When the day is done
God bless our love
God bless our love
Spending our lives together
Man and wife together
World without end
World without end
Grow old along with me
Whatever fate decrees
We will see it through
For our love is true
God bless our love
God bless our love.

INDEX

Page numbers in *italic* refer to illustrations.

John Lennon is abbreviated to JL, and Yoko Ono to YO, in entries other than their own.